BEING FICTION:

Short Stories

This is for Beverley

BEING FICTION:

Short Stories

by

John Moss

Tecumseh Press
Ottawa, Canada
2001

Canada

We acknowledge the financial support of the Government of
Canada through the Book Publishing Industry Development
Program (BPIDP) for our publishing activities.

Canadian Cataloguing in Publication Data

Moss, John, 1940-
    Being fiction

ISBN 1-896133-25-8

    I. Title.

PS8576.O7863B44 2001   C813'.6   C2001-900045-6
PR9199.3.M66B44 2001

Cover by Bull's Eye Design, Ottawa, Canada;
using images/design as in acknowledged in p. viii.

Printed and bound in Canada on acid-free paper

Contents

Acknowledgements

I am indebted to my old friend Jack Morgan for using his convalescence from a temporary setback to my advantage. He read rough versions of these stories as a captive reader at his home overlooking Georgian Bay when I'm sure he would rather have been out on his boat, the *Miranda,* messing about in the freshwater sea. His fine critical intelligence and gentle candour gave me much to think about. I did not always pick up on his queries or follow his suggestions and this book may be the less for that. But it is certainly much better for the comments I took to heart, the problems I endeavoured to resolve, the pretentions I subdued. The dinner I promised is small compensation for the unfettered imagination and informed love of literature he shared in his reading.

Thank you as well to Mary McGillivray for invaluable feedback and to Robert Kroetsch, Gerald Lynch, and David Carlson for their generous encouragement. Thank you to Laura for her objective advice and thank you to Julia. Thanks, of course, to Beverley, who has accompanied me through every twist of personality and turn of phrase on this adventure, and to whom this book is dedicated.

Slightly different versions of "Waves Break Stone" and "Temagami" appeared, respectively, in my book *The Paradox of Meaning: Cultural Poetics and Critical Fictions,* published by Turnstone Press in 1999, and *Visions and Voices in Temagami,* edited by A.W. Plumstead and published by Nipissing University Press in 2000. "The Reconstruction of Forgotten Dreams" was first read at Queen's University on Nov. 7, 2000. "The Juxtaposition of Alice" was first read at the University of Manitoba on August 11, 2000. "A Romance for Barbara" was first read at the Convegno Internationale, Universita' degli Studi di Udine, May 20, 2000. "A Move to the Glebe" was first read at The McLuhan Symposium, University of Ottawa, May 5-7, 2000, and will appear in the book edited from the proceedings. "Temagami" was first read as "Grey Owl in Temagami" at the "Visions of the North, Voices of the North" conference sponsored by Nipissing University, Temagami, May 13, 1999, and in modified form as "A Grey Owl Narrative" for the Trent University Canadian Studies Symposium at Wanapitei Wilderness Centre, Temagami, September 24-26, 1999.

Cover image, "Arctic Beach," by Beverley Haun Moss
Cover design by Beatrice Winny

The greatest illusion of all is authenticity.

—Jorge de Cuchilleros
The Invention of History
trans. Manuel de Medeiros
Madrid: Prado Editores, 1984

Thomas, Tess, and the Kamseh Confederacy

Sometimes I think I speak Italian. In Toronto ristorantes I listen to the animated conversations of my fellow diners and whatever language they are speaking the context enlivens them and they gesticulate with flourishes that rattle the tables and their voices dip and soar like operatic arias. Even the tight syllables of English loosen in the cacophony of table talk to a sonorous buzz, and real Italian spoken from the shadows thrills like parmesan. When the waiter comes to take my order, I order in Italian. In Toronto, I am indulged although the waiter usually confirms my order in English. On the few occasions when I have visited Italy, waiters never know what it is I'm trying to say. Invariably I resort to pointing out items on the menu that catch my interest and then I mumble and look quizzical. By reading the waiter's response I nod my request or pass on to something else. Lingering over multiple courses, I imagine understanding everything being said around me. When I leave I shake the waiter's hand, no matter how casual the service has been, and declare loudly enough to be overheard by patrons in the vicinity of my egress, gracie molto, gracie molto mille, creating the impression I spoke Italian all along and wish to include them in the conspiracy. I smile indulgently and then depart.

We live inside scenarios, constantly reinventing our lives. Whether I am being a Roman food critic undercover in Siena, or living la dolce vita in Toronto over a plate of tagliatelli al funghi, supported by a quattro litro of chianti, I am the creation of my own contriving, under continual revision, a writer, as I sometimes imagine, in the midst of

1

an astonishing oeuvre.

I have never actually left a restaurant in Italy the way I described. The closest I have come to speaking Italian is reciting Latin declensions for Miss Collip in Grade ten. I am not a writer, I work in a large metropolitan office, doing office things. You have to imagine these words being spoken; we are acquaintances. By permitting me access to your time as a listener you pay me a great compliment. Why don't we choose a context where we will both be comfortable and you will not feel hurried. I know a small Persian restaurant where they have magic carpets on the walls and offer strong Iranian coffee, where they serve women and men equally with courtly deference. Because it is not smoke-filled you can smell the antique wools from the tribal rugs in an intricate medley mixed with the odour of fresh-ground dark-roasted arabica coffee and the opulent scent of herbs and spices from the small open kitchen at the back and a warm smell emanating from the floors and walls, even descending from the painted pressed-tin ceiling, the smell of another era, when these premises housed a shoemaker's trade at the turn of the last century. It is dark, despite the mid-day sun glazing at the windows, and we have time.

We do not know each other well. You have an interest in reading and so do I. If I was not afraid I would be intruding on your privacy, I could tell you things about yourself. Nothing new, but in confirmation of what you already know—like a fortune-teller in a second-floor room over an exclusive dress-shop on Queen St. West. How we tell our stories is in direct response to the audience we envision. I envision you a generous person, not gregarious, with a good mind you sometimes suspect is not functioning at full capacity in your present life and you are mildly ashamed, with a quick imagination, a refined sensibility, although you might be hard pressed to define either in exact terms, and an empathetic soul, although you are not religious and assume by soul I am not alluding to theology and transcendence. You have had relationship problems in the past and have known tragedy; you are a strong person and believe everything will work out, one way or another. You resent assumptions being made too readily by people who think they understand you. You reinvent yourself in many disguises, as you have done to join me in our Persian sanctuary from the office world outside.

There is something I want to talk about. I thought I heard you ask a question, the same that someone else asked me only last week, how does *Tess of the D'Urbervilles* end? You need to know that I would respond if I could. I have read the book twice, most recently about twenty years ago, and I have seen the Roman Polanski movie, and a recent BBC serialized adaptation, but I cannot answer. Tess and Angel Clare are vivid in my mind, along with Jude the obscure and the mayor of Casterbridge, but I do not recall the ending of a single Hardy novel. They are brooding, disturbing, enthralling, filled with sound and fury, but there is no closure to any of them in my recollection. You nod assent but at the same time reveal the trace of a smile, suggesting you already knew my answer before you asked, and perhaps the end of the novel as well. It was some kind of a test.

I divert your attention to the carpet on the wall across from us. We are each defined by esoteric knowledge: what we know in common affirms our similarity, it is the unexpected things that assert our difference. For years now I have been making a study of oriental carpets. Most of the better rug merchants in the city recognize me as a familiar, and while I seldom have sufficient money to buy more than the occasional antique bag-face, they are usually congenial and on slow days especially in the dead of winter they offer me coffee and we talk. It is always a pleasant smoke-free atmosphere, vital colours splayed and

rolled, subtle scents of Anatolia and Iran and the Caucasus and Turkistan; no-one who loves piled wool or kilim
would stain the air with tobacco in their proximity. We
talk and I learn, I read books, I haunt the smaller shops
away from Avenue Road, sometimes spending hours in
the lovely depths of Indo-Armenian Rugs Ltd., on Queen
St., Georges Yeremian, President, an Armenian with an
ageless face whose sweet and solemn manner suggests
memories of worlds long gone but still evoked in the rugs
surrounding him, deep in his store, like ghosts.

This perhaps is my test for you. You cannot get a
good perspective in these confined premises and the light
is subtle, more like being inside a tent than in the glare of
day. That particular rug hanging opposite was in its prime
when Thomas Hardy was a child. See it hanging with its
surface worn, the colours vibrant, suggesting it has not
been long retired from usage. Given its origins among the
Kamseh people, in the household of a tribal leader—all
this can be told by the border imagery of splayed scorpi-
ons and angulated flowers, by spandrels of botehs with
the eyes of dragons, but especially by the small rampant
lions in the field among random birds and floral discs
whimsically abstracted around a trilogy of irregular medallions—a large rug, it was probably used for successive
generations by people who trod gently on it over dry earth
and is likely a rare recent import from Iran, perhaps never
walked upon in Canada.

Like my memory of Tess, the story of this carpet is
open at the end. Of course, if I asked you, we could round
out Hardy's plot in a sentence or two. But I would forget
and have a disposition against holding in my mind experiences that deplete me. That is why I have never risen
above mid-management in my office. I am not executive
material. Endings seem too much reminders of my own
mortality. That makes me inefficient. In reading, it is the
process I want, not to reach an outcome but to fill with

another consciousness the mind of the persona I invent for myself as a reader, not Thomas Hardy's but his own creative emanation, Tess.

Sometimes I think I speak Italian. Sometimes I hover as a sort of loving witness over the shoulder of a tribal woman absorbed in her work on a horizontal loom in the lea of her tent in a far-off place I only know by reading her design. Ah, the colours, the texture of the wool, her concentration, the play of personality against the borders of convention. Wessex could not be more authentic, nor Italy more enthralling. I know her in each rug I experience, and in each she is a different person.

Look carefully at the Kamseh rug. As you trace it in your mind, you recognize a rhetoric that is both intricate and eloquent, speaking to you the way music does, from inside. When we first came in, the carpets on the wall created an exotic atmosphere, as if we had shifted worlds. But observe, we are surrounded by separate compositions, each played out in colours, shapes, and lines. Your gift to me is opening yourself to what I see. If I were to read *Tess of the D'Urbervilles* over and over, I might have a different experience each time, for my readings would reflect the ongoing progress of my life. I might pick up nuances I had previously overlooked. But there is no reason to expect I will comprehend it any better, without someone teaching me. I need someone like you to bridge the gap between apprehension and understanding. No matter how receptively we take in the world, we all need help in making sense of it.

This is the first time I have brought someone here. I never learned to share my enthusiasms and have never had a friend. I am anxious now about losing you, despite your kindness as a listener. You flinched a little when I implied that I could be your teacher. I meant to suggest you could equally be mine. Perhaps we can allay the sense of oppression that threatens both of us if I come

clean and make it clear why I brought you here, and why
I need to talk. The truth is, I am turning invisible. No-one
sees through me yet, but it is happening.

I first noticed when I started forgetting how things
end. Several months before the person at the office who
took me by appearance to be a reader asked me about the
fate of Tess and Angel Clare, to which I only replied that
I would not give away a plot that Hardy had worked so
passionately to construct, I began to suspect I was fading
like a character on newsprint in the rain. It was a feeling,
nothing more. Then I realized I could not remember the
conclusion of a single novel I had read, of the many that
got me through an isolated childhood and dreary adolescence. My mind is filled with doors opening into vivid
worlds created by Robert Louis Stevenson, Charles
Dickens, Mark Twain, and countless others. I can easily
present myself at these myriad doors and enter. But there
is no way out the other side. Each has its own reality
unlike those of any other, so that you know by the quality
of the air, the feel of the ground, the intensity of your
presence, whether you are about to encounter Becky
Thatcher, David Balfour and Blind Pugh, or Pip playing
with Estella in Miss Havisham's garden. I am contained
by each, I have all my faculties but am a disembodied
spectre. Only through careful concentration can I resolve
my personality, look back to my absent being in the
world, and extricate myself. Now I seldom venture into
narrative unless someone inadvertently compels me there,
unwittingly asking me the very thing I do not know.

I have always liked to imagine I speak Italian, although I have made no effort to learn. It is a matter of
wishful thinking, not pedagogy. I want to be someone
vital. Instead, I am becoming transparent. You are experienced in such things. As a reader, you cannot alter the
course of events. You observe with real eyes yet you have
other eyes outside the text, where you have power. You

have no control within the narrative yet you can close the book at any time, your power is absolute. The difference between us is that you are comfortable as a witness. I seem to lack the necessary empathy. I can only see what is before me, and that seems insufficient to give me substance, and I am fading.

At my office people sometimes talk about me as if I were not in the room. On the subway yesterday a fat man who smelled of cigars sat squarely on my lap and I think he only noticed because I yelped. At stoplights, drivers look through me crossing with the green and make right turns and I am forced to leap aside. Last night at an eatery on the Danforth, when I ordered dinner in Italian, the owner-waiter did not bother to verify my order in English and served me something strange. The generalizations within which I live are collapsing around me. Soon waiters may not bother to serve me at all, perhaps they will seat others at my table as if I am not there, maybe not see me as I struggle to catch their attention, will bus their own dishes, sweep the floors themselves, turn out the lights, and leave me in the dark.

I have asked you to accompany me to a small Persian restaurant and you have been accommodating, listening to my words because I asked you to imagine they were spoken. Look at me. Is it only the atmospheric lighting, the play of shadows across my face, or are you having trouble seeing me? When I was a child my stepfather carelessly but not maliciously called me 'nondescript.' It was on my eighth birthday, the beginning of my ninth year. There was a curious delayed reaction while I looked up 'nondescript' in our thirteen-volume Oxford Dictionary, and then I was devastated. From that time on, I stopped looking for myself in mirrors. When I inadvertently confront my reflection on an unexpected surface, I do not see a face but a word, the same word that now lies between us and cannot be rescinded. When I wash and shave, I con-

centrate on the parts being administered, and avoid my
eyes. Look at me. If you will take advantage of your facility for transforming invisibility into sensible experience,
you will see I am still here.

On the wall beside us is a Shahsavan. It is behind me
but so indelible in my mind I can describe it without turning. It is rare. Let me write it to you, speak of it as if it
were a Hardy novel you already know. We can plunge in,
there is no beginning. It would be absurd to start at the
bottom edge and work our way upwards, describing line
by line of weft, as the lines of warp control our upward
progress. Only when you have finished reading can we
explore. If you were describing Tess to me you would not
begin with the opening sentence. You would say, there is
this woman, then according to the ways her world engaged you, you would proceed. If I knew her well already, it would be you I would perceive.

Contained within a bold red and black border of what
could be interpenetrating arrow-heads or chains of landscape, a series of four bright medallions float against a
field of golden camel fleece, yet paradoxically as you
relax the medallions recede, opening like windows into
other worlds. The indigo especially, in two of them,
seems to be the evening sky, reaching under the medallions, beyond the borders of the rug itself, intimations of
infinity, and in the other two, one madder-red edged in
white, one edged in black, are gardens. In the golden field
are many flowers. These are neither symbolic nor realis-
tic, innumerable small tablets of blues and reds, strewn
randomly yet with precision. And among the flowers
where the medallions meet are small herds of twenty-
seven deer in all, all of them but one facing the same way.

This rug, which hangs from the high ceiling to the
floor, is very old and the black wool has corroded, but the
colours are vibrant, the palette as rich and balanced as
when a woman in the north of Persia chose each of its

tens of thousand strands one by one from skeins of dyed wool and camel fleece and tied them each with equal tension to achieve this perfect play of casual formality, of tradition and invention, necessity and lyric inspiration. She has been dead perhaps seven generations and still her soul lingers, softly but not unknown. The single deer facing in its own direction, once you see it the rest becomes a context for this to happen. There is a conversation between you and the tribal woman of the Shahsavan, who made this deep pile rug when the other women around her were weaving kilims. It is not a conversation of words but when you look at that one deer, the two of you connect.

You can see me better now. As you observe my narrative, scanning the carpet, letting it fill your mind, my features emerged briefly into light. Perhaps it was how you adjusted your posture to get a better view. Perhaps it was while you descended in your imagination through the thick depths of the coffee aroma into a more receptive state of consciousness, or possibly it was because you know Toronto, recognize the streets we travelled to get here, east off Yonge and south of Queen, and feel comfortable in an Iranian establishment that defines our new and cosmopolitan dispensation as well as Eatons' Georgian Room or Frans defined the old. In any case, you caught the look of excitement in my eyes, saw my lips shape words, saw my nose as strong not podgy, my entire appearance as pleasantly coherent.

Yet, no sooner do I celebrate my opacity than the symptoms of invisibility return. It is not your fault. I have tied my enduring presence so much to material things that they displace me in your mind. You may think of me, but you envision carpets. This was how it was in what I fondly call my dating period, which as you might imagine was not of long duration. Because I could conjure nothing much to say of interest about myself, I would prepare for dates by studying. I always asked girls and women to go out by telephone. A surprising number acquiesced. I think it was because they could not place my voice, but since I seemed to know them from school or, later, from work, and they had time, they sometimes agreed. Trying to anticipate what their interests were, I would cram by memorizing whole issues of *Vogue* or learn the scores of every match that year at Wimbledon or immerse myself in opera to the point of nearly drowning. It is also surprising how many thanked me at the door for an edifying evening and explained that they were actually involved with other people. Eventually I stopped trying.

Some things we take for granted and one of these is that class knows class; you and I are both of the reading class and so I did not ask if you know Thomas Hardy's novels. I assumed you do. However different you and I may be, we are of the educated middle class, by virtue of being schooled in a country that admits no possibility of an upper class and elevates the working poor by the condescending rubric, lower middle class, as if the 'middle' tag lends compensation for their inferior status. You and I are beyond class, ourselves. That is the nice thing about being a contemporary Torontonian, you are not burdened by class. The moment I started talking to you, I knew you were a reader, familiar with Atwood and Munro, Conrad, Hardy, Austen and the Brontes, Twain, Fitzgerald, perhaps Borges, Marquez, certainly Dostoevski, Balzac and Cervantes. I took many of the same courses myself.

You have been able to accommodate the worlds created by your reading in your life, as you have the worlds of film and theatre and all the other arts. Your personality provides perimeters to the galaxy these worlds formulate inside your brain, whirling among the infinite dark recesses of your skull. My own life has been uneventful. It is those worlds I have read that made me who I am. I did not make them happen; they created me.

You can imagine then why Thomas Hardy has been

so important. He seizes the receptive personality and draws his reader headlong into other lives. To appreciate the turbulence of destiny in his characters' existence, you must relinquish hold on your own. Reading Hardy is like falling through a life, I could plummet through with Tess or Jude and leave my world behind. I would go to the office and do my office work, but in reality I would be hurtling through Wessex, perpetually falling. Until recently I read a lot, I always have. It's the only way I could connect. Not with the character. I am not deranged. But with the reader reading, the persona of myself. Perhaps I used to read too much, or too much Thomas Hardy, or perhaps I simply reached a point of saturation where I poured everything I was into novels, trying to find myself, and there was nothing left. Perhaps it was only because I reached that certain age, going through a change of life. In any case, as my own existence became more and more intangible, I found myself forgetting how the novels end.

I stopped reading Hardy, stopped reading much of anything. But I was too late. Even though I functioned in the real world, as we like to call the world of blood and concrete, I would drift from one book to another in my mind, and none of them would end. Only among carpets in the rug shops around the city did I emerge as my own person, and then ironically for my esoteric appreciation of the culturally uncommon.

That is why I brought you here. I thought if you could see me surrounded by these tangibles I love, perhaps your sensual engagement with the subjects of our discourse would lend me substance. I have shown you a Shahsavan and a rug from the Kamseh Confederacy. We have sipped our strong coffee and in the dull light looked at each other across the table. You are against the light and I am in shadow, so it is difficult for each of us to distinguish separate features. We could almost be the same person. While I do not confuse myself with Tess, I find that she is animated by my experience of the world; just as I expect you find yourself in me. I wish I had more to offer. To both of you.

Behind you on the wall is an Akstafa with a field of indigo. It is the only rug in the restaurant not Persian but perhaps it came to be here through Iran; it echoes others on the wall, the Qashqa'i and the Afshar, with its eloquence of colour and design. Yet it could not be mistaken. Lean forward and turn your face against the light, you can see the soft and supple way its fibres catch the diverted sunshine, reflected from the office windows and cement surfaces outside. Lean away and you can see the geometric chains of abstract birds in madder-red, pistachio green and blue indigo against a band of natural ivory from undyed wool in a border so intricate it is vibrantly austere. Think about this, we are in Toronto, this rug is not an artifact, an arcane reminder or souvenir of Other, a talisman of foreignness. Lucky us, this Toronto, this rug as inevitable as in a Turkish merchant's shop in Istanbul or warming a rough floor in the Caucasus of the great grandchildren of the woman who made it when her people still lived in landscape, long before the Soviets settled them in awkward villages.

We are lucky to be here, you and I. An unobtrusive waiter serves us sweets which take the bite of the coffee from our mouths. We both ask for water. You do not drink enough water and although you watch your diet and build exercise into your days, refusing to take elevators for an ascent of less than fours stories, descents of less than six, and you do not smoke, if you were a smoker we would not be talking now, I worry that you do not drink enough water. I care for you and not only because you are my designated witness. You remember the endings to every novel you have ever read, every film you ever saw. You have substance and you have power; you handle power with generosity. You could get up and leave, make my transition to invisibility complete by turning a page, refusing to listen, looking the other way.

Look! Let me take you into the Akstafa. I speak with the authority of an enthusiast and not a scholar, but I have studied. You once read critics who told you things about Thomas Hardy's Tess that did not accord with the Tess of your own imagining, and Tess was not diminished and your understanding was enhanced. I know about dyes and knot counts and the itineraries of nomadic peoples of the Orient. I know how colour is made from crushed beetles and ground flowers, and how looms are constructed, and how court rugs may display astonishing levels of craftsmanship, but only tribal rugs born of the hands and mind of a nomadic woman working alone in the open air can achieve the level of art. I can show you in a single carpet the evolution of form, where magnificent peacocks posture beside ancient swastika patterns made from a nexus of elongated birds' heads. We can share our delight in finding two human figures of equal gender who reveal, if we look carefully, that one is the forbidden figure of a woman, for the other has a few pale knots suggesting a penis protruding from the bottom of his identical tunic.

Stand, I will show you the three shields that float upon the indigo field with its abrash of colour that ranges abruptly from night-blue to azure, and how they contain trees with symmetrical branches of birds' head abstractions and how each is surrounded with dozens of heads protruding like quills or a palisade into the blue which is speckled with animals the size of flowers and small birds within birds and arrangements of rectilinear petals, some no bigger than insects, and whimsical checkerboard patterns like matchbooks arranged with precision to defy the organized mind. This is the most formal of the carpets I have shown you, and the most enigmatic. It is also the most relaxed, a perfect harmony of innumerable knots, like printed letters on a page, and the artist's vision, more splendid perhaps than she could have dreamed. Or perhaps she had the genius to know she was becoming art, and understood exactly what she did.

   We are on our way out. I have shown you nothing you could not have seen on your own, but at least you gave me the pleasure of sharing. Let me cover the cost. It is my treat. The proprietor speaks Farsi, not English, and a little Italian. I enjoy negotiating the bill with him; he regards the restaurant as a gathering place and tries to charge for time. You go ahead. You are a good listener, and have an excellent eye for detail and design. You have much to do in your life. I will stay behind and watch as you enter the bright glare of light outside, and I will think wistfully about you as you disappear into the world.

A Move to the Glebe

I stopped reading books when I turned fifty. Under the aegis of Marshall McLuhan I determined the impact of print on my life was antithetical to living well. Not being a zealot, I have not given up reading in dailies or weeklies the captions under photographs, or print on signs or cereal boxes, or printed texts emblazoned on screens. Nor, when I made the conversion from print to experience, did I consign my library to a ceremonial pyre; I am not a fanatic, nor given to grandiloquent gestures. Instead, I boxed up the vast collection of leather-bound books I had acquired as an avid bibliophile and all the paperback books I had accumulated over the years as a literary academic, and donated them to the Salvation Army. Having done that, I bought a small house in the Glebe and moved out of my capacious condominium with its spectacular view across one whole wall of the Gatineau Hills. I work out in a gym off Bank Street, and in the evenings I watch television. I have not read a book in ten years now and find my teaching has improved, I am in excellent condition, and I know what is going on in the world.

Of course I often listen to radio. As with many who live alone in this country, the CBC is my surrogate family. When Barbara Frum died, I was devastated. Gzowski's retirement took over a year to assimilate. Michael Enright's shift from "As It Happens" helped ease the anxiety but Shelagh in the morning was inevitable. "Quirks and Quarks" is my science and "The House" is my politics. Understand this, if you are not familiar with Canadian things, I no more feel bound to explain these allusions than you would, to explain why your sister has a strange physiognomy or your grandfather was shot for desertion.

Some things are simply authentic and must be accepted.

No-one has noticed my eccentricity—and I regard it as such, for everyone in my field of endeavour is surrounded by books, fortified from the actual world by a palisade of books, inured from experience in a garrison of books. I walk through bookstores now and am amazed at all the people. In the giant stores they swarm like inversions of bees, taking away from the honey-combed cells their vital nutrition, to read in isolation, each reader on his or her own. Circulars come through the mail advertising all manner of book clubs. People give books as gifts, they decorate their homes with books, impress their friends with table-top tomes too big to stand upright in cases manufactured for the average-sized volume. Books are as ubiquitous as air, yet no-one notices that I do not read.

Giving up books is not something I would recommend to a younger person. My reasons for saying so bring me back to McLuhan. Books were important to me as a child. I grew up in an orphanage and did not discover until my mid-twenties that I was not a foundling. My parents decided while still a young couple to sail around the world; a baby, weaned and unwieldy as I was when they left, was a dangerous encumbrance. At some sacrifice they gave me up for adoption, leaving me in the care of The Church. Since in Quebec at the time the birth-rate was still so high as to be considered a progenerative act of God, and I had neither blue eyes nor blond hair and was circumcised, there were no takers. I spent my early years free of familial impositions. Only by the strangest of circumstances did I eventually discover my parents were alive and living on Vancouver Island with my two brothers and two sisters who, being significantly younger than me, still lived at home.

We have encountered a problem, here, inherent in the narrative text: print occupies time. I set out in the previous paragraphs to relate my life without books to Marshall

McLuhan. If I had been telling my story to the ear not the eye, the medium of our discourse would be air—sound waves, which at close quarters are virtually instantaneous. Or personalities; the medium of my story would be the interface of our separate lives, the sustained contemporaneity of our common experience. To imitate the immediacy of speech, I write this text as if it were written in the perpetual present. The illusion is a convention. As soon as I commit words to print, I immerse myself in a parallel world where time is subject to invention. As you listen with the eye not the ear, you too enter another time, a continuum governed by syntax, by rhetoric, by narrative design. Speaking, it would not have been necessary to give you an account of my life. Background would have been carried sufficiently on the occasional inflection or gesture. But text attenuates consciousness on a linear plane, denies simultaneity. In print, everything connects; not in concurrence but in consecutive sequence, whether overt or implied.

Given my invocation of McLuhan to justify behaviour that perhaps was ordained from the moment I opened my first book at Immaculate Conception Orphanage, it is surprising that I have not been more strident in differentiating between print on paper and print elsewhere. They are not at all the same. Some day I shall write about electronic print and the mind, about how they relate. For now, I am caught up in the memory of that primal experience, my first book, which I recall with indelible clarity.

It was not a picture book but a text with large block letters, suitable for the ill-sighted or the novice reader. I placed my hand on the page to feel the letters, expecting an evanescent quality of heat or texture since I had observed others draw from books a variety of ecstasies. There was nothing but the flat cool of paper. I spit on my hands and rubbed them together to make them more sensitive, the way I had seen older boys do in the dormitory before they retreated under the covers to secretive delights. Still nothing. I spit again and again, my fingers fairly dripping, and rubbed and rubbed. At last the page yielded nubbins of gray residue, damp bits that fell away from my trembling hands as the saliva adhesive gave away to the force of gravity. Anticipating I know not what, I looked at the text and was shocked to observe a brambled blur. Thus, even before I could read, I learned not to trust the stability of print on the page.

I was punished, of course, with a memorable beating—a rite of passage that marked the onset of literacy, for having been discovered as the destroyer of books by the ink on my hands, I was banished to a bare subterranean room for a full month with only a pail for a toilet and an Eaton's Catalogue for toilet paper, from which I taught myself to read by searching out pictures with alliterative labels and comparing first letters, thus learning 'c' from canoe, camera, corset, cup, and 's' from socks, saddles, and stoves. I was astonished at being in solitary confinement, although at five and a half years of age I did not comprehend that this was not the way to maturity. Motivated by a desire for the power that could invoke such fury from my keepers, I dedicated myself, in that sad hovel within the bowels of an institution dedicated to the promulgation of faith and right reason, to books. From thence forward, I would be in their thrall.

And so I was, until my fiftieth birthday. I read through childhood and adolescence with a precocity that displaced the normal experiences of growing up, but in their stead gave me breadth of awareness and depth of understanding belying my untried condition. In my early years I was little affected by notions of a continuum or of duration. So much was I immersed in the discontinuities of text, so intrigued by the submission of time to the innocent act of closing or opening a book, that while other children were playing in the snow, leaping to keep warm into drifts piled by the long driveway, I was busy as a volunteer in the library, ecstatic among the innumerable moments held in suspension around me. It was not the knowledge contained by the books that intrigued me but my own potential to make the past real, simply by reading. I never learned to form angels in the snow or to build snow forts, nor how to play hockey, but I was not unhappy. After I left the orphanage, for a brief period I seemed to have entered time the way I had read about it, as sequential experience, which heretofore had only been measured by the expanding extent of my reach to inaccessible shelves in the library. I had grown up without really noticing.

At the University of Toronto I enrolled in a course by McLuhan. It was this that saved me from drifting like flotsam on the river of one-moment-to-the-next. Nothing else could account for the rapid shift in my notion of consciousness from swirling vortex, in a library where books were arranged by colour and size, to linear cascade to fathomless deep. To adjust my analogy somewhat—once enrolled as an undergraduate and away from the orphanage, I found I had tumbled out of a mirror and into a maze, neatly constructed but baffling if I did not follow the prescribed pathways of inquiry and discussion. I found myself looking back through the mirror at the chaotic splendours of my childhood sanctuary, and charged with adopting systems of patterned responses that would bring them to order. Only McLuhan taught me to look at the glass itself, and from the glass to the frame, to consider the nature of frames. From there, it was a small step to look past the mirror, to the unmirrored world of authentic experience where mazes were memories, reminders encoded of where we have been.

I was a desultory student in the first couple of years and with the arrogance of the largely self-tutored thought Professor McLuhan merely the most bizarre of a bad lot. Not until after I moved to Victoria to pursue doctoral studies in practical criticism, something I did not recognize as oxymoronic until years later, not until then did I come to realize it was he who had saved me from confusing the mirrors and mazes of the academic fun-house with life itself, as so many of my colleagues have done. The day I received my final degree, while others were celebrating with family and friends, I spent the evening alone in my cluttered office writing McLuhan a letter in longhand to express my indebtedness. I told him how books had been my refuge and consolation when I was a child, and under his tutelage had become objects of desire. Nothing gave me more pleasure than to be surrounded by books, shelves of books, neat stacks and tumbling piles of books; their content was immaterial. Books existed in the real world; their content did not. When I finished writing the letter I tucked it into a copy of Blake's major prophecies and there it remained until by chance I found it the day I turned fifty.

On a sunny afternoon during my second summer in Victoria as I sat on a bench by the harbour in front of the Empress Hotel a young woman walked by and I fell in love. Never before, nor since, have I had any interest in my own sexuality. I have not found members of either sex particularly attractive and were it not for the occasional wet dream when I was younger I would have said my hormones were dysfunctional. I think now, looking back, I simply had no conception of intimacy beyond what I read of in books, which from an earliest age I recognized as words typeset on paper and therefore illusion. As the young woman walked towards me I recognized in myself the literal symptoms of love, and immediately that she passed I rose and followed her and introduced myself, which we both took to be the most natural thing in the world. After a few moments, we adjourned from the sunlight into the Hotel solarium for scones with clotted cream and a steaming pot of Darjeeling tea.

I have no desire to create suspense but only to acknowledge the extraordinary coincidence of our meeting. We quickly resolved that our mutual attraction was due to our exceptional similarity to one another, not to that complementarity that one would expect in an affair of the heart. It was not long, however, before the unusual flutterings in my viscera subsided as by a process of interrogation and elimination I determined that we were in fact brother and sister. She herself was born on the boat that I discerned was my parents', a ketch with a wood hull, harboured in Kowloon at the time. The young woman invited me to go home with her for dinner, which I agreed to do. The strange feelings of excitement at finding someone so perfectly like myself gave way to trepidation as we approached her family's house. She opened the mock-Georgian door and as we entered a middle-aged woman emerged from the shadows of a library off the living-room. Without looking at her directly I turned away, as if I had forgotten something just outside the door, which I closed behind me as I walked through and was half-way down the block before I heard it open again and a middle-aged woman's voice call after me.

Somehow, in our first moments of intimacy I had neglected to offer the young woman my name. Nor had I said exactly what I did, apart from the fact that I was deeply involved with books. So that was the end of it, the closest I came to having a family. I have sometimes wondered what it would have been like had I stayed. Would the middle-aged woman have embraced me or recoiled? Would my sister and I have been tempted by incest, the gentle lust of our likenesses being always between us? Was my father still a sailor? These queries would needle me through the decades to come, every night as I would drift off to sleep. And every morning they would dissipate into the events of the day.

Not long after graduation the offer of an assistant professorship came through from the University of Ottawa, and my only alternative being a post-doctoral fellowship at Queen's, I accepted. I bought a fifteenth-floor condominium high over the Ottawa River. For the next twenty years I taught and I taught. I wrote the requisite books to become an associate and then a full professor. And I read. I read to myself and aloud to my students. And as I taught and I read and I wrote, I accumulated a sizable library which sprawled through the three bedrooms of my condominium, shoving my austere furnishings into obscurity as it did so. On holidays and sabbaticals I travelled to bookstores, especially in Britain, wherever books were honoured as artifacts and sold as items. I bought many books but I had no need to catalogue my collection. It was enough to know the books were there. I could open a few at random and read a line or two from each and set up the most astonishing conversations among them. Sometimes even unopened they made such a din I could hardly hear myself think. My life was simple. By some lights my life was austere.

What print inscribed on paper ceased to be of great interest to me while I was still enrolled at St. Michael's in Toronto. That was McLuhan's gift: by inviting us to look beyond the text to the book, and not accept books as incidental to the text and the experience of reading, I was drawn into time as an ocean. As I am a creation of consciousness and creature of language, my initial experience with books at university gathered me into a torrent of words channelled to run the mills of academe. I could leap from one flume to another, but always the flow was one way. My experience of the world attenuated into lines of force and direction. Living within books as I did through my childhood, reading voraciously and at random, time had been wondrously fragmented and frangible, swirling around me like a whirlpool that both held me secure in its grasp and kept me from drowning. I did not like the new linearities, and when McLuhan opened my mind to the estuary I entered the ocean, I left the parsing of knowledge, the parting of waters, behind.

My conceit is obscure. And not entirely honest, for I have earned my living in the very institution I claim to have abjured. Let me clarify two things, then I will proceed to the events of my fiftieth birthday, the murder that may have occurred, and an explanation of why I gave up reading in books.

Time is a mathematical concept, a theoretic construction. Print is a method of encapsulating fragments of consciousness and removing them from what we experience as the temporal continuum. The past in print becomes more authentic in the reading mind than the personal past, which is encoded in memory and is empirically unstable. The present in print is instantaneous, as in actual experience, but unlike actual experience it may be sustained for perusal or returned to, again and again. The future in print is all that remains unread on a particular reading, even if the reader has read it before. The future is fixed and finite, determined and accessible on the turn of a page. It can be visited and made to recede as often as the reader wishes. The future in actual experience is indeterminate, unknowable, and by definition beyond reach.

Bear with me a step further, then we shall return to the text. Time is the medium of mental activity; print allows time and the mind to merge. Time does not exist in its own right. It is important to understand this; it is a matter of perception and measurement. One moment ago or to come, a billion years in the past or the future, these concepts have no meaning except from a present perspective. When we are dead, there is no more present. Does that mean time stops? It was never moving, never more than a projection of consciousness on the dimension of existence we have elevated to special importance because it is coincident with the mind that perceives it and sets us apart from all other beings, so far as we know. Print reconstitutes time in discrete particles entirely subject to human control.

That should clarify my first point: it is print that allows us the illusion that time is a tangible thing, by segmenting it off into retrievable chunks. The second point of clarification is this: books do not contain time, for time only becomes real in the reading mind. Books are a site of negotiation between reader and text, but, as McLuhan argued if I understood him correctly, they are reservoirs only of ink on paper. They do not hold words, but only the potential for words; they do not hold time, but only the promise of an exploded continuum. They are things, and as such, to be valued as things.

On the evening of my fiftieth birthday I opened my latest acquisition that had arrived the week before from a favourite bookseller off Charing Cross Road. Hoping for a sense of occasion, I had waited to unwrap the parcel until my birthday, the brown mailing paper being a subdued substitute for the gift-wrap one might have preferred for the occasion. I was not alone. On my way home from the university I passed the unfortunate derelict who seemed to wait at the end of my block every night just for me. I had become accustomed to giving this wretch whatever change I had in my pockets each evening, sometimes accumulating extra through the day for the purpose, if the weather was miserable. It being my birthday, I felt magnanimous and invited him up for a drink. He resisted at first. Then, warily, he followed me into the building, onto the elevator, down the hall, and into my apartment. Drink in hand, still shrouded in the all-weather hood he wore like a cowl, he watched me open my gift to myself.

My hands trembled as I unwrapped the parcel with surgical precision, as if I were stripping away the funeral bindings on a mummified corpse. I forgot about my strange companion as I drew a fine copy of the *Sylva*

Sylvarum by the Right Honourable Francis, Viscount St. Alban, into the Canadian air. *Sylva Silvarum: or, A Natural History. In Ten Centuries. Whereunto Is Newly Added the History Naturall and Experimentall of Life and Death, or of the Prolongation of Life.* "Published (I thought rather ironically) after the Authors Death by William Rawley, Doctor in Divinity one of his Majesties Chaplains." "The Seventh Edition. London. 1658." My visitor, who had drawn my facsimile edition of Blake's prophecies out of a pile by the sofa, reached forward from his own shadow and took the volume from my hand, which I readily relinquished for fear of harming the pages. Blake, he let fall to the floor. A folded letter slipped into the air and in the instant I knew what it was, my note to McLuhan, but my attention was otherwise addressed.

My companion handled the *Sylva Sylvarum* carefully —and revealed herself in these close quarters to be a woman, for in her effort to read the faded script inside the fly-leaf and on the title-page she held the book to the light and her cowl slipped back. For only a moment was I nonplussed; then I too became absorbed in the handwriting. We could easily decipher the name William Lock, and a hand-written date, 1693. But there was other writing in a more diminutive hand, Marie Rush, three times repeated, then altered to Mary Rush. Then some modest flourishes of a capital M, over and over. And parts of words. The end-papers had been used it seems for a writing exercise.

Upside down on the same page as Marie or Mary's name, there was a tightly written quatrain in a spidery script, only the second line of which was decipherable and read, "For time is no time when time is past." Running slant-wise across this verse as if to efface it was a signature in yet another hand, Thomas Rush, to which was appended as if in a gesture of pride or defiance, Not One of Family.

My companion looked at me and for the first time since I had encountered her on the street some years back, she spoke. "How much is that worth?" she said. It did not occur to me to be disingenuous and I answered, "About two thousand dollars." She looked deep into my eyes, as if a revelation were at hand. She could not be my long lost daughter as I have never consummated a sexual act. She could be a descendent of Mary Rush, but this seemed improbable. She smiled. "That is a lot of money," she said. "I wonder why Marie became Mary? I wonder if Thomas Rush was a poor cousin, or a bastard child, or a presumptuous servant with education beyond his station? I wonder that their writing is worth so much and so little."

She continued, "I would like on my gravestone, 'For time is no time when time is past.'" Then she added, "You are not an unkind man. I too was a reader and life passed by. Then I stopped reading altogether, and I have not been unhappy although I have been unsure who I am, more and more as the days become years. Now in your book for two thousand dollars I have found myself, my whole life, in a woman's name. Repeated in celebration, long after she died."

I had no idea what she was talking about. I held my new treasure close to my chest as she walked to the balcony door, stepped outside and gazed across the river from our fifteenth storey vantage. Then as I followed her and began to speak she leaned forward into the air. It was a cool evening, I was born in November, and I breathed deeply and listened for the sound of her body on the lawn below and was disconcerted to hear nothing over the soft rumble of the river's flow.

I looked down on the brief activity as she was gathered up and carried away. No-one came to my door to investigate and I made no effort to volunteer information about a situation I did not understand. After a day I stopped trying to sort out what had happened and went to the city morgue where I claimed her body, identifying her as Mary Rush, originally of England, I imagined, and in spite of her street-weary appearance my closest friend in Ottawa. I had no explanation for the hand-written note addressed to Marshall McLuhan they found tucked up her sleeve. I arranged to have her buried with a stone inscribed as she wished. I'm not sure the Salvation Army had any idea as to the value of the books I donated and I think they probably discarded the older ones as not worth the effort. Sometimes I miss reading books, but there is enough print around me that I am not bereft. I miss Mary and what we might have been. I sometimes feel that I killed her, and sometimes that I set her free.

Reading to Borges

Observers would see parallel computer screens reflected in the lenses of my reading glasses if I were to look in their direction. This is misleading since if I had visitors I would not permit my computer to function; unless, conceivably but not likely, I did not notice being observed. With the light behind me, I can see myself mirrored on the surface of the screen. I perceive language through my own image, which due to the inverse perspective of mimesis seems to have depth the print lacks. This makes it easier to comprehend my place in the story while I am writing than if I were inscribing my text on a page.

With the instruments of modern technology print is no longer fixed but fluid, everything you write becomes narrative, you can dance with a word through a sentence, shift phrases, delete, save, write hidden texts. The act of composition is no longer a paradigm of the temporal continuum. Moreso than ever, you are part of the story, perhaps only in a matrix of syntactical tensions or perhaps in a parade of allusions, or even in the narrative construction of a personality much like your own. The story is yours but not you. You are so deeply embedded among the intricate designs of whatever you write, once the words have been set in place, no matter how busy the conversation among them, no matter how preoccupied they are with their own relationships, you could not escape if you wanted to. That is the paradox of writing; authentic as you become among words, you cannot slip away, you cannot write the self real in the world outside of the text.

This discourse, if it may be called that, might seem an oblique way to start something offered as an entertainment. My title should have served as a warning. You chose, after all, to read this because you had certain expectations. Perhaps you knew Borges was blind in his later years and Alberto Manguel, a Toronto writer, when he was a child in Argentina had the good fortune to read to him on a regular basis. That is the literal precedent for the gerundial allusion. Couple the act of reading with the notion of Borges and it is hard to resist the suspicion that something more could happen than has yet been imagined.

Reading aloud to someone is a curious anomaly. Imagine yourself reading to Borges. The voice you hear resonating in the shadows of the room, the shutters closed to keep the midday heat outside, is your own. The old man listens with an air of distraction. It is not you he is listening to, your voice against his eardrums has become another's, he hears the words themselves, the sound of language resonating through the corridors of his mind. You could stop reading and for a while he would not notice. The dust motes in the lamplight would cease swirling in the silence. The tendrils of hot sunlight that made their way through the louvered shutters stir restlessly on the Qashqa'i carpet. The dark odour of books and lemon oil distracts your vision, and for a few moments you see nothing. Then the old man stirs but does not ask you to continue. The text has been shelved in the endless passages of the infinite library through which he wanders at will in the brightness of memory.

When you read to yourself—which was, according to Alberto Manguel's celebration of literacy, *A History of Reading* (New York: Viking, 1996), a mental trick still rare when St. Augustine recorded his astonishment at an encounter with St. Ambrose, in about AD 383, wherein the latter's "eyes scanned the page and his heart sought out the meaning, but his voice was silent and his tongue was still" (p. 42)—you are imposing yourself within the text. Much more so than if you read aloud. The heart finds meaning that the voice, which must still the words for coherent transliteration into sound, cannot convey. Aloud, ambivalence and ambiguity are pinioned by the moment of their utterance, pinned specimens in a diorama within the listening mind. In quietude is the excitation of language most apparent, for as the eyes scan, as Augustine observed of Ambrose that day in Rome, words dance the quadrille, and simultaneously they rock and roll.

Only the boundaries of personality, the self that lives within the configurations of your own life, limit the possibilities of the silent text. As you draw out the words in your mind, you set them free from the stasis of print. In the chaos and clamour, the lovely disinclination of language to submit quietly to arbitrary design, come infinite evasions of meaning. That is the essential paradox of language: words alive in the mind move, not towards singularity but away from it, towards endless allusion. It is only the rational persona, the exterior mask, the shadow that is cast by the self in the temporal world, who forces them into conditional submission.

Imagine Borges reaching to the switch by the mantle, turning out the lights so that now you are both blind. Or imagine him rising from his leather chair beside the empty fireplace, walking into your voice, grasping the exposed nape of your neck with fingers like talons, and with the other hand swinging the reading lamp on its axis so that the glare fills your vision with shards of astonishing pain. You learn about silence. He cannot read to himself except from the books in his head. These, he has decided on this particular afternoon, are more than enough. You walk out into the wheeling subtropical sunlight, feeling unappreciated, perhaps dreaming of a Canadian winter.

The old man settles into the darkness of his leather chair, reaches to the wall and extinguishes the light or turns it on again; it is a rotary switch so he cannot be sure. Among the bright corridors of his private landscape a nearly forgotten excitement returns as he slides a dust-rimmed book from the shelves of his mind, opens it to the map that is folded inside. It is a map of gardens, the paths forking among flowers and low shrubs, smelling of blossoms and honey. Here between sunlight and shadows he contemplates the absolute red of a single hibiscus, tears of the morning not yet dry on its petals; perfect beauty that echoes a loved woman's passing and draws her to life. He is old and distracted; this wraith of a woman finds only his longing. He waits at an ocean, for all maps are oceans, but is lost between grief and the limitless shore. She recedes unrequited on currents of air so gentle he takes them to be his breath rising against the high planes of his cheek, and he drifts into dream, the book now abandoned, returned to the stacks, the map refolded, the scurried dust already fallen back into place.

Reading is not, to writing, an opposite, but rather, like the image in a mirror, a free-standing likeness utterly dependent on its antecedent, its every aspect in reverse.

Be wary of mirrors. In the reading room at the Borges apartment there is probably a large mirror over the mantle. It has a gold frame with rococo filigree and the gold is mellowed with age to a dull sheen. Sometimes the blind old man stands in front of the mirror, knowing his reflection is looking back at him. It is a curious sort of vicarious vision and amuses or depresses him, according to his mood. He turns this way and that, knowing the image follows suit, a bust cut off from his body because of the mirror's height on the wall. He reaches a hand forward and touches the glass surface where he imagines his eyes to be. He knows behind the glass the silvered plane that allows this illusion is aged far more than himself and inscribed with the delicate patina of innumerable seasons, more lined and transparent than his own sallow skin. And beyond is a shadowed room familiar to memory, a set within a shifting proscenium that changes as he moves this way and that, altering perspective. He knows he is among the shadows in the mirror with more certainty than that he is in the room itself. If I move away from the mirror, I will disappear, he thinks. It is like closing a book; if you return to it you will find yourself there, but closed, you are absent.

Who is this woman we have invented—we, for I may have slipped her into the discourse but you accepted her, you've been wondering about her as much as I have. We are in this together. Lewis Carroll had it right. We cannot follow Alice through the looking glass and be spectators at the same time. You do not observe the mirror, you enter it, a different world, its coherence controlled by perspectives outside, in the world you left behind. Lewis Carroll, Dodgson if you prefer, understood the conspiratorial nature of the writing-reading coalition and turned anarchy to art.

The woman in Borges' contemplation at the confluence of a map and an hibiscus in full bloom can be anything we want. Figure in a tragic romance, sad ghost of furtive passion, indefatigable souvenir of a love that never was. Real or imagined? And by whom? This Borges emerged full grown, an old man, from imperfect recollections of an icon being read to in a text by Alberto Manguel. A literary phenomenon. I have read much of Borges, his wondrously contrived fictions. How these have stayed with me, the remnants of bewilderment and delight, this has informed the Borges we now share with subtextual vitality, with soul. Myriad sources mostly forgotten, these give him an authentic presence in the world; a photograph in the 'People' section of *Time*, his name seeded carefully in a cultural happenings column of *Vogue*, or perhaps it was *Bazaar*, an obituary reference at the termination of some other life, the obsequies at his own, a critical discussion, his name adjectival. Perhaps a thousand times the name Borges entered my life, passed before my eyes, often while I was looking for something else, perhaps only diversion, sometimes. It is within his mind, this old man, such as we have made him, that the woman emerges, a fleeting reminder that our Borges was not always old, not always enigmatic in the labyrinthine shadows of a darkened room.

A person in the present moment is not the entire self. We do not live our lives but live within them, each of us a narrative under perpetual revision. In silent reading we are released from presence, from our habitual posture upon the surface of the surge of time. Through illimitable evasions of meaning within a given text, we encounter as fiction a more authentic version of ourselves. It is not the story, not the content, that contains us but the words, moving towards coherence and simultaneously resisting, words in the excitation of infinite potential, that set us free. Being there, we draw the little buggers into restive order, make them yield sufficiently to our needs. We do not read ourselves, but personality evoked makes reading possible.

So too with the writer. The writer as person, writing, is a momentary shell, carboniferous residue, fleshy carapace, visceral cerebrum, remnant of the authentic personality informing a work from the entirety of a lived-in life. Caught in the maelstrom of words and intent, the self as a fiction creates. Writing it down, whatever is written, does not make the words hold still, the language submissive. Rather, it fixes in script an opening or portal, inviting a reader to enter for a while, to share and endure the lovely inexhaustible storm.

Perhaps I am naked in a dry bathtub observing the passing world in a mirror, through an asylum window. You have only been told this now because I only now remembered. Although the concept originates in a novel by Robert Kroetsch, it is a direct steal from *The Studhorse Man*, it happens by coincidence to be my own situation.

Such is life, that it will hazard the absurd, sometimes replicating art with larcenous absence of originality. The truth of what I am telling you can be corroborated (Kroetsch, Robert. *The Studhorse Man.* Toronto: Macmillan, 1969; New York: Simon and Schuster, 1970, p. 45 *et passim*.). As a reader, you have accepted more implausible conceits without blushing.

A further coincidence is the Marat/Sade paradigm, which, while of peripheral interest, bears little on Kroetsch's fiction or on me. Marat's bath was brim-full of soapy water so that, when Charlotte Corday plunged her knife between his clavicle and jugular, opening holes in his body through which blood surged like steaming syrup to seek the level of the water, the crimson suds overflowed the tub's edge and gleamed in a spreading pool across the marble floor. And de Sade, of course, is no more pertinent than the bedraggled corpse of Marat, his writing censured as it was with such severity.

You might wonder where John Irving fits into the already crowded tub. In *Setting Free the Bears* (New York: Ballentine, 1968), if you can believe Irving, Hannes Graff lends territorial status to a bathtub as a locus of contemplation and interpretation. You begin to appreciate the problem. Carelessness about my condition in the world is not related to a sense of displacement, but rather to its relative ordinariness. The tub is full even without Archimedes, whose resounding expletive, Eureka, I quote to myself every time I step ashore. There are three men in the tub, an owl and a cat, and so much more. Digression is Borgesian.

I can imagine Robert Kroetsch amused at the multiple allusions. It is more difficult to imagine John Irving who remains an American although he lives in Toronto. As an American living in Toronto, Irving probably knows Alberto Manguel. Both have read de Sade, perhaps to each other, perhaps to themselves from a shared copy.

Perhaps they have never met, and yet they have de Sade in common. Kroetsch might smile at that, being familiar with de Sade himself. I have never actually read the Marquis de Sade apart from the Classic Comic abridgement when I was the same age as Manguel when he read to Borges. Perhaps he read de Sade to Borges from a hidebound copy, the smell of dried flowers slipping from the antique vellum to permeate the darkest corners of the room, echoing the garden patterns of the carpet undulating on the floor between them. You see how everything connects.

I forgot my situation for a very good reason. As I explained, I subscribe to the notion that writing, like reading in silence, allows the whole personality to engage in the act; it summons the presence of self. Outside the text your personal history is subject to the vagaries of memory. Among words, the chronology of your life falls in chaotic splendour out of sequence; the present moment, as you read or write, submits to priorities as evanescent as the stars on a perfect winter night. You know yourself out of time; and there, in the cosmos of your own personality, it is easy to forget, not the past but the present, to forget that you are sitting in an empty bathtub, buck naked, gazing periodically through a mirror that is poised like the moon overhead, to take in whatever your perspective allows.

My stints in the tub are limited by battery longevity. Even though the tub is dry, they will not let me plug in my computer. The electrical outlets are sealed in this room, to remove temptation. In order to recharge, I must go back to the bedroom which at present I share with no-one. To do this I must dress. They will not let me walk through the corridor unapparelled. It is a very short corridor but we are a co-ed institution. I could surround myself with yellow sheets from a legal note-pad or with three-by-five index cards, stapled carefully, but I do not use either, as such instruments make writing a public activity. My computer is private, the words hidden inside or instantly erased. Fortunately, the toilet and sink are in an adjoining room, accessed separately. I am not, in other words, forcing discomfort on others. When someone wants a bath, there is a polite knock on the door and I am asked temporarily to vacate my sanctum sanctorum. My insurance company pays a lot of money for such consideration.

If you have read aloud my use of the term 'buck naked,' the image no doubt seems raunchy, perhaps crude. If you read it to yourself, it probably came across as a revealing cliché, perhaps with a wry touch of bathos. Either way, it suggests that behind the pseudonym under which I write there is a nude male. It seems unlikely a woman would use the term buck to describe her nakedness. Unless, of course, purposely leading you astray is her narrative design. But that would imply intentionality that is beyond me, right now. You have to trust me on this. It is enough that I write and you read within a common field. The parrying of syntax and diction will create all the misdirection we can handle. We are not jousting but reaping. Neither of us needs arbitrary distractions, to be thrown like peelings of potter's clay askew from the turning wheel.

I would like to see the mathematician, whose claims to elegance thrill me with their naiveté, who could in a polyhedral universe approach the complexity of the elusive metaphors just dealt to us in the preceding sentences. There is nothing true about numbers beyond their intentional deployment. Insofar as they are beautiful there is no truth for they are simply projections of consciousness, ciphers of desire. As they are truth, absolute in their unyielding disposition, there is nothing beautiful. But among words, truth is beauty, beauty truth. So said the dying poet. He had access to the infinite and eternal, as time closed down his utterance, the brief cadence of his lovely verse.

Perhaps we share our madness, you and I. There is something like religious ecstasy in the madness of your encounter with your reading self, your personality or soul. Rather than evasions of language through ritual prayer, mantric perseveration, strategic glossolalia, mortification of obdurate flesh, you have chosen literal immersion. You have entered the text, been renewed each reading in a world that precedes you. Once, in infancy, you learned language, entered into consciousness through words. Now through words you enter the authentic self invoked by their eclectic promiscuities. This is madness, the natural madness of the reader, reading. Not assumed, like Hamlet's, mirroring to expose or to illuminate. Natural, like Lear's, where reason and emotion together lead to unexpected passions, sometimes folly, sometimes, poor Lear, to insanity. And sometimes to revelation—then is our madness comic, its pleasures manifold, manifest as we emerge.

Notice I differentiate between insanity and madness. As I sit sprawled against cool porcelain in this overheated room with its groaning radiator, pale green walls, and single-glazed window, for a moment my attention wanders. Why is there no storm window? It would not obtrude upon my vision which, as it is, in the coldest weather is obscured to the limit of opacity by layers of frost as steam from every bather rises in its turn, curls around the room, condenses to a fine mist against the glass and freezes, until, at last, an insulating thickness is achieved, at which point droplets gather and descend in crooked patterns to the window sill, where they pool, and then. And then. Of course I do not add to this pellucid residue, except at the brief time each day when I am compelled to wash. I would have baths of my own accord. I do not need instruction. But I like being told what to do. Then I can choose to do it or not. I always do, but the choice is mine.

Mine is a fine madness. I pity the insane. I have taken up the dialogue of self and soul with indiscriminate enthusiasm. It is an excellent pursuit. The Irish poet whose joys and fears and irritation at his own mortality, set down in verse, convert the austere spirit into something beautiful—I refer to Yeats, but you knew that, recognizing the aforesaid dialogue as the title of one of his poems, just as you recognized the beauty/truth truth/beauty line from Keats; I assume your level of literary acumen by the fact that you have read this far; we are both snobs of a sort, drawing pleasure in dropping, or in your case, picking up, literary allusions—Yeats, then, was less inclined than I to see the self and soul as mirror images of one another. From the perspective of either, the other is a reflection, a disembodied emanation. Both are real. Only the mirror is illusion. Sitting in a dry tub, contemplating my laptop screen, occasionally glancing at the outside world hovering overhead, or down at my genital region which, with the computer in place, refuses to reveal my sex, I have equal access to both. Remove the mirror and they are the same, the self and soul, a single entity.

In the shadows of his room, darker in contrast to the strands of midday light against the antique carpet, white strands on indigo and madder red, Borges is annoyed at himself for sending away the boy who was reading to him. Alberto Manguel. Borges has been thinking much of death in recent days and on this particular day it seems incongruously both a doorway and an intrusion. Tomorrow it will be a place where the idea of place is no longer possible, an activity in which all activities cease. It is a game, the contemplation of death, in which the rules implied by precedent have no meaning. What he knows of other deaths is only of dying, or as a metaphor. About death itself there is nothing written. Riffling through the bibliography of his mind, the capacious planes and endless passageways, he cannot find a single reference to death as a condition. As the afternoon proceeds, an arrow of sunlight plunges slowly up the entire length of his body. When it reaches his face he stirs as blood rises to the warmth on his cheek. He contemplates the carpet which is now in complete shadow so that time-set colours are muted and the small details obscured, although the design he cannot see is strong, even in the dying light.

In that carpet a century ago a Qashqa'i woman tied knots innumerable like the moments of her life. Medallion and spandrels, borders and field, these were determined by ancient habits of her tribe, just as the major events of her life from birth, through maidenhood and marriage, motherhood, old age, and death, all played out within the confines of established ritual. In the comings and goings of nomadic existence, structure is necessary to maintain continuity. Here and there, when there is time, she will unroll her rug, set up the horizontal frame outside her newest home, then draw from skeins of dyed wool dazzling strands of colour, each choice deliberate and spontaneous, and tie one after another to the separated warps before drawing a new weft, at intervals determined by the carpet's width, firmly into place. The palette is her own. The integrity of the knots is hers. The small figures she allows to enter, whimsically or with much thought, some geometric, descended from dragons and birds, flowers and trees, some merely the play of imperfection on implied symmetry, some wry allusions to her private world, coy revelations of her fantasies, these assume their places in the field. Generations later, you recognize her people in the over-all design; you see this unknown woman's soul in the details.

Borges thought of this. In his blindness he could see and share her separate universe with exhilarating clarity. He drew himself forward in his leather chair, slipped down onto his knees, and slowly the old man unfolded lengthwise along the carpet. Its close-worn pile thrust myriad bytes of colour against his face and fingers, like a play of signatures in braille. Eventually he succumbed to a profound and perfect sleep. Myself, I marvel that I can see the carpet and Borges and my computer screen all at the same time. If I look up, I can see a Home Hardware calendar on the wall. The picture above the block of numbers is an hibiscus, with light falling on it preternaturally from all directions. With mathematical rectitude the numbers lined up below 'Tuesday' read: 2, 9, 16, and 23. Since 30 does not conclude the column, I infer it must be February even though the month itself is obscured by the glare of the recessed ceiling-light. The flower is a form of denial. So much for arithmetic and the perfection of numbers. I once owned the Borges rug, on which I have allowed him to expire.

Not dead, he is merely resting. Alberto Manguel has yet to grow to manhood, Toronto is not yet in his future; by any small act whatsoever its inevitability could be voided. He will read again to Borges. He will emigrate to Canada. Borges will die in time, on October 31, 1986. He only passed away for us because I release him from our fiction. I have the power to do that, and you, the power to let him go. We work together, you and I. Why does my computer screen go darker when I first boot up, then light? I can risk asking you, I feel we are that close. Given the option of staying with me, naked in an empty porcelain tub with lions-claw feet settled deeply into gouged linoleum, or remaining with Borges, reading to the old man while he wanders through the labyrinth your spoken words invoke, would seem to leave you caught between two stools. Yet you have chosen to continue, chosen me. I am flattered by your madness. I feel the heavy weight of narrative responsibility.

My keepers sometimes try to see what I am writing. There is no lock on the door—not because this is an ancient edifice that once had more dignified business than housing pampered emotional pariahs like myself, and had no need of locks, but because we cannot be trusted on our own, for fear of masturbation or suicide. I therefore keep a towel draped on the side of the tub to cover, on the rare intrusion, not my nakedness but the computer screen. Generally there is time to scramble my words into a code I devised for the purpose, which may be invoked on the depression of the bitten-apple key and one other, in quick succession. At worst, I delete all. As I have not uttered a word in public since entering this institution, the assumption among the staff is that I write gibberish. There is nothing wrong with my hearing.

When no-one is around, I sometimes read aloud from my own text for the sensory experience. When you read to yourself, perception and memory are simultaneous. When you read out loud, you see words unreel before your eyes, listen to their sounds, process the cadence of their syntax, the melodies of diction. Later, you remember reading more than what you read; if your parents read to you when you were a child as mine did, you remember the rooms, the affection, the resonance of voices. In contrast, what stays with you from silent reading may sometimes in retrospect seem more authentic than the inchoate flutterings in memory of actual events.

Let me try to explain silence. It is the condition of our meeting: I, a sad man writing, wandering through sentences like a convict on parole, and you, my solitary companion. There is quietude in our conjunction that reverberates with more clarity than choirs of noisy angels, as our souls play. You are not Sancho to my doleful Don, astride his Rocinante rocking-horse. You are not a straggler, sycophant, or acolyte. Perhaps if you committed literary criticism and conversed openly about our mutual adventure, you might be. But in the silence we share among configurations of words as they are, we are equally authentic personalities, each a reflection of the other, while, perhaps, only the mirror between us, the text, is real.

Let me explain silence again, and address you as my lover. Let us succumb to poetic devices. I am filled with longing, as the morning mist is rising and the perfect day is dawning, for the stars and wheeling galaxies that are dying in the light. You were yesterday in mountains by the brittle waters dreaming and I was drifting downwards, caressed by drowning asters in the phosphorescent night. On the road that we are travelling, while the flowers by the gutter, flung by careless tourists in an endless stream of colour, are littering the snow, I am cast among the mountains by the surging waters dreaming, and the night I yearn is thronging with the light of rushing torrents that I will never know.

You must recognize from the rhythm, dear lover, silence is my only option. That was romantic contrivance, a road poem filled with private meaning. I wanted you to find pathos in the obscurity of my allusions, to love me for my aesthetic sensibility. I am afraid of losing you, I therefore hide. It is a common practice.

The truth is, I speak to no-one, here. Sometimes volunteers read to me, usually on public holidays. I am polite and accommodate them with an appropriate air of distraction. This allows fulfillment of their missions more than if I attended to them carefully. There is satisfaction in offering a crust of bread to a starving idiot, I think, not found, sharing a feast with a philosopher. I listen, but do not appear to hear, thus pleasing both the readers and myself.

I learned silence the way some people learn to throw pots, as a form of therapy. There was not a singular trauma. It came to this. I once had seven children whom I loved deeply, one for every day of the week, for every circle of being, and when they were grown up I needed them to listen, but they would not hear, not because they did not love me but because they loved another with more urgency and desperation. The details are unimportant. When I tried to explain, there was no room for words to displace the pain that filled my children's lives. They attempted not to understand. Words that penetrated the barriers of their anger were discarded, like spent bullet casings. I considered suicide—how could they resist my truth in a letter of absolute good-bye. I spoke righteously, then softly. I wrote in solitude. And when my offspring would not receive my words, there seemed nothing more to say.

After a while I found myself here. It is a nice place. I like the food. My room, despite the soporific wallpaper, is pleasant. I am treated with considerable dignity. No-one is concerned with details. The bathroom is my sanctuary. The shaving mirror extended on a metal arm above the tub lets me observe the world I left behind. My computer, a Macintosh Powerbook 180, gives me access to another world, transcendent, if you will, the only one I now desire. If Borges had his endless corridors of books and could find the spent time of his life redeemed among their illimitable announciations, I can plunge through the screen before me and discover, awaiting my arrival, words in furious anticipation, prepared to slip the bonds of ordinary usage and build with me whatever wonders we together can contrive. Here I have discovered or per-haps recovered my spiritual self, my authentic personality or soul. It is a secular thing, and not immortal. But it is very nice to have, to be.

I want to thank you for bearing with me through this, you the perfect reader whom every writer most desires. I have left, turned out the lights, shut off the power. You have decoded everything. It is your story. If I cannot give my progeny the words of my life, if they will not receive my truth, then, finally, only silence is enough. In the mirror world beyond the screen, there is nothing that can happen that has not already happened, nothing as our spirits merge you cannot imagine or conceive. I wish my ashes scattered in the asylum garden, thrown at random among the forking paths. As for yourself, beloved reader, I wish you well.

Signals from Elsewhere

Some lives are irrevocably changed by an act of good fortune and some are hardly touched by good fortune at all. When Sarah James won $78,000,000 in a lottery she resolutely determined that she was to be among the latter. Instant wealth and the sudden fame that was bound to come with it were so unexpected the shock effectively closed down her horizons so that all she wanted to do was sustain being the person she had been up until now. At her first press conference she announced that there would be no difference in her life. She planned to buy a car and a house for her parents, who had always lived in rental units, and for her siblings, both of whom were underemployed at the moment. She planned to buy a house and a car for herself. But she would go on living exactly as she always had. Perhaps she would lose some weight. Otherwise, she was pretty much as she wanted to be.

Sarah worked in a shopping mall. Twenty-seven years old and she had been a clerk at five different stores but always in the same mall. She was never fired from a job but one thing or another, seasonal fluctuations in staff requirements, the trickle-down effect of corporate mergers, displacement by a relative of the store manager, meant that Sarah thought of the mall as her employer rather than the individual stores. Over the last decade The Country Heritage Shopping Centre had displaced her parent's house as her home, as her benefactor, as the centre of her life. She had become attached to the mall and dependent on it for her emotional as well as financial well-being. Lunch in The Food Court was the most important meal of her day.

Sarah James was a covert reader. She sometimes read

45

poetry, mostly in anthologies. Usually she read novels. She never took a book to work, to read on her breaks. None of her friends at the mall read books. No-one she knew was a reader. She read secretly. It seemed to her something a person did in private, like going to the toilet. She thought of the branch library near her parent's house as a sort of communal bathroom, where everyone moved around in relative silence and pretended not to hear the noises made by others, and settled into cubicles and carrels or in quiet corners to pursue their own business. She never read in the library; she timed her excretory functions to be performed before and after work in the family bathroom at her parent's house. Peeing was more casual, like browsing through the tabloids; she did it as required in the public restroom at the mall—until recently, poised above the seat. This was something that had become harder to do as she gradually accumulated weight over the last decade and lately she had taken to sitting on her hands, then washing them thoroughly afterwards. As her friend Emily said, it's easier to wash your hands than your bottom. Emily read the tabloids as serious literature, sometimes trying to engage the others at their table in esoteric chatter on the collapsing in trash journalism of distinctions between fact and invention. Emily chose not to read books on principle. She used to, she said. Reading was for people who worked in offices and for teachers, people who could afford not to be engaged in real life.

The closest Sarah ever got to having a literary conversation was in The Food Court when she and Emily were waiting for the Cineplex to open. Emily said she was named for Emily Dickinson. Sarah said she was named for Henry James. Emily, sensing a joke had been made, smiled enigmatically. I love Emily Dickinson, she said. I read everything she wrote, she said, before I stopped reading. If you've read one Emily Dickinson, you've read them all. Frivolous people read novels, she said. Sarah looked carefully at Emily for some indication of how she was meant to respond. Sometimes Emily's smile was inscrutable. In slow stages Sarah grew restive. She had thought Emily Dickinson wrote poetry. She was certain she had read everything published under the name of Emily Dickinson. Perhaps her novels appeared under a pseudonym. That is the kind of thing this Emily would know. Sarah was uncomfortable in the silence, not being able to hold up her end of the conversation, and grateful that Emily let the subject drop.

Sarah suspected there were other secret readers among the people she knew. Not long ago at The Food Court she became mildly flustered after dropping the name Jane Austen into a conversation about the breakup of Brad Pitt and Gwyneth Paltrow, but no-one winced or looked confused. As she recovered her composure she thought the lack of response a tribute to the educational system, although some of her lunch companions had not been to school for decades. She then considered how smug she was, to assume she had overextended the boundaries of polite discourse. She spent the rest of her lunch break on her own, apparently window-shopping, in reality observing the mall itself, contemplating the nuances of architectural confectionery reflected in the glass. Here was marble for the masses, an effusion of materials and detail far beyond the domestic experience of its patrons, an infusion in the ordinary lives of shoppers and mall personnel of opulence not unlike the cathedrals of Europe she had never seen but thought of, for the most part, as extravagant grotesqueries taken over time to be icons of good taste.

Sarah never bought lottery tickets. She had books to nurture daydreams. From what she observed it was mostly people of restricted imagination who enriched their lives with the uncomplicated fantasy of spontaneous wealth, who poured money into the statistical vacuum, and who seemed to be rewarded vicariously no matter who won. It was always someone just like themselves. Sarah did not daydream of wealth but after buying a ticket she was surprised to discover herself entertaining in off-moments the alternative lives it could buy her. She did not really think of herself as leading those lives, but rather of reading them, of being comfortably ensconced in her bedroom, observing them from a comfortable distance being written expressly for her. To think of herself as a witness, to project her own being, such as it was, among words, this was as far as she allowed fancy to carry her.

She did not recall seeing anyone buying a lottery ticket and a newspaper at the same time. Usually, it was a lottery ticket and a carton of cigarettes. When Emily insisted she get with the game, the jackpot was so large it was positively sprawling, Sarah pointed out the odds were no better, in fact worse, since so many people were going after the big one. It was as if the regular payoff of ten million or so were not incentive enough for the daydreaming poor, but now the jackpot was really worthwhile. Emily, who bought one ticket a week on principal, showed her how to let the computer pick her number. Since computers selected the winner, it seemed best not to intrude on their internecine negotiations.

While Sarah took modest pride in her own imagination, nurtured as it was by the range and depth of her reading, nothing ever showed in her behavior to suggest her mind sometimes wandered into exotic realms beyond anything she had experienced in Preston. Sometimes while she was reading in bed, propped up with pillows on top of the covers in late summer, she would take a peach selected for its resilient ripeness in one hand, the book in the other, and gently roll the peach across her bared stomach, sometimes as she read allowing it to roll up under her pajama top and around her breasts so that the fuzz nipped against her skin until eventually in distraction she would put down her book, bite into the swollen flesh of the peach, devour it, placing the stone carefully in a tissue on her bedside table and without brushing her teeth would turn out the lights and will herself to sleep and to dream. In winter, she would sometimes remove her top before trying to sleep because the flannel sheets against her nipples reminded her of summer and peaches.

Sarah felt no guilt about what she recognized as a mild eccentricity, nor did she ever feel inclined to experiment further. She was happy enough to observe lovers in books and to awaken some mornings exhausted with the exhilaration still swarming within of having made love through much of the night. Sarah had never learned to be inquisitive but she was never bored. If her mind occasionally threatened to fill with emptiness she would immediately turn to a book that she had already read, to be in familiar territory, filled with excitement at knowing what events lay ahead in the characters' lives. She learned to read Emily Dickinson when she was sad, as occasionally she was. Her inexplicable encounters with sadness were usually turned into pleasure by reading only a few lines and finding herself distracted by the profound simplicity of Dickinson's style.

Sarah was reading in her room when Emily called to tell her to switch on the draw. Sarah was in the middle of a time-travel book about a contemporary Englishwoman with American tendencies who was anxiously awaiting word of her husband's fate at the battle of Culloden that was raging in the background, this being a different husband from the one she left behind in present-day England who had by now presumed her dead and was on the brink of marriage to another woman who might or might not be a descendent of his wife's offspring born in the eighteenth century lowlands of confusing paternity, he being one of the two possibilities. It was not Jane Austen but was good reading, at least as plausible and equally engaging. Sarah

turned on the television to appease Emily and had returned to her book when Emily called back. I think I have
the same numbers, Sarah told her. Emily, who was younger and on principle never swore, said no shit. I think so,
she said. I didn't write them down.

Waiting for Emily to call back again after she checked
with the television station, Sarah James looked wistfully
around her room. She did not want to be a winner. She
liked the chintz chaircover and the floral bedspread and
the swollen folds of the matching curtains with their effer-
vescent flounce across the top that had been there all her
life and the renaissance etchings on the walls and the
hooked rug her sister had made in therapy and the bedside
table her brother had manufactured in machine-shop
before his accident. She liked things the way they were.
She did not want the phone to ring, she wanted to read, to
be in Scotland and to discover the outcome of the battle at
Culloden, hoping against all common sense that things
would work out for the better. Later that night she wrote
out a post-dated check to Emily for one million dollars.
She imagined that would be enough. In the morning she
crossed out the one and wrote five.

I regret interrupting the narrative flow but I do not
think I can go on. Emily is beginning to interest me more
than Sarah. I lifted Sarah from an incomplete novel, a
project I abandoned several years ago. The original Sarah
was nothing at all like this one. She was an inmate at the
Prison for Women in Kingston. She was serving hard time
for killing her infant daughter, even though it was inad-
vertent, to protect her from a brutal husband-father whom
she murdered wilfully although not with premeditation.
This Sarah James would skip out on a day pass and return
to Toronto where she was convicted, disguised as a man,
and there she would secure a job as gardener-chauffeur to
the judge who had sent her to prison. She would become
close to the judge in spite of herself and he, a widower,

would be tormented by the inappropriate longing he felt toward her, who he thought was a young man, and when he died she would become friends with his estranged lesbian daughter, with whom she becomes intimate. Their friends think they are a straight couple but peculiar. Two thugs, both young lawyers, hang around with them, drawn to the deceased judge's residual influence. The three men bond; that is, Sarah as a male and the two men bond. One night at the judge's cottage in Muskoka the four of them drink too much. When one of the lawyers makes a pass at the judge's daughter, she reveals she is a lesbian. The two men are excited by the revelation but humiliated by their gullibility. They make abusive advances. Sarah intervenes. Compromising her masculinity to protect the judge's lesbian daughter, whose name is Emily, Sarah denies they have ever been intimate. Enraged by apparent betrayal, Emily proclaims Sarah's sex. The two men beat Emily into unconsciousness, beat and rape and murder Sarah. Emily expires. I could not decide whether to end with a police car pulling up behind the cottage, having been summoned by neighbours in response to the screams, or to have the men leave, return to Toronto, and read in the paper the next morning of the brutal suicide-murder of quarrelling lesbian lovers in the heart of cottage country.

My new Sarah is not as thematically complex and this Emily has little in common with the judge's daughter. Yet both originate in the earlier narrative. You would not have known this if I had not told you. Have you ever wondered how often this happens? You think you understand a character because you can comprehend her, see around the edges, when really there may be hidden within her alternative worlds, life stories, that are accessible only to the writer in moments of introspective candour. Of course, I hold with the critical dictum that the writer is not in a position of privilege in relation to his or her text. I

have learned never to trust writers. But just the same, they
know about what they resisted. Sometimes, when you
read Emily Dickinson, you suspect what she did not write
is as important as what she did.

Sarah James has the opportunity to reinvent herself,
but does she have the incentive? Does she have the imagination and desire? She has not been unhappy. Why
should she descend into the world, abandon the style
which defines her life, austere as it may seem, for the sake
of change. But change is inevitable. At a series of press
conferences the lottery people flaunt her ordinariness. But
whatever she is, she is not ordinary. Having $78,000,000
in the bank, or the residue after taxes which amounts to
just over $50,000,000, makes her unique. She has never
met a millionaire. She has read about rich people, but she
no more relates to their wealth than to the conditions of
their lives, being urbanites or adventuresome or sexually
insatiable. They are imaginary, even the ones photographed in *People* and *Vogue,* and she is not imaginary;
and yet, oddly, their world seems more real than her own.
Preston, she thinks, with franchises and chain-store outlets, at the intersection of numbered highways, the random interceptor of signals from elsewhere, is disengaged
from geography and history, from space and from time. It
is a floating island in a sea without shores.

When Emily took the cheque with a dramatic show of
disappointment, Sarah recognized that she had moved into
a realm of reality previously inaccessible. Emily said, I
practically bought the ticket for you, and Sarah immediately told her she could have half, after taxes. Emily said
thank you and accepted the money but they were no longer friends. They had been close and always considered
themselves alike, both of them accepting that Emily was
slightly superior, but now they were very different, each
was rich in her own way.

In less than a month after her windfall, Sarah was

fired in a most kindly manner. Managers at the other shops were equally pleasant in telling her they did not need anyone at present, but they would keep her in mind. Even The Hosiery Store with the sign in the window advertising help-wanted had nothing. Her brother was too busy driving his new car to offer much consolation and her sister was emotionally committed to salving her newest boyfriend's wounded ego, with whom she had bought her new house as tenants in common. Her parents could not get past effusions of pride to be of much help. On receiving a cheque for her share, Emily had faded like the Cheshire cat so that all that remained of their relationship was an incredulous grin as she scurried off in opposite directions. In a world that suddenly seemed imponderable and restricted, Sarah needed a role-model. She drew forward from abandoned files in her mind the stories of women with whom she had once been enthralled, mostly fictional. Unfortunately, Emma Bovary and Anna Karenin and Catherine Earnshaw and Amelia Earhart did not offer lives to be emulated. Sarah retreated with a six-quart basket of peaches to her room in her parents' house, which she had bought from their landlord at fair market value along with all the familiar furniture and appliances; they had already moved to Bluejay Crescent. Nothing in their new house was more than a month old.

At present Sarah does not recognize why she is toying with a series of peaches, distractedly recalling her impressions of the women she has met among words, all of whom seem more real than anyone she actually knows. As an inmate of the P4W Sarah James did not have the same needs. She was fiercely self-reliant, in the end a battered victim of her refusal to submit. To what? To the boundaries of gender and class, to the vagaries of fate and the vicissitudes of circumstance, to changes in her life not the result of her own personality. This Sarah knows that Sarah, although so deep within she is inaccessible except as a vague feeling of suppressed and directionless envy.

Jane, she thought. Jane Eyre. Jane Austen heroines. Yes, there are women who do not die broken-hearted. But proof of their worth seems always in marriage. Sarah had never had a boyfriend. Once, after her good fortune, she went out on a date with the manager of a donut shop. They drove to the municipal boundary, an imaginary line through the litter of pressed-plastic storefronts and parking lots and neon, a line indicated only by a sign to which had been appended a smaller sign which read, "Home of Sarah James ($78,000,000)." The sign indicating it was The Home of the Three-Time Peewee Regional All-Stars had been removed. From his satisfied smile, Sarah knew her date was instrumental through his role on the executive of the Junior Chamber of Commerce in having the sign changed. He had been an All-Star in his day and she appreciated the extent of his sacrifice. Nevertheless, she asked him to take her home and once inside her empty house she cried and for the first time in her life she was desolate with fear of the world and loathing for herself.

Sarah decided to organize her days. She missed who she was but that person was irretrievably gone. She knew she would have to become someone else. In the mornings she read, trying to find someone to be. In the afternoons she went to The Workout Club in the basement of The Country Heritage Shopping Centre. When she would pass former colleagues on the way in or out, they would either ostentatiously ignore her or flash covert smiles and then turn away. She had already lost weight and in six months she plummeted from a size sixteen to a size ten. In the evenings she rented videos. For a while she could not decide whether to be Thelma or Louise. She was growing to look more like Susan Sarandon although felt more like Geena Davis. But she realized a freeze-frame suspension of narrative over the Grand Canyon was an inept paradigm for seizing hold of one's life. There was always gravity; once you entered the flow of time there was always the gaping of space below. Susan and Geena might grow old but Louise and Thelma were dead.

As she gradually turned beautiful, Sarah assembled a new wardrobe by catalogue. At first she bought transitional clothes. Catalogues poured in through her mail slot. She bought exciting clothes. She bought a conservative sweater set from Victoria's Secret. Then she bought raunchy underwear. She looked at herself in the mirror, wearing the underwear from Victoria's Secret, and she became vain, and in all innocence loved her own vanity. At the end of a year she stopped looking for herself in the women she read about and started looking at the men who loved them. She stopped eating peaches and bought a vibrator by mail-order. It was uncomfortable and she donated it anonymously, in the dead of night through a drop-off box, to the Salvation Army. She bought a dozen more vibrators and donated them as well. It occurred to her this was something Emily might have done. But Emily was dead.

I do not want to tell Emily's story. I want to displace it with Sarah's. Emily as the judge's lesbian daughter was an interesting foil for Sarah, whose life and tragic death were redolent with thematic possibilities. Emily was a device, but not intrinsically engaging. You were appalled when she was beaten, but when Sarah died you felt yourself under attack, you experienced the horror firsthand. This Sarah is not so immediate, but as she becomes more and more authentic in her own eyes, she takes on a palpable presence that you, or at least I, would find hard to deny. She does not grieve for Emily, she has already done that, but she pities her. Emily does not die because she deserves death as punishment for the way she treated Sarah. She dies because the same arbitrary principles on which she stood to claim a share of Sarah's windfall led her to spend stupidly and die from an overdose of a drug she had never even heard of before their good fortune.

Sarah was puzzled when she read that Emily had died, but she was not surprised when she read in the paper that a massive legal battle was under way concerning the dispersal of her estate. Sarah decided to leave Preston. She sent for travel brochures. Soon her living-room was alive with pictures of frolicking couples in every corner of the world, on the slopes of the Himalayas, under the waters of the Galapagos, on the various beaches of Club-Med, in the cathedrals of Europe, the small streets and markets of ancient villages. Among them, inadvertently, a brochure appeared for a university not far away. She could get in as a mature student. She could afford the tuition. She had read many of the books prescribed by the syllabus. I would like to talk about them, she thought. On the front of the brochure there was a photograph of a woman not unlike herself, wearing a sweater-set from Victoria's Secret. She was holding in her hand a worn copy of Emily Dickinson. In the background were buildings and trees. People were walking about, although in the photograph they seemed still. I will begin my travels there, she thought. She was already beginning to fall in love.

Temagami

Whenever I am in Temagami I think of murder. Not abstractly, and not with pathological intent. It just seems to me that if I were going to murder someone, this would be the place to do it. When I round the corner on the highway driving north and first catch a glimpse of the town-site opening ahead of me—rising from the shore with roadways and buildings set in angular response to the primordial lay of the rocks and the water—my mind immediately turns to the disposal of bodies, the choosing of lethal devices, the selection of an unsympathetic victim. At my present age, I am not likely to kill anyone; it is enough to cope with my own precarious mortality. But I am a writer of fictions. If I were going to write about murder, this is where I would set my story.

Nothing in my life prepared me for getting old. It was inconceivable to me at twenty that I would ever be sixty, just as it is inconceivable now that the world will not be appalled at my death. Facts we know with certainty often remain unreal. That is the difference between true and the truth. It is true I will die; but the truth is I cannot imagine my absence. I can envision a world without me in it, but it is only imaginary, a projection of my own mind. If I were not here, it would collapse into nothing. And therefore I write. To make the world real.

Perhaps only now, while there is still time in my life, has the desire to shape the world into being achieved such urgency. Perhaps only in Temagami do I associate place so strongly with murder, where intimations of mortality first entered my mind when I would struggle against sleep as a child on our rocky one-acre island, in a tent pitched over a soft patch known as 'the Englishman's grave.' If my brother left to go into the cabin or into the shadows for a nocturnal pee, I could feel the corpse beneath me drawing me downwards into the dark mossy earth. This was the only spot on the entire island where the soil had depth and it took on a sinister character when my father refused to dig the hole for the new outhouse there. That was his way of honouring the story that passed like a rumour from his own father to him before I was born that this was a place of interment. Instead, the outhouse was straddled across a small crevasse on the far side of the island with a spectacular view through the open door down the northeast arm.

Even when Richard and I were very young we would drive the kicker into Temagami for groceries on our own. We would land at Ernie Smith's and take our list to Doughtie's Store, then walk to The Store of Little Things for popsicles, circle back to pick up our groceries and ice, then drink glasses of well-water which Mrs. Smith would have waiting for us, along with a smile that she would hold effortlessly and without words the whole time we were there. Then we would climb back into the five-horse outboard for the long trip home. Richard would drive; he was older. I would sit up against the half-deck at the front and watch for shoals.

One summer, when we arrived from the south and scrambled out of the car which we parked beside the canoe-works shed at the Smith's, Richard and I listened while Ernie told Mom and Dad that we would have to buy our groceries somewhere else this year. Mr. Doughtie had killed Mrs. Doughtie and Mrs. Doughtie's mother. He had set fire to the house and then shot himself through the head; and the fire had smouldered for days before they were found, the three of them smoked dry like pemmican. Mrs. Smith served us cool drinks of well-water on the front porch overlooking the dock where the kicker was gassed and ready to carry us with our new baby brother down to island 108. We never had a name for the island other than its registry number, although Ernie and my grandfather, Austin, and his friend, Archie Belaney, and a man from the States had built our cabin two generations before and it was teeming with stories through our childhood, until Mom and Dad sold it in the mid-fifties and bought a sailboat on Lake Ontario which could be moved from place to place on a whim and the wind.

Old as I am, as the narrative voice I can be as young as I wish. When the Doughties died I was six or seven. Since Steve was a baby I must have been six. The melodrama of their deaths seemed awesome and exciting at the time, overheard on the Smiths' porch. I could see through the trees the roof of the house next door where it happened. I could not imagine anyone else living there again, with the smell of smoked flesh embedded in the walls, but another family moved in. From that summer on, no matter who was living in the Doughties'old house, it always looked empty to me, as if the gravity of past events had more weight in my mind than the present. The summer I returned with my own children, after an absence of years, to see if the Smiths were still there, the Doughties' house was gone. It had burned to the ground the previous winter with no-one inside. Mrs. Smith, I was told, had died, and Ernie had retired from making canoes to live in a small house down the highway. When we found him I introduced my children but Ernie spoke only Ojibway by then so we left after a few minutes and proceeded on the canoe trip that had brought us there.

Every story must have a setting. Today I am in Temagami. I write that down and the fact becomes fiction, a truth to which you accede by narrative convention—you, by convention, lending your life to the text to affirm its veracity. The story at this point is simple; it is about me in Temagami contemplating murder. But nothing has happened. I have established a location in your rational mind, but probably not yet in your imagination. I have indicated a temporal context—today—although it will always be today in my text, so time is elusive. I have seeded your curiosity, perhaps, with a passing reference to Archie Belaney, a name which gained much prominence years later when it was associated with the man who became famous as Grey Owl. I have suggested emotional conflict, my concern about age; I have shared my implicit intention to ground consciousness in the world through language, simply by acknowledging your presence in my discourse. Of greater significance to us both, I have proclaimed my desire to make the world authentic through fiction.

If you are offended by solipsism, consider: it is the poets and painters who shape where you live. As you look out the window in northern Ontario you see tall pines, the cedars and birch, articulated by Tom Thompson, as surely as crystal on linen is ordered in your mind by Vermeer, sunflowers by Van Gogh. The equations proliferate. Do you remember that evening you spent drinking red wine by lamplight on Piazza San Marco, or is it the geometric precision of Canelletto you recall? The first time you visited England, sitting on a train sliding through English countryside, the windows framed Constable landscapes. When you went to the Arctic and each time you return, you see echoed the paintings of Lawren Harris and Doris McCarthy, Tony Onley and David Blackwood, and you wonder what Americans see.

Before you dissent, proclaiming yours to be an untutored sensibility, pristine or unpractised, consider: painting, like grammar, brings a random vocabulary to order. The fact that you do not know parts of speech, cannot parse a sentence, does not mean you do not speak words that Shakespeare spoke, contemplate thoughts that Milton wrote. Print and paint have etched in your mind deep structures of aesthetic response; you only see what has already been seen.

From the perspective of Temagami I realize my life has

increasingly become a struggle to keep on the surface of time, without flying off into dream. At an age when memory so often distracts from experience, no place seems more than a projection of my own personality. The world has become a protean concept, its myriad forms in my mind more substantial than my present location. That is how I know I am old: places from the past seem more real than the present. That is what Temagami has made me realize, because Temagami is the one place in my life where time is ephemeral, flowing by me like mist on a wind, while I remain constant, as inseparable from the land as an inlet or a promontory. Place here is the constant, and time is unreal. In such a setting, murder seems possible, although my choice of a victim, even in fiction, from this point seems arbitrary. It is like going to sleep and no matter what you intend to dream, the dream will determine what's dreamed on its own.

Let me sum up, for summations should never be left to the end. Those versed in such things may find echoes here of Husserl and Heidegger, Saussure perhaps, and Wittgenstein, and even Derrida. For the rest of us, more comfortable in the libraries of our minds among volumes less weighty than those that the vestiges of these men inhabit, all of them but Derrida being presently deceased, I will attempt clarification

Temagami, the lands of the Tema-Augami Anishnabai, is so much a part of my sense of self, when I am among the lakes and rocks and trees I am most truly at home with my mortal condition, a creature of consciousness inseparable from the immediate world around me; and when I am away from the bush, the vital waters, the outcroppings of stone in the sunlight, I return to their configurations as landscape in my mind to locate myself where time and space merge, the one place in the world I am real.

Temagami is without boundaries or limits, although maps may put edges on it, which land-claims dispute. It is seen by outsiders as empty, although there is not a trail through bush, a route over water, a cliff-side vista, that has not been experienced by humans for thousands of years. Temagami is vast and intimate; I can travel its terrain for months on foot or by canoe and always, the tree I lean against to ease my burden, the lake I cross to make my way, the rocks I shift to set my tent, are so familiar, I seem to be their holy emanation, not they projections of my personality as humanists would have it.

Descartes founded all knowledge on the immodest premise that consciousness is proof of existence, a proposition not unlike my own declaration to write the world into being. I designate Temagami as the place where objective reality and I, as its human witness, converge. Temagami transcends my own life or my death. Some places precede us in the world, and others only exist as we become aware of their presence. Think of an English manor house and Agatha Christie. Think of Tombstone and the Okay Corral. Think of a tall ship caught fast in Arctic ice. Death, whether as diversion, as American melodrama, as the force of indomitable nature, imposes on the imagining mind a powerful sense of place. Certain settings anticipate our discovery of the deaths that occur in their midst. Then by the efficacious logic of a well-turned corollary, a place that is most splendidly real invites the contemplation of death, as the human activity that most engages individual consciousness with the implications of being alive.

Nothing affirms our authentic being in the world like a reminder of mortality, and nothing reassures us so much as confrontations with death contained within narrative design such as we find in a well-wrought story of murder, mythic violence, or the indifference of nature to the vainglorious aspirations of human endeavour. If I write about murder in Temagami, I had better do more than describe the eruption of the Doughties' domestic dispute—even when offered from the oblique perspective of a child, it seems a violation of privacy to give the terrible fate of those people a context of fiction that might place their suffering within a spectrum of understandable behaviour.

Domestic violence does not necessarily make good fiction. That is true, but of course King Lear is a domestic tragedy. Much fiction originates in or reveals family life —what makes it good, however, is not domestic revelation; it is the design of the story, the moral and aesthetic structure by which the violence achieves meaning. In my account of the Doughties, there is only artlessness. I remember in Temagami the time a woman drowned her two children in the boat-house slip, then tied an anchor to her feet and drowned herself. I knew the family. There was no meaning to this event, either, no story to redeem the lives lost, no narrative absolution. Only the stunning finality and the infinite pain.

To make murder tolerable, to make it cathartic or exciting or amusing, it must be placed in an unthreatening context of moral coherence, described in a context of narrative closure. Story, in other words, must be sufficiently removed from real life to make sense, yet anchored in experience enough to engage. If I am to situate a murder in Temagami, the one place in the world more real than the past, then I must provide you with character and plot as incentives to remain with the text.

Plot: I am suddenly old. Character: think of me as a spectre from another dimension. I can lie dormant indefinitely in a configuration of words. I am able to cross over successfully from potential to being only so long as I can hold your attention. If you have ever watched *Star Trek* or *The X-Files,* you will know how it works. I have no qualms about my fictional status. Whatever I am while I arrange these words, in their arrangement I am something else. Like Descartes, my presence in language has more substance than my life. I have already suggested that you have become fiction yourself, insofar as you permit yourself to participate in my rhetoric. You have the advantage, of course, the power to annihilate me as a textual entity by closing the text, refusing to listen or read. But I would remind you, the butterfly and the carpenter see different trees. Why not give my being as fiction its due.

What we need to sustain a relationship is common ground where you and I are equally authentic. I propose Temagami. But suppose you had never been here before my words urged the necessity of your presence. You need story, you need facts. You need atmosphere and perspective. You need time. The present, where the past and future divide, depends on when the text is revealed. You need a temporal axis to locate yourself, for when you enter a text it is like stepping away from the north pole into a time zone determined by the direction you choose. Once committed to time, you will need parallels of latitude to determine location. These come from story and place.

As an astute reader you will be wondering impatiently, haunted perhaps, by my early reference to the Englishman's grave on our island; wondering why the word Englishman was seeded with meaning and then seemingly dropped. The problem is, I do not have a plot in mind which I intend to reveal as the fiction progresses. The opposite is true. Fiction will create plot, not reveal it, from memories evoked by the Temagami landscape in conjunction with the urgency by which I measure each passing moment as the murder of time.

There were two Englishmen in my childhood. My grandfather was one. He died before I was born. He was my father's father. My mother's family, and my father's mother's family, were Canadian hybrids of Mennonite and Mohawk, Presbyterian, Lutheran, United Empire Loyalist, Viking. My father's father and his friend, the other Englishman, met in Toronto early in this century. Austin had been a ranger in the Boer War. Archie Belaney was younger, an idealist. From our perspective they were practically pioneers. In their own era, they found Toronto an inhospitable fusion of the new and established, and within a short while after their arrival in Canada they fled paradox, north to Temagami, where they both found refuge from the New World amidst the vestiges of a civilization as ancient and elusive as the one they had left behind in England because it seemed more the subject of books than experience, and here they embraced native culture in which people and place, the sensibilities of the people and the authenticity of land beyond any consciousness of its presence or worth, were indivisible.

My grandfather and Archie teamed up with Ernie Smith, who liked them because, for their different reasons, they were both eager to be just like him. They built canoes together and Ernie tried to teach them Ojibway. When a handsome hawk-faced man from the American southwest appeared, he was hired to help with the work, chopping wood for the rib-steamer. After a season of apprenticeship he became an equal partner as it did not seem right to have three bosses and one labourer. The stranger learned Ojibway which he spoke softly, quite unlike the two Englishmen, and soon spoke it better than them. Ernie said he was an Indian. The man said nothing to confirm or deny his origins, except to speak earnestly sometimes by the dying light of the boiler fire, late at night when the men would share a mickey of rye, about being born out of death, that he had been cut from his mother's womb as they prepared her for burial. I know this because Ernie would stay over sometimes in the cabin on island 108 and tell us stories in the flickering lamplight, and that is one of the ones he would tell.

In those days, a trickling of tourists moved into the area in the summers and even after the Great War, as the trickle turned to a seasonal torrent, it seemed that the vast open arms of Lake Temagami could embrace everyone. When Archie and Austin returned from the War, the four partners resumed their business and prospered, and were soon building cabins for outsiders as well as canoes. Things changed when kickers arrived. Suddenly the drone of outboard motors severed the silence. That, of course, is speaking poetically, for the land is never silent, the lake breathes with a resounding and subtle dissonance of wind and water, and you can hear the sky. It is only poets who hear nothing in nature but the sounds of their ear-drums beating and the yodel of the loon.

When I was a young man I worked as a bush guide and we used Temagami cedar-strip canoes, some of them old enough they might have been crafted by the original team which broke up long before I was born. We sometimes paddled past cabins they had built; you could always tell their cabins by the way they were set among the trees and the rock like natural events, not propped up on cliffs or crowding the shoreline. Of the four partners, I only knew Ernie. Austin died the year after my Mom and Dad were married. Archie Belaney died in various ways, depending on which story Ernie chose to relate. The most chilling was the one he sometimes refused to tell, sometimes sending us out to our tent on the Englishman's grave so terrorized by his reticence that we would try to stay awake all night. The stranger from America married a local woman, Anahareo. He took an Ojibway name and did some writing. It was he who became known as Grey Owl.

Now if you were attending carefully, even before my sentence came to a full stop you were thinking of murder. All my life, I have been wondering the same thing. I have never said anything about this, not even to my brothers. I have heard nothing about it from anyone. What actually happened, the years closed over. Time itself is a conspiracy. If people in Temagami registered interest or alarm, nothing of their concern is recorded. Four partners went out to build a cabin on island 108. They hauled their equipment over the ice, including a boat, the prototype of their new line of outboards based on the classic Peterborough design. After the break-up, only three came back.

Years later, following his own death, Grey Owl, who had become a famous Indian, was revealed with considerable fanfare to have been the manufactured persona, some would say fraudulent persona, of the Englishman, Archie Belaney. When I first heard that, my impulse was to write fiction, to correct the record. But I thought about Ernie and realized he would be amused, or more likely would think the confusion not worthy of comment. I remember once asking him, when I was still working as a canoe-trip guide, who Grey Owl was, since even then there was some confusion about his authenticity. I used that word. Authenticity. Ernie ignored my query. Not exactly ignored. He weighed it, and left it unanswered. But Mrs. Smith spoke; it was the only time in all the years I knew her that she ever said more than a greeting. I had no idea how much English she knew. She said, "His name is Wa-Sha-Quon-Asin. He is 'authentic.' He is Indian. I knew two wives. Anahareo, she is my cousin. Her husband tells good stories."

Since hearing that Grey Owl and Archie had apparently become one and the same, and the existence of the American had been extinguished, whenever I am in Temagami I now think of murder. Place here is more knowable than time. If there is a world that does not need to be written to be real, it is here. When I return, even in imagination, it is always waiting, just as it was, although the particulars change. If I went to island 108 I know what I would find in the Englishman's grave. Archie Belaney would be saturated with bogwater in a mossy cleft deep under the soft dry layers of pine needles and fragments of lichen that are matted from years upon years of tents being pitched over his earthly remains.

His skull would be split and the bandage that was used to hold it together would fall away, if his grave were opened, and the two halves of his skull would come apart in the air. He was not killed by Ernie or my grandfather. If he had been, we would never have grown up knowing our island campsite as the Englishman's grave. The secret would have been absolute, with no room for irony. It was the stranger who killed him, the man who took the name Grey Owl. The man who after his own death was given Archie's identity. It was a quarrel. It was about Archie try-ing to be Indian, and the stranger, refusing. Ernie and Austin would have returned from the mainland with a load of stripped saplings for chinking the logs and found the murderer sitting against the giant white pine in the middle of the island, cradling Archie across his lap, staring into his empty eyes, trying with both hands to hold Archie's head together.

This revelation is not an epiphany. It is, after all, part of a fiction. I am older now, and no longer text. I have gone on to other things. You may linger a bit in the today of your reading, to contemplate the implications of being present in a fiction that offers itself as a witness to murder. But it is Temagami this is about, not you, not the pathos of a man who killed his mother-in-law, his wife, and himself, ineptly, not about a hawk-looking stranger who became, perhaps, what he had always been, and not about an Englishman who perhaps said the wrong words at the wrong time, and has become more a part of Temagami than the real Grey Owl could have imagined. It is a story about arriving finally at a certain age and discovering I would rather be in Temagami than old. It is about shifting identi-ties through time, and about the efficacy of place as a plot device; and it is about the presence of death as an absence in your life, like a grave on an island in the back of your mind.

Understanding Shakespeare

What I need to know is, how could Shakespeare happen? There are many things I do not understand; I have grown accustomed to the mystery surrounding my own ignorance. I have no problem not understanding infinity or eternity—the illimitable limits of space and time. I can suspend disbelief; and belief as well. Of those things I know, the origin of art is not the most certain; but I am comfortable thinking that Wordsworth wrote his poems in ways not inconceivable to an inquiring mind, and Whitman wrote his in like manner. Theirs are not accomplishments beyond comprehension; academic careers are given over to speculating on how they were done. I can imagine *The Divine Comedy* working its way out of Dante, and *Paradise Lost,* out of Milton. The Brontës seem plausible origins for their fictional confections. And so on. But how Shakespeare could happen, that is more than I can conceive.

Let us deal with solipsism right off the top. The fact that I cannot reconstruct in my own mind even the possibility of a mind like Shakespeare's does not mean I question whether or not he existed. Obviously, he did. And so do I. My problem is that I cannot reconcile the two, his existence and mine, as somehow co-equivalents in the world. Dante: I can imagine imagining what he imagined; I can from his writing interrogate its informing intelligence. The Brontës of Haworth, their house looming over the dapple-gray churchyard, Branwell's pub cradled in the church shadow like a prodigal son perpetually dying in the memory of a churlish parent, the town on a crease in the dales leading out to wild bare landscape, haunting even in brilliant sunshine with promises of heartrending solitude, they are easy to envision behind every writing. Milton most of all seems almost inevitable; there had to be John Milton between Spenser and Blake, survey courses and the sweep of cultural history demand his presence, and reading him we experience a visionary personality turned inside out, as it were, on public display in his texts; Milton as God, and Lucifer as well. It is only Shakespeare who seems unreal, far more elusive than Homer, a life more incomprehensible than Emily Dickinson's.

I cannot picture William Shakespeare looking at himself in the mirror, what would he see? I stare into the glass and catch my image in the present moment, hovering at a particular angle, caught in the arbitrary design of a reflected world. The mirror is framed by its edges so that everything within it, while I am looking at myself, seems intrinsic, authentic, and all that surrounds it bleeds off into peripheral inconsequence. Could he have looked in a mirror and seen only himself, or would his own image transform into an infinite window, and the window into convolutions of language, simultaneously words and all they could possibly mean.

He could not have been indifferent to his own mortality. Sometimes in the mirror I try to imagine my absence. When I was small, I would sneak up on myself, crouch below the mirror and leap suddenly, catching my image as a blur of colour. Later, I would approach by stealth in the darkness, then flip on the light and surprise myself staring into my own eyes. By my teens I would play a game over and over, knowing I could not win, yet enthralled by the impossible challenge; I would glance away quickly, then back, trying to catch myself looking away. At twenty I discovered my profile; in a men's shop for the first time I confronted myself in an angled triptych, and looking at one mirror could see myself looking away in another. From then on, mirrors became metaphor; I dwelt in a house of mirrors for that was my most authentic locus of being. Or else I thought of them as a practical device, an instrument for grooming and a diversion while brushing my teeth, like leaving the water running. Now, at this age, older than Shakespeare when he died, I sometimes look in the mirror and try to imagine cellular cessation, the absolute stillness of death.

It is impossible. I can imagine myself expired. But I cannot see myself as a corpse, a cadaver, a dead thing, something not happening. Not when I look at my reflection, not without imagination conducting a macabre, emotionally-charged ceremony in which I am the central attraction, and my remains, the agent of much sorrow or guilt and therefore with a life of their own. I am uncertain about why I try to see myself dead. It is not because I am in a hurry to get there; I think it is perhaps to get used to the idea, a sort of rehearsal, the way we anticipate any inevitable event in our lives, sometimes as consolation in advance and sometimes to give ourselves the best lines.

The curious thing is, lately when I have tried to confront death lying dormant beneath my reflection I have thought, perhaps I am trying to work magic, imposing on the mirror the metaphysics of Oscar Wilde, so that my image will expire while I remain alive. I have been wondering about that, and thinking, too, that the person I see is not me. It is William Shakespeare; he is in my disguise. He is mildly amused. He is curious, perhaps, at the display of benign desperation. But he is as inaccessible as ever.

Sometimes I dream I am Shakespeare. I dream through Shakespeare's eyes. He has invaded my unconscious peregrinations in the dead of night, as well as my consciousness, the observer of my reflections on mimetic transference. The strange thing is, I do not in these dreams issue diadems of iambic pentameter from my lips as you might suppose. I do not think great thoughts and utter memorable aphorisms bound in their time to become pleasingly familiar clichés. What I do is to putter about my room, it is the study in my home in our small university-town in central Canada, not in my Stratford house or in London, on the south bank of the Thames. Sometimes as Shakespeare I sit in front of a computer screen and scroll through what appear to be dictionaries on the web, sometimes encyclopaedias—I know this is what they are because if I slow down the scanning sufficiently I can see knowledge before me in discrete and diverse chunks. Although the print is always in English, I cannot make sentences cohere from their beginnings to their ends, but nevertheless I achieve satisfaction at having it all so nearly at my command. Sometimes I daydream in my dreams, but not about kings or enchanted islands or charming confusions of sex and identity. I know I am daydreaming, but about my own life as a dreamer, not Shakespeare's, who in my dreams is the dreamer dreaming about me.

Since I have no special insight in these dreams, no great capacity for parsing emotional complexity into its constituent parts, how do I know I am Shakespeare? That is the pleasure of dreams; you know things there that you do not know elsewhere, and with a confidence that when you awaken seems disconcerting, as your knowledge slips over the edge of forgetfulness, falling among everything in your life that you have forgotten, most of it irretrievably lost. I once had a dream where my father, through the entire intricate narrative, observed from the sidelines, looking like an eponymous pen-sketch on a Smiths Brothers cough-drop box, which looked nothing at all like him in real life, and at the same time, another version of himself, looking like he did when I was a child, behaved in the dream like someone quite different. I never doubted, in the dream or afterwards, that the Smith brother was him. It simply was, and so was the person who acted so strangely. The same with Shakespeare. I know it is him, because I know. I see the world in that other kingdom through Shakespeare's eyes. I avoid mirrors in these dreams which might compromise us both.

Before I go on to develop a plot, we need to deal with the implications of what has happened so far. From your perspective as well as my own, in a different way, I am the creation of language. Shakespeare transformed a concatenation of medieval words into the stable and eloquent language we now live within. There is no boundary between my awareness of myself and the language that he invested with soul in which I am aware. To comprehend Shakespeare is like asking Adam to know the God who gave him voice and the power to name, thus erecting an insuperable barrier of consciousness between them. After Eden, Adam could only guess at his creator's existence. The trick for Adam would be to remove God from time—in order to experience an infinite and eternal presence, to separate God from language. I am not Shakespeare's Adam, not even a prophet. I am a shambling Ishmael, reborn from Exodus and *Moby Dick,* a wanderer driven by his author to satisfy someone else's obsession. I am molecules of air expanding, and Shakespeare is the membrane, the balloon holding it all together. Can the contained know its container? I suspect only in mirrors and dreams.

I implied a plot. That would necessitate character. So let me begin. There is Shakespeare. There is me; I do not mean 'I,' as I would prefer to cast myself in the objective case. And there is Beverley. This is a love triangle. That means character *is* plot, with 'is' in italics. All else is diversion. You can expect a certain amount of narrative development, with events occurring in a sequence that will necessarily be distorted in order to play anticipation and recollection against one another in the service of irony, suspense, and possibly catharsis. If faithfully rendered, this triangle will generate a vision in your mind of perfection, disparate elements in perfect harmony, and at the same time will husband the notion of compromise, the need to love wisely in the real world.

For background perhaps we should go to Saussure, Ferdinand de Saussure (1857-1913), the founder of modern linguistics. We will consider him in order to validate by an appeal to authority the concept that we are all creatures of language, our consciousness co-extensive with the capacity of words to connect in their myriad ways. But already we have left Saussure behind, for he was so absorbed with words as separable entities that he overlooked the illimitable extent of the conversations among them. We must move ahead by reaching out to Shakespeare—to his written legacy, not himself, who is impossible to comprehend as a singular being since all experience known to us, seemingly, passed through his mind, so much have his uses of language clarified consciousness in the English-speaking world, in the way heat clarifies butter, or a lens, blurred vision. Reaching to Shakespeare is not reaching back but reaching out all around us.

You can see the problem. Beverley and I courted through e-mail. Language unencumbered with social proprieties or epistolary conventions was the medium of our enveloping affair. From a brief encounter where we exchanged addresses, innocent of romantic intent, we swiftly become best friends, intimate confidantes, then virtual lovers, all in words held in binary code on a spun disc, flung into the electronic ether with sweetness unknown in analogic reality. From the beginning, however, I suspected another. Her language was pure and fresh and yet so familiar I was sure it had been refined through the sensibility of a mutual acquaintance. This did not seem reasonable since although we had quickly discovered we knew certain people in common, as all people do, we knew no-one so well that our language itself would imply his or her presence between us. Yet someone was there, haunting our diction, pulling us back from excessive vernacular, maintaining syntactic decorum, slipping in lovely allusions, sponsoring puns, playing out meaningful ambiguities, there was someone else there, not a force or condition; an inescapable unknowable third.

I wrote nothing to Beverley about this. I am obsessively wary of being labelled paranoid. For six months we chattered along electronic corridors, cast softly our most secret words onto the internet seas, and the third person with us seemed to me as real and as spectral as we did ourselves. Beverley was a young widow, relatively speaking, and I was in the throes of painfully intricate negotiations for a divorce. Not surprisingly there were ghosts and wraiths in the interworld where we discovered ourselves playing with the innocence of children. But this was not an apparition of the living or the dead, this third; not a figment of memory, or of guilt or fear. It was nothing counterfeit but wholly amorphous, and it coalesced when we met in the flesh for the second time, when we left our strange semblance of passionate childhood behind and became real.

My first look at Beverley's library explained much. The matching sets, one cluster bound in crimson leather with gold titles embossed on their spines, one in hardcover blue with silvered columns of spidery letters exposed to the eye, and two sets of paperbacks, the familiar two-tone design with black print naming Shakespeare the author of each volume, and all forty volumes of the multicoloured Arden Edition, fresh off the press, these among dozens of linear feet of books of all sizes and textures, in room after room, proclaimed Shakespeare my rival. I knew she liked older men, I am older myself, but this seemed bizarre. How, as an obscure academic with my few jottings on the most esoteric of topics, how could I compete?

But compete I would, for I was now refigured by love so much that what might have sent me scurrying in the past to my study, to meditate safely on great subjects, now inspired me to turn my existence in time and space to advantage. I spoke Shakespeare's language so I was not in complete disarray. I would learn what he offered, how he seduced my beloved and continued to hold her in thrall. First I would re-read all his works. To be truthful, there were some I had never read: *Pericles, Timon of Athens, The Winter's Tale, The Two Noble Kinsmen,* some of the royals, *King John, King Henry VIII,* and Part 3 of *Henry VI.* I cannot remember reading *Cymbeline, Coriolanus,* or *Titus Andronicus,* but I imagine I have. Probably I read *The Merry Wives of Windsor* at some point; it seems likely. Without detailed reminders of which one was which, I confused *Love's Labour's Lost, All's Well That Ends Well, The Comedy of Errors, As You Like It, Measure for Measure, Much Ado about Nothing.* On the other hand, I had seen eleven different versions of *Hamlet,* could recite passages from *MacBeth* and *King Lear,* and entire sonnets, on reasonable notice. As an undergraduate I studied *Troilus and Cressida.* I once witnessed Richard Burton and Elizabeth Taylor in *The Taming of the Shrew.* I knew my way through the passages of *Romeo and Juliet, Othello, The Merchant of Venice;* was a familiar in *Twelfth Night* and *A Misummer Night's dream:* knew *Julius Caesar* enough to appreciate parodies; and had been enchanted by *The Tempest* beyond repair.

Yet having done the reading, the entire canon, nothing changed. We did not sit by the fire in the lingering evenings of our first long winter, quipping lines of iambic pentameter. We did not rent Olivier videos, nor attend movies by Branagh, nor watch Pacino twist cruel Richard to the shape of his own peculiar genius. But Shakespeare was there, an unarticulated palpable presence. You need to understand: the problem was not that Shakespeare came between us. This was a triangle: consider for a moment the geometry. Nothing comes between each point in a triangle and either of the other two points, the other two people involved. If someone does come between, that is not a triangle. To call it such is a misapplication of mathematics.

Ours was a true triangle, rare but not unknown in literature and in life. Since my relationship with Beverley, like an enchanted garden, had bloomed into extravagant flower, the pathway between Shakespeare and myself had become increasingly familiar, and between them, was surely as worn. To clarify, let me be esoteric for a moment.

William Blake had a vision of perfection; one facet of the vision ordained it could be achieved through the perfect balance of action and passion. In this vision, Jerusalem is aroused in the arms of her sleeping lover by a poem of incomparable beauty that expresses the absolute harmony of the poet with the splendour of inspiration and the drive to create. He awakens, they become one, and the world comes into its own. There is more to it than this, of course. But stay, this will be enough. The poet, Blake names him Los; he is male in conformation to stereotypes of the time, and inspiration is his female twin, Enitharmon. But they, together, are born out of the womb of Enion, who is the female side of Urthona, the generative principle on a higher plane. Los and Enitharmon are the offspring of Urthona, but also his embodiment in the physical world, and he is not pleased, for all that remains of him, there and then, is a Spectre of his higher self.

Blake's model is determined by both gender and sex, by conventions and biology. On a level of being not much elevated above our own, he has devised a triangle that, if passions are requited and constraints overcome, will issue perfection. Los loves Enitharmon but she is his sister. He is strongly attracted to the Spectre of Urthona, to possess such a fine rage for corporeal being, but that invokes a powerful taboo against homosexuality. Now consider his twin; she loves her brother but there is the taboo of incest, he is too much herself to make love. She loves the Spectre, but his lack of a body makes consummation unlikely. Think about Urthona, or the force of his absence. He loves Enitharmon, and is enraged they cannot be lovers; but he is also attracted to Los, for the poet's gentle acceptance of his place in the temporal continuum, and for his embodiment of the Spectre's ineffable urgings.

The perfect triangle. Each bilateral pairing is a complement to the other two, each, the essence of love, each, fraught with imposed limitations. The poet, slowly expiring in time and space, struggles to reconcile the dissociative rage to create with his soul or other self, awaiting articulation. His beloved sees in her love for him the reflection of herself, and yearns to be possessed by another. The other, harrowing down the long corridors of the poet's ambition, longing to make love to his sister, thrills them both with desire. Caught in the infinite moment of their impossible embrace, words achieve presence, and perfection is born.

The problem with this model, of course, is that as a psycho-aesthetic construct it may not be quite appropriate to the actual situation. True, Beverley loves the elusive infrangible Shakespeare and I am as confident she loves me. True, I hold Shakespeare in high esteem and, without reservation, love Beverley. And true, through the infusion into everyday English of his own ineffable personality he makes love to us both, one to one, his spectral emanation haunting, caressing every node and cranny of our own illimitable minds.

Sitting together in front of a birch-wood fire, this third winter of our shared life, I try to explain all this to Beverley. She responds with disconcerting serenity. I think she must not understand, but she does. We sip our sauternes, a half-bottle of 1967 Chateau d'Yquem. This is reputed to be among the greatest of wines ever made and I want the revelation of my anatomy of love to be splendid. Anticipation and satisfaction are invariably at odds. The wine swells in taste, its complexity and depth overwhelming, the swallower swallowed. But it could never be all that I expected, even though it evokes, as it resonates through the mouth, such images of sun-soaked grass and ancient vines, and the ripeness of frost, the leathery richness of earth, that a gallery of images to outdo the Louvre fills up my mind like snow falling in a forest, or the sound of instruments filling the score of a symphony.

I ask her to abandon serenity and talk about love. We use the language of Shakespeare; we consider the implications of triangularity. She points out that homosexuality is no longer taboo and incest implied by the twinning of our two souls in absolute love is absurd. Gently, she points out that the sexist conventions which served Blake no longer apply. But she undermines her own argument by observing that I am as much an inspiring force in her life as she is in mine; and I say *precisely,* as if the word were in italics. Blake uses now-discredited stereotypes to illuminate universal truths that lend themselves readily to explication through paradigms which oppose them. We inhale deeply, in tandem, the residual aroma of sauternes in the clear crystal stemware bought for the purpose in Ireland, and devour the damp crumbs of the Stilton brought like booty home from Fortnum and Masons on Picadilly Street, London, SW 1.

I am not trying to say we do not speak for ourselves. Shakespeare refines the sensibility, expands our emotional range, articulates my innermost self. But I am still me, born into the language he infused with vitality, pouring blood through its veins, giving it soul. I speak my own words, we connect in our private vernacular, the language we live within stands on its own.

The triangle persists. I am not jealous; if Beverley

loves Shakespeare for the beauty of his imagination, I love him equally for the nuance and ferocity of his poetic expression. His love for us separately is implicit in how we use language to make love to each other. Not jealous, but I am still mystified. How could Shakespeare have happened? To us? Or at all?

Beverley has gone to bed. The fire is waning, the flames slowly sink into embers that shimmer like shook foil. You see the problem with words! Gerard Manley Hopkins. I know he wrote this image first in a poem, shook foil, before I conjured it here. Do you imagine he was the first? Not likely. But he connected it with the grandeur of God, and that made the difference. I use it now to give resonance to drowsy reverie, before I drift into my Shakespearean dream. There are only so many images possible, but their connections and contexts are without limit. Twenty-six letters make a dictionary in English; words in dictionaries make all the books ever written. The images Shakespeare put in the mouths of his characters, the lines of his verse, are so precise they astonish and yet open the mind to the unreachable limits of language itself.

Asleep I am Shakespeare; I avoid mirrors. I am in love with two people, one a man and the other a woman. They are in love with each other. This could prove interesting; it might make a light comedy, possibly a tragedy, more likely a problem play where the resolution is a matter of wit more than will, although Will's be the wit, and wit his will. With a hey and a ho and a hey nonny no. There is no doubt I am Shakespeare, no-one else except Ella Fitzgerald uses nonsense like that so adroitly. But if I am wretched in love, why do I feel on top of the world? Because I am the dreamer dreaming as well as the stuff of his dreams. From the dreamer's perspective, asleep on the blue sofa in front of the cold fire, my presence defines his continuous surprise at finding himself at this stage of his modest life so in love. I have given him words to savour his love, he gives me the flesh to be real in his dream.

She, our beloved, re-enters the room. Although I cannot see her in this other kingdom, I know she has come to take him away. They have talked about me tonight. He will awaken and walk sleepily with her to bed. I will remain by the fire which will rise into flames from dead embers for an hour or two, then by morning it will expire and I will vanish, and never again will I enter his dreams. I can no longer conceive myself as a person, especially incarnate as a tenured professor at a mid-rank university in central Canada. She will not dream of me either, my beloved Beverley, for I have no form in her capacious mind beyond the words of my roaring. She will remain serene. They will be happy together, and I will always be there, spectral as a theoretic point, on the line between them that keeps them connected yet holds them apart, whatever they might choose to believe about triangles and the perfection of love.

Peggy Be Good

It is interesting how many of my generation have never grown up. Not that we remain children through arrested chronology, for we have aged apace; nor, in our part of the world, by succumbing to waves of famine and pestilence. Rather, we resist what we were taught was maturity, the condition of emotional and intellectual and especially social stasis that served our parents as a buffer zone between the turbulent years of their youth and their declining years, as they called them, when their bodies and minds slowly shut down. Maturity in my generation is something that happens to government bonds and good bordeaux. It is not that we choose an alternative. It is just that growing up never happens, only growing old.

There are few of exactly my generation, of course. We round out years into decades and decades into eras. We identify with those a little older or a little younger as time washes over us and we are caught in the ebb or the flow. Sometimes we are the youngest of our peers and sometimes the oldest. Of the six billion people presently swarming the surface of this small planet, a few hundred perhaps were born at exactly the same moment as yourself. On the instant of your first breath, they too began breathing. You will die separately, of course; some already are gone and a few will outlive you by many years. These are your true generation; others only overlap to a greater or lesser extent as you proclaim or accede to a collective identity.

Myself, I emerged with querulous reluctance from my mother's womb, from my own womb within my mother's warm soft body, at precisely the second, minute, hour, day, and year that Margaret Atwood rent the air of a delivery room some miles away with her primal utterance, the first of innumerable that have since passed through her fine thin lips. As far as I have been able to ascertain over the years without being obnoxiously intrusive, we are virtual siblings, synchronic twins. It is a fact of our lives and thus far has proved no great advantage to either of us. She, of course, does not know of our relationship. I have been appropriately discreet. Given what my life has become, it has turned out to be a kindness on my part to keep distance between us.

At the present time I am reading one of her novels, *The Robber Bride*. I keep thinking as I read, isn't it strange and wonderful, we've never grown up. We'll be sixty this year! I know she was younger when she wrote it, in her early fifties, but that is the genius of print, it confounds the passage of time—which, of course, is only a figure of speech since it is we who make the passage, not time, although that is what it feels like, like time is passing right through us and ripping at our entrails along the way. At almost sixty, we can both relish an allusion to The Shadow, he who knew what evil lurked in the hearts of men, it was 'men' then, when we listened as children to Lamont Cranston's spectral alter-ego rasping through the radio speaker; and we both get a kick out of allusions to Captain Marvel and Mary Marvel, and to Capt. Marvel Jr. wearing blue instead of red in his fight against the evil Sylvana, all three of them conjured in comics from civilian life by uttering the single word, Shazam.

Atwood does this *thing* with casual references to the cultural details of our childhood that enforces a pleasurable bond between us transcending the text. She would right now correct me about Shazam—Billy Batson said the name of his mentor, Captain Marvel, to transform from crippled newsboy to juvenile superhero. It was the other two who said Shazam. She would know that. And we would be grateful to have been shown where we went wrong. An exhilarating mark of her genius is that younger readers seem not to feel excluded but, rather, privileged at being exposed to the myriad small revelations of our lives. There are few readers left who are older, if you allow that our generation now extends to the near side of senility.

You will have read about me. I'm sure she has. I would not be surprised if some version of my notoriety finds its way into one of my shadow sibling's brilliant stories. It often happens that way. You see a photograph of John Torrington's mummified corpse, I think it was in *National Geographic,* disinterred from the permafrost of Beechey Island by forensic pathologists, and you think, there must be more in those lugubrious frozen youthful-ancient features, somehow pathetic and macabre at the same time, than science could possibly reveal. It seems no sooner do you think that than out comes *Wilderness Tips* and there he is, a figure of fiction. You visit Dylan Thomas's grave, you remember a love that expired like air seeping through the walls of a neglected balloon, and then you read about both in "Grave of the Famous Poet." She reads the papers. She will know about me. If she can write about sin-eaters and rape fantasies, how could she resist turning me into fiction as well?

Whatever you do or think or read, she seems to have noticed the same things you did, and she puts them into her narratives. You read in *The Robber Bride* about historic battles and new-age crystals, about menus with attitude and about soap bubbles and funky clothes and atonal melodics, and you are giddy with excitement because it seems everything she knows is being jammed into the novel for your personal edification and delight and it is stuff you already know for the most part because you live in the same world but she has put it all together, arranged it in a coherent narrative, so that the most trivial and bizarre details acquire significance beyond signification, numinosity if you prefer, and the familiar becomes un-nervingly exotic.

She will have read of my humiliation with glee, not because she is a cruel person but because behind the carnivalesque emotional extravagance of my ordeal she will find traces of the ordinary, and it is this that will capture her imagination and make her my unknowing advocate. In writing me into fiction she will make the case better than I could that I am not a monster but simply mis-understood. She will write as my sister, my twin, because the coincidence of our being simultaneously conscious in the worlds we share leaves her no option. She will see beyond the garish front page of the tabloid story, she will find me in the comics, in the letters to the editor, among the columnists and stringers, in sports and the cultural features sections, in the sprawling chain-store advertise-ments and among the classifieds. As she did with Grace Marks, giving a long-dead and possibly demented mur-derer humanity, a gift she shares with passionate precision in *Alias Grace,* so she may do for me with even more empathy for we are more alike than she and Grace, we have more in common.

Continuity is in the details, this incapacity for grow-ing up. Our parents did not forget their earlier selves but they disowned them, it was a social necessity, they patronized them, it was a mark of their maturity. I spent some time with Margaret Atwood's parents once. With her as well. We travelled together in a small group, ostensibly to bird-watch. For a week we explored the backwaters and forests of Cuba, looking for additions to our life-lists. Of course I did not have a list. Margaret Atwood was much more famous even then than I am now, and I watched her. (It is all I can do to resist metaphors about plumage and field habits and flicks of her glittering eye.) What I noticed especially was how infuriatingly similar her parents were to my own, and her behavior

towards them to mine towards mine. They struck me as
charming; they had dignity. Whatever their flaws, they
kept them obscured by an aura of casual gentility. If they
were occasionally difficult, as we imagine the parents of
all talented people must be, they showed nothing of this
as we plodded our way through the Cuban landscape by
rickety bus and rickety boat and in cars held together with
coathangers in search of errant warblers, recalcitrant spar-
rows. I might have been with my own mother and father,
whom I knew in more detail but no more depth. In fact,
given my covert sibling relationship with their daughter,
I thought of them secretly as if they, too, were mine.

After Cuba I never saw her parents again. My own
died and I read one day in *The Globe and Mail* that her
father had passed away. That is an expression their generation used, passed away. As if death were transitional,
the same as when they passed irrevocably from young to
grown up. In our generation we moved through years, or
the years washed over us, and undeniably we changed,
but unlike them we never had the need to let go of the
past, to leap the abyss of our own dissociated sensibilities,
to break from the chrysalis of youth and become speci-
men butterflies adrift in formaldehyde. That's how we
saw them, and we turned from the predictability of metamorphosis, with its occasional mutations of genius, to the
affirming progressions of infinite nostalgia. Old age will
not be a shock to us, just a broadening or narrowing of
perspective. We will not pass away. We will simply die.

Sensibilities such as ours find nothing too trivial to
savour in memory, nothing of our past so inconsequential
or silly that we cannot find and appreciate a present context in which it will glow with an intrinsic evanescence
we may have missed the first time around. That is her
genius, to make the details important. In this, only Jane
Austen is her rival. And perhaps Nabokov. We did not
become friends after Cuba. For a brief time I called her

Peggy, she didn't address me by name, we drifted apart. By the time the plane landed back in Toronto, neither of us could remember having met.

I wonder if she recognized me when my case first hit the papers. It would have caught her attention. Not every day, at least in Canada, do children sue a parent in open court, especially adult children, especially for a misdemeanor so obscure and obscene. Obscure is how the defence described the situation: these charges are frivolous, nebulous, unquantifiable, indeterminate, elusive, obscure. The tabloids said my putative crimes were obscene. But would she have known it was me? I imagine her, after following the court proceedings for a few days, pausing over her morning paper, staring in distraction at two houseflies copulating in an empty juice glass—that is what we suppose they are doing when they buzz around in their brief orgasmic fury. There is a slight fibrillation of the cerebral cortex, a flickering acknowledgment of familiarity with the protagonist of the piece, namely myself. The flies lapse into post-coital torpor. She returns to the newspaper, having decided she knows me only from the convergence of previous reading and a narrative imagination already reworking the story for future use.

How will she know everything about my world the way she does those of her other characters? How can she know everything? My immediate problem is that I can't tell whether I like *The Robber Bride* best or least of all her novels. How does she convince me she knows everything about Charis, so much that I suspect Charis is an authorial persona, and then about Tony, or first about Tony and then about Charis, and then about Roz? They cannot all be their author in textual disguise. It is only the perfidious Zenia we know little about, the wicked, wanton, predatory, perfidious Zenia. She, I realize, has all the power precisely because we know little about her. Zenia, who can be anything she wants, it is Zenia who is the authorial persona, the persona of all authors, of every text. Perfidious Zenia.

When she writes about Tony, the diminutive history professor for whom warfare is a religion and battles the liturgy, she is at home in the university environment and you think, yes, of course, she was an academic herself. When she describes Charis's profound flaky spirituality, you wonder, how does she know so much about numerology and New Age stuff, auras and vibes and talismans? But she is so sure about the details you figure she must have gone through a phase and you think you remember pictures of her wearing black capes and long black dresses. Then she gives you Roz's world of corporate power and you assume she has made so much money as a writer that she now occupies that echelon with as much aplomb as if she had been born to it. As Zenia draws each of the other three into the open, and steals their men, you assume the author herself must have survived awesome romantic catastrophes. Or caused them. But how will Zenia draw me out, how will her author inhabit my life?

There will be an element of paranoia. There always is in Atwood's characters. It is a trademark. Charis, for example: "anything with an awning intimidates her," and "when there's mist you can't see what's coming." Usually they are not so vulnerable as Charis, more edgy, bitchy, flippant, clever. It always makes you feel she's sharing attitude and, generally, you feel grateful, relieved to be on side. Occasionally you are put off by the cleverness but then, invariably, you end up realizing antipathy was supposed to happen; even when you're off-side, you're off together. There will be a lot of word-play. No matter whose the mind, she cannot resist cluttering it with cunning puns and runs of silly homonyms, syllabic quips, deliciously inappropriate vulgarities. She uses the word snot a lot. For the sound of it, for character revelation, yours not hers.

It is ironic that I am not effeminate. She must be intrigued by that. The photograph favoured by the papers emphasizes my masculinity, showing me in a sultry half-light that makes my features appear coarser than they are. Of course, it is context that makes their real point for it shows me with the SkyDome looming in the background, which the tabloids take as proof of manliness. The truth is, I have never been to a professional sports event in my life and I do not drink beer. Still, their point is made. The more normal I appear, the more bizarre my situation.

I do not identify with Grace Marks. You never do with an Atwood protagonist, especially when the protagonist, like Grace, murdered people and then seems to have carelessly misplaced her grasp of the event. Or with Zenia, who robs women of their partners, exploits their pathological dependency on men. Or Offred in *The Handmaid's Tale* who is so much the powerless victim that when she virtually deconstructs before your eyes in the postscript you are both infuriated and relieved. As a reader, especially now, I identify with the author. This supratextual coalition between the writer and her reader is where Atwood differs from most of her contemporaries and from virtually all her predecessors. Perhaps in her first novel there was room enough and circumstance to see Marian as a textual emanation of the author's personality and an alter-ego of your own. But Atwood kept you at a distance, shifting voice and shifting tense and seeding caustic comments through the narrative that would sting you if you got too close to their objectives. Even then, in *The Edible Woman,* she made you want to be the trusted confidante behind her eviscerations of convention, her blistering righteous public wit—like two wicked children peering down through the landing balustrade on the grown-up world, one of them with all the good lines, and one, you, with the gift of infinite appreciation. Like, friends.

And you, like Zenia's victims, flattered by the friend-ship.

There was talk of murder but it came to nothing. I concede that I dishonoured my wife and that may be contemptible but it is not a crime. Not unforgivable, or at least I wouldn't have thought so. I meant well. I can honestly say I meant well. When she died I tried to take her place. Because her death was ignominious, I denied its happening. That, I think, was my biggest mistake. To deny someone her own death is like burying her in a pauper's grave, leaving her body to rot on an open battle-field, sweeping her desiccated remains under the opulent carpet of misdirected charity.

Had I not been sufficiently endowed by my ancestral inheritance and had not my children's mother been a whinging sailor, all this might never have happened. They were very young when she set out to sail around the world by herself. Sean had just been weaned and Pat was not yet toilet-trained. Their mother, I cannot bring myself to say her name, complained about everything in her life as if consciousness was the ultimate affront. She sailed. She said that was her only consolation. The children and I would go down to the private ferry sometimes and see her off, on her way across to the RCYC on the Island where the boat that had once belonged to her father was docked. We would then rush to the Western Gap or the Eastern Gap to see if I had guessed right, and, if I had, we would wave when she went through. She always sailed alone and would never say which way she intended exiting the harbour for the open lake. Since it was generally an on-shore or an off-shore wind, the choice was arbitrary.

She spoke in a ragged high-pitched voice and almost no-one would sail with her. Anyone who offered, myself included, she didn't want. She was in finance, a mid-level executive in the bank where her father had been Chairman of the Board until his death. Debentures. It surprised everyone when she breast-fed. When she decided on a solo circumnavigation of the world, no-one was surprised. When her boat was discovered drifting off Toronto Island, fully stocked for an extended voyage, without anyone aboard, unmanned, as it were, it was assumed that she had been drunk—it was known she drank—and fell over the side. The fact that the main anchor and anchor rope were missing confirmed in most people's minds that she had got herself entangled in an inebriated state and when she tried to set the anchor in deep water, it hauled her over and down and she drowned somewhere out in Lake Ontario, having characteristically started off on her marathon trip in the middle of the night. No-one would have been surprised when I chose not to have a memorial service but instead donated her boat to the RCYC Members Fund, sold the Rosedale home, took the children, and disappeared.

You won't remember that part of the story since there was no story. Margaret Atwood will research it, for she is an indefatigable researcher, relentless and daunting, as readers of her more recent novels will avow, but she will not find even a death notice in *The Globe and Mail*. My children's mother's passing away was a private affair. There was, in fact, very little interest at the time among our acquaintances and neither of us had surviving relatives close enough to care what had happened. The appropriate papers were filed. That was an end to it. The children and I moved to the old Sunnyside area of west Toronto, settled into a nice duplexed house which I bought and had renovated and then rented out the upper half to a series of pleasant tenants while the children were growing up.

And grow up they did. After twenty years of Sunnyside—they both lived at home right through university—they moved to The Annex, which must have reminded them of their old neighbourhood with its tree-lined streets

and neo-Victorian brick houses with bicycle-laden veran-
dahs. They moved into separate one-bedroom apartments
within a few-minutes walk of each other. It seemed
propitious at that point for me to abandon Sunnyside to
the ghosts of the amusement park that older residents still
remember, as the roller coaster, its final vestige, was not
torn down until the fifties and the stone bathes are now a
public swimming pool. Having taken their mother's place
for so long, it now seemed reasonable to resume my own
life, to live, as it were, for myself.

As anyone who has read Atwood knows, nothing is
ever that simple.

I wish I were reading *Surfacing*, or even *Survival*. The
problem with *The Robber Bride* is that I am amused, I am
engaged with the background of the characters' lives,
what happens to the characters themselves brings a chill
to the bone. But can I trust what I feel about people whose
emotional complexity is conveyed by the itemization of
artifacts that surround them, actual and psychological,
remembered and observed? They are not superficial; they
are fully individuated within the narrative; they are their
author's creations. Sometimes, the absence of an author
is essential in a modernist text. It gives the reader the
chance to be absent as well, so that the characters come
fully to life within words, free of you both. That is what
The Robber Bride is, modern; there are none of the tricks,
the self-conscious authorial reconstructions or conflicted
motivations that you would expect of a postmodernist
novel. Sometimes the relentless almost breathless attention to detail generates at least in this reader the feeling of
oppression. I am not seduced but saturated. In *Surfacing*,
a much earlier work, the fusion of authorial presence, narrative reality, and reader response perfectly conveys the
convoluted peregrinations of the protagonist's mind. I
miss that. *Survival,* of course, I threw in as a bonus.

You might ask what all this has to do with my story.

You must have noticed the absence of detail in my description of the Sunnyside years. Despite an incalculably pernicious subtext, those were the two most unimaginably bland and uneventful decades I was able to devise. Sean and Pat and I lived together in familial harmony. Sean would sometimes cry herself to sleep in my arms, but she did not remember the mother she was missing, she cried night after night for an absence that, holding her close, I tried to fill. Pat's childhood was happier. As a teenager he did teams sports and dated smart girls who wore just the right amount of makeup and he thought he might become a sportscaster, although he became an engineer. Sean studied law at Osgoode. She is a criminal lawyer. The suit against me was her idea.

You can infer, I am sure, the importance of Atwood in my life. I did not work, I tended the house, I looked after the children. Not once did a visitor set foot in our home. Only service people and sales reps and the tenants, once a month. By choice, I had no life of my own. The one exception, you might say aberration, was my trip to Cuba. Years before, when I was just out of university and back from my requisite hitch-hiking tour of Europe, which meant, of course, Western Europe because in those days none of us travelled east of Berlin even if we had been able to, I was looking for something to do in Toronto, some sort of job that would make me seem interesting; sometimes I went to poetry readings at the Bohemian Embassy. That's where I encountered Margaret Atwood. Other poets our age read as well. Dennis Lee was solemn, mesmerizing; Gwendolyn MacEwen was menacing and vulnerable, dangerously sincere. But Margaret Atwood's ominous quiescence, atonal insinuations, the strange familiarity of her wit, did something with attitude and language that changed my life. Even then it was delivery. She made words real. Not what they meant or described. Words themselves. Suddenly, in those smoky coffee

evenings, just off Yonge near Gerrard or maybe Welles-
ley, language was not a barrier between me and the world,
it was the world. She made words an environment, the
extent of existence itself. I read everything she wrote after
that. When I discovered, years later, a place open on her
Cuban expedition, I leapt at the opportunity to extend my
life-list of her works to include, just for a vicarious week,
her life.

Something you may have noticed about Atwood's
canon, especially if, as I did, you read each novel or collection of short stories or poems when it first appeared,
paying hard-cover prices when necessary, you may have
noticed that the dominant narrative perspective is always
from the age she is at the time of writing. The precise age
we are, together! That is unusual. Lucky for me. In a generation that doesn't know how to grow up, in a life so
cunningly devoid of detail as my own, it was pure seren-
dipity that the writer who first named my world into being
and, inadvertently, me, dare I say it, into the world, that
that writer should be the one who would articulate our
aging sensibilities with such relentlessly thorough conviction that I had no need for two decades to have first-hand
experience beyond my Sunnyside home. That made the
other, my putative crime, which I thought of as self-de-
nial, not martyrdom or sacrifice but benign generosity, so
much easier to sustain, to endure.

My inner life through those years was rich and varied,
while my quotidian life was prosaic, to all outward ap-
pearances uninspired. Even before my wife's demise I
read *Lady Oracle*, I daydreamed new twists to the plot.
The appearance of *Bodily Harm* seemed preternatural,
coming out as it did so shortly after her death. Yet by then
we were already living in an alternate reality. It was no
surprise when *The Handmaid's Tale* came out. Having
explored the limits of romance and the metaphysical
potential of the murder mystery, it seemed inevitable that

both Atwood and I should find ourselves ready for speculative fictions on gender and sex. I didn't forget *Life before Man*. It was the only one of her novels I read in bits and pieces. It took a couple of years, reading in bed; it was too honest, even the title made me restless, the relationships disturbed my normal patterns of sleep. How does she know so much? Then came *Cat's Eye* and the answer. That was my life in that novel, even if she disguised it a bit. There was no question, this was about me.

I read the short stories, of course, but I usually waited for the paperback since I had read most of them in periodicals before they were collected in books. I read the poetry and worried, sometimes, that she revealed too much about our secret lives. I read the essays and worried, especially about *Strange Things*, that being clever is not always enough. Stringing the details together into arguments is not like laying them down in a fiction. The essays didn't satisfy, playing with the facts in a world not of their own making. Sometimes, reading the essays in bed, I would get up, put on my robe and slippers, and sit in front of my dressing table, staring into the mirror, as if I were trying to confirm that I was really there. After a while I would hear Sean and Pat stirring in their rooms and I would feel the rightness of things, and go back to my bed, take off the slippers and robe, crawl under the covers, flip off the light, and go to sleep.

Only once, in images of drowning, did I think of my wife. I read other writers, mostly Canadians, mostly novels and short stories by women. Alice Munro. Sometimes in *The New Yorker*. Sometimes from the library. Books gave me all the life I required. And my children. I do not think they thought of me as a boring person although that is the demeanor I had chosen, the mantle I had donned, so to speak. I was simply there. The house did not clean itself. Meals did not get cooked of their own accord. Laundry had to be sorted and washed and ironed and folded and put away. Eventually they shared in the domestic chores without being asked. Pat was better at it than Sean. She was more inclined to do things for herself but let communal necessities accrue to her brother and me. Her own room was always immaculate, precise. We were close, affectionate, but there was no more intimacy in our relationships than between a favourite toaster and a good breakfast.

I am not Irish. Sean and Pat were named to irritate my long-dead mother-in-law who took her own life in a fit of pique after the death of her husband, my father-in-law with the berth at the RCYC so snug to the Clubhouse that the hot afternoon sun in summer was swallowed in its immense baronial shadow. I look a bit Irish, it's from the McCorkadale side of my family who lived in Belfast for a couple of generations, and now that I'm back in the heart of the city I sometimes go to an Irish pub on Bloor St., where I linger in the background and drink long lugubrious draughts of Guinness because I read once that it is good for you. Occasionally a middle-aging woman will settle in beside me in the semi-darkness, looking for company, assuming I am as lonely as her. Why would a handsome man, somewhat slight and small, perhaps, be on his own, just so? Of course, as their eyes accustom to the murky light they invariably recognize me. They finish their drinks politely, excuse themselves to go to the washroom, and never come back.

I wonder, when Margaret Atwood writes my story, and it has occurred to me that she might not, she might find it offensive, she is a mother, after all, and women, especially, seem to find what I have done more reprehensible than men, a trivializing affront; she might not. Men find it frightening, a testosterone challenge. How, if she takes up the project, will she bring everything into the open? It will have to be a dramatic scene, poignant, thrilling, blood-chilling, and precariously hovering between funny and sad. She will know how to do it. There is such synchronicity in our lives, among our generation, she will take what was a trite if not trivial event and make it real as kitchens.

Her biggest problem as I see it, and I am her avid reader, not a writer, myself—as an existential emanation of her probable imagining, it seems to me her problem will be to take a story already well-known and make it original. But that is perhaps what she is best at. Like Sophocles, she taps into the profound depths of things familiar, she makes consciousness a revelation. She will exploit the obvious. How could my children not have known? She will provide such a sweep and depth of detail, it will seem impossible for them to have seen through my disguise. She will observe that I attended so fastidiously to every aspect of my transformation, it would never have occurred to them that things were otherwise. She will have me buy sanitary pads of several capacities, and tampons, every month. I will dispose of these accoutrements of menstruation with overt discretion. She will have me feign PMS or use it as an excuse to give in briefly to my normal bitchiness. Before Sean and Pat leave home she will have me exhibit early signs of menopause. Mostly by rapid mood swings and occasional bouts of aggressive distractedness. I will rise early, shave, put on my make-up, and have breakfast on the table before the kids are out of bed. I will shave in the afternoon before they come home from school. And put on afternoon makeup. I will be careful to give them air-kisses and to hug them always so that we avoid awkward contact. I will never wear slacks, trousers, pants, only skirts and dresses and never shorts. I will not be too feminine. I will be inseparable from their notions of home, quietly efficient, always there, the hoarder of recipes, the arbiter of clothing, the keeper of secrets revealed in the laundry, in offhand conversation and nocturnal confession, the perfect mother. I will be their one living relative, the only mother they know.

She will expose their humiliation on the page, as it were, from my perspective. She will see them as I do; she can't help herself. But she will show what they are going through from the outside with so much urgency, such sardonic compassion, you will swear after reading that she has been inside their minds. Read again, carefully, you will discover it is herself on display, her own inner turmoil at dealing with my hidden realities, the small anxieties and triumphs of my years of deception, my bewilderment at their response to my exposure as a rather ordinary, quite pleasant, unprepossessing, even diffident, male, the only father they have ever had.

The tabloids made it all sound sleazy and sinister. What happened was this. They visited me once after I moved into my high-rise condo overlooking the Bloor St. viaduct, the Don Valley so far below me that the trees looked like a pen and ink drawing and the stream, the Don River, like a ragged cut in the paper. They wanted to make sure I was really there. They didn't know I had thrown out all my dresses and skirts and sweater sets and lingerie and blouses and costume jewellery, that I kept only the outfit I wore for their visit and enough makeup to get me through the day. They had no way of knowing the pleasure I took in outfitting myself in a complete new wardrobe, mostly from Harry Rosen, a Giorgio Armani blazer and half a dozen shirts, all of them white, a couple of Collezioni jackets, three pairs of Mani slacks, a couple of Emporio sweaters, and a drawerful of F/X underwear and socks. They had never seen me spend money on myself. I always bought clothes privately. They assumed we were at the 'careful' level on the economic scale, with enough to get by but not enough to squander. They both worked part-time and in the summers through university.

I was not clog dancing the night I bumped into them at the Irish pub. I was not wearing a shirt open to my navel, flaunting my chest hair, I was not wearing a gold chain draped across my collarbone. I simply stepped up to the bar for my second Guinness and there they were, Sean with a strapping young man hovering so that I didn't see her until I literally entered her shadow, Pat with an attractive young woman standing beside his bar-stool, leaning into him in that way women have, breast against tricep as if it were nothing at all. "Good evening," I said. "Mother," they said, simultaneously. Their dates looked at me, a middle-aged man immaculately attired, dressed inappropriately for an Irish pub, but that was an anomaly I enjoyed, a luxury I earned, and they laughed. The dates laughed at what they thought was a joke. Each of them said, "Hello, mother!" and they laughed some more. Pat fell into Sean's arms and began to weep. Sean glowed a dull crimson with absolute rage. Their dates, laughing hysterically, fell into each others arms. I excused myself and went back to my table.

What will Margaret Atwood do with this? The story, I imagine, is not in what I did. That was two decades of cautious banality. It is in my children's reaction. I was not who they thought I was. Their personalities were shaped, they had lived their lives, sometimes to spite me and sometimes to please me but always in response to my presence. Pat grew to manhood neither frightened by his own masculinity nor enamoured of it. He had a sound relationship with his mother, gender affirming. Now what? Sean was the woman she was, in good part because she kept bumping up against me and that was what she did not want to be—but if I wasn't me, then who was she? She felt violated, or so she said in court. Pat said he felt emasculated. Sean said she felt cheated, her childhood was a sham, unreal. He said he was robbed of a proper father, his mother stole him away. Neither of them were much concerned about their real mother. She was not the issue. I was.

I accept that I have been the author of my own folly. I was a good mother in ways I could never have been a good father, although sometimes to be good in one respect means to be not so good in others. I hope never to grow up. This will blow over. It has been cataclysmic, like a natural disaster; there's the inevitable debris that wants tidying. I think I was a good parent. If Margaret Atwood writes my story, my one desire is that she be as good. I think I can trust that she will, Peggy will put it all into meaningful order. So long as hurricane, cyclone, typhoon, or authorial initiative do not stir the waters too deeply, everything will fall into place. Sean and Pat will come home. They are already more mature than I am. They will become fond of me. I will forgive them. They will watch me grow old. I am the only parent they have.

Good-Bye, Matt Cohen

Matt Cohen has died. At what point does the shift in grammar occur and we submit to the copula. There is no verb in English for being dead. We are going to die, we die, for a brief time we have died, then after a period of grief we are dead. In the syntactical refusal to acknowledge death as a verb we insist it is a condition in the ongoing present. Dying is one thing, death is another. Before Matt died, before I knew he was dying, death was a noun. It was easy then to write about him as fiction, to imagine someone within the known parameters of his life as a creation of consciousness, his and my own. Afterwards, after, my solitary friend, the principal witness to my adult years, he remains in the present until I too die, and we become fiction together.

I'll be honest with you. I'm surprised you're reading this. Not because you don't know who Matt Cohen is. He is a Canadian writer. If you are reading this in America, as Americans like to call the United States, you are less likely to know his work. If you are Dutch, and reasonably literate and eclectic, as the Dutch often are, you will almost certainly recognize the name. He is a best-selling writer in Holland, in translation. In Italy as well. Here and there in a global crazy-quilt pattern, he is celebrated or ignored. Only in Canada could he be described as somewhere between, the moderately famous Matt Cohen.

I'm surprised at your attention for another reason. Not because you don't know who I am either, or do, and find me unattractive. It is because I am not writing this for publication. These passages have been perhaps retrieved by a literary executor I haven't thought to name yet, in which case you have me at a disadvantage. You know

better than I whether or not I am alive. Of course, I might
have changed my mind and published under an opaque
pseudonym. I've always admired the monosyllabic symmetry of the name John Moss and it is sufficiently obscure for my purpose. I want this to be about Matt Cohen,
not about me.

Let's share the assumption you have no idea who I
am. Still, you already know more than most. You will
have picked up on the emotional austerity characteristic
of a committed academic postmodernist, my indifference
to public acclaim may surprise you, you have probably
accepted my friendship with the eponymous Matt Cohen.
You will have inferred that my commitment to a progressive agenda is not categorical. I am an anarchist, not a
fanatic. If my friend persisted in writing fiction that plays
on the emotions and appeals to the intellect with word-
play and wit that compel the reader's attention from one
page to another, from first page to last, I am not immune
to the generosity of his anxieties. I am not untouched by
his need to be read.

If you suspect this is a phenomenological ploy, what
I am doing here, that I am really the posthumous voice of
Matt Cohen, writing about myself, forget it. True, I use
commas as conjunctions as he did, and sentence fragments as if they were whole. But so does Margaret Atwood. These are minor eccentricities and the mark of
possible genius. You will have to come up with something better than that. If I were Matt Cohen I would be
comfortable enough with my own good mind and excellent canon. I would have no need for subterfuge. There is
nothing I could not say directly in fiction, if I were he,
that I must resort to dissembling. The implication that the
author of my discourse is the creation of its principle
subject, I, the writer assigning attitude to Matt Cohen's
persona, find demeaning.

Perhaps I should set the scene. While plots are passé

(a remnant of Euro-egotism indicating the valorization over chaos of Aristotelian hegemonies of order and consequence, and characterization is redolent with neo-American ideologies of self-love and self-loathing, the legacy of Puritan individualism), place is still important, establishing the scene is essential. Face it, there will be no plot. And if you insist on character, read Cohen. But if you want a good setting, a believable uncompromising locus, where you will find Matt Cohen a spectral presence among words and yourself his friend, then read on. Admit it, stopping at this point might indicate you are not up to the challenge, too much the victim, conditioned by old-fashioned narrative, a weak person, a literary luddite, a humanist crank. There is no shame in completing what you began in good faith simply because it refuses to toady to superannuated conventions of aesthetic engagement. Read on. Please.

Picture a house in the country. Picture me in the house. What kind of house is it? That is a trick question. It is too early to say. Imagine me as a character in a Matt Cohen novel. If you have not read anything but a few of his short stories, so much the better, for now. In short stories he is adept at quick character delineation, a few strokes of idiosyncrasy, a touch of the familiar, an ominous hint of the grotesque which gives the comic context an aura of unreality, a sad context a sense of the absurd. Just because you and I don't believe in the efficacy of character does not limit his ability to create them. Let us say I am a character he has not yet found a place for, a narrative home. Now you can begin to imagine the house.

Why am I here, why am I writing, is it my house, am I writing for pleasure and profit or out of desperation? For any sort of thematic progress, the house has to be in shadow at least part of the time, in the mornings and then again in the late afternoons. This means there are big trees in the yard, on the east and west sides. The house must therefore be old. It is facing north, probably fieldstone with dressed corners of cut limestone blocks, a feature often incorporated into the work of Scottish stonemasons after they finished the Rideau Canal which was to protect us from an American attack. It didn't do much good since between 1812 and 1814 the Americans burned down Toronto twice. In 1813 we burned the White House to the ground.

This stone house was built facing south but the fourth or fifth generation of occupants turned it around. They filled in the front door space with its half-circular Georgian transom before the turn of the last century. They replaced the twelve-over-twelve front windows with Victorian sashes and put a fireplace where the door had been. At the back of the house a French door was forced through the outer stone wall of the attached woodshed which became the livingroom and that opened onto a verandah which overlooks the new road that was built to the north when a subdivision took over the pasture. The verandah has been modified in recent years, closed in with sheets of glass and a pressed-steel door that looks like wood panels painted metallic. The whole effect is of an attractive mongrel, with its rump in one era, torso in another, and its head in the present. Frontier, colonial, contemporary; the effect is postmodern, especially since there are no other houses like it in the area for comparison.

We seem to be dealing with a bifurcating personality. I've told you this is about Matt Cohen, then tried to pass myself off as his avant garde writer-friend and now as an unused character in his imaginative pantheon. *Mea culpa. Moritori te salutamus*—I remember that from Grade 10 Latin with Miss Collip. I have a history. It was Port Credit High School, that was before they were called Secondary Schools, before the fire that rumour had it Red Vetero started because he was given a detention and was late for his job at The Record Bar on Lakeshore Road; it was when Miss Collip's room smelled of chalk and old varnish and Jergens Hand Lotion, before we moved to the portables. I could go on, but I don't know whether to trust my memory. Matt Cohen characters always have a past, each of them has. But so do his friends.

Plot is a plot. Think about that. From the foregoing it is easy to see why character is problematic. But at least character is only a vestigial imperialist intrusion, or as one pair of critics so aptly described it, "a passionate supremacist totalitarian fantasy...where the subtle presence of a castigating power ensconces itself." Putting their words in quotation marks goes half way toward giving these critics authority; not naming them throws my own authenticity into question. Character, hard to avoid, is the recrudescent residue of a discredited notion of narrative voice. Plot is more sinister.

Think of Matt Cohen writing fiction, a short story. It is happening still, the proof in his words. He talks to himself out loud in his head. An observer would witness only silence and an attitude of distraction. But in the vast chambers and corridors of his skull, in the amphitheatres and stadiums, among the sky-rises and suburbs and wilderness trails, the cabins and libraries and galleries and sacred places, there are infinite conversations all happening at once. So many, so resounding and lucid, he can hear them all, turning attention to any one of them at will, while the others carry on, all as accessible, all as articulate. It is the writer's mind I imagine, limited only by language itself and the capacity of consciousness at the time of creation. Plot is what happens to the words when they emerge in the open, how he strings them together. Plot is the tyranny of linear time, our mutual submission to meaning and order. Plot is the conspiracy of metaphysics to subvert the pleasures of our infinite hearing. The pleasures of dissonance. Aristotle's revenge for a forgotten wrong.

This is about my friend Matt Cohen. You will notice I do not insert a comma, placing the person and the concept of friend in apposition. I am not setting up an equation but, rather, indicating a unified phenomenon. There is no plot here; plot is an alien notion in the lives of real human beings. It is the way we arrange elements in our various stories to make us seem more or less than we are. We take a single event, the time Matt and I fell through the ice on the Depot River, walking side by side, huddled close to project our voices over the winter wind, until suddenly he plunged through up to the knees and, simultaneously, I plummeted into watery depths, so that, twisting against the sudden rush, when I looked up through screaming panic I could see the underside of the ice, radiant and lethal, and at eye level on a ledge leading to the shore Matt's boots, motionless for an interminable instant as he tried to assimilate my disappearance into a logical account of what had occurred. We give such an event a beginning and an end, we set limits, in our conditioned desire for coherence and implication, we reinvent a brief episode in the illimitable life of the world to make it accessible.

But it wasn't that simple. Matt reached into the icy depths, I stretched my arm upwards to the light, we connected. We had both removed our mitts, Matt to keep his dry and I to feel the water, make direct contact with the medium enclosing me like an imploded crypt. Our hands touched. It was like the garish image by Michelangelo on the ceiling of the Sistine Chapel, God and Adam reaching to each other. Before ten minutes had passed we were sitting in front of a Franklin stove, drinking rum, something God and Adam likely never did before their falling out, and certainly not after it, although Adam's descendants suffered a deluge of their own and most of them perished.

You can see what I mean about plot, it is insidious and grandiloquent. We can move into the small details of our relationship, how we used to walk together through inclement weather, sharing nonsense and secrets. Or we can pursue implications arising out of the familiar allusions, and perhaps write ourselves into the great Western mono-narrative as *agents provocateur*, our brief episode a metaphoric paradigm for subtextual undermining of the foundations upon which our precarious culture advances, like walking men on thin ice, exemplars of the post-christian neo-hebraic coalition informing the new reality.

I cannot recall in detail Matt Cohen and I doing things with other people. It was always the two of us. He would come to the country and we would do things together. He had other friends in the area but these friendships were like separate galaxies wheeling in the distant night. The implication that we occupied the firmament in a constellation of our own may seem romantic, we were not Wordsworth and Coleridge, but we had stellar times, the two of us. From his perspective it might have seemed I had no other life.

I did, of course. Beyond what he could know. Or it seems that way in retrospect, as I construct the past. I have given myself no family, so inevitably I am now alone. But I have memories, a house, history. I have given myself a pleasantly diffident personality and permitted myself talent, the drive to create, and a radical will to renegotiate the rules of narrative for the liberation of oppressed and manipulated sensibilities. I give you, my reader, my trust, for although I did not anticipate your presence I will hold nothing back. Should you discover things about yourself while I expostulate on Matt Cohen, you have no reason to hold me responsible. Nor him. Even if you suspect I am his creation. You cannot blame us because your talent is reading.

Myself, I am Matt Cohen's perfect reader, as you are

mine. In the early days of our friendship he would show me manuscripts. I am not an editor. He would show them to the indefatigable Dennis Lee in the city and get pages of feedback, but for myself, my responses were so deeply internalized they would not appear when I summoned them forward, would not submit to articulation. I was perhaps too close to withdraw sufficiently from the undifferentiated candour of our relationship. I preferred reading the published works in which I could, exempt from the creative process, look for myself. He read my writings in turn, but with so little equivocation I felt sometimes he was my ghost, writing me. That was the beginning of it, of my questioning my own palpable existence in the world between us.

I have never really got used to mortality. Perhaps none of us does. Whether we spring from the generosity of an author or from copulation, most of us find life disconcerting, knowing as consciousness dawns that our ends are capricious, the darkness inevitable. Erasure absolute. We butt our way through, from paragraph to paragraph, like blind stallions in heat, no, like earthworms on the sun-baked surface of a garden in August, squirming in random directions until we expire. No, we wander from sentence to sentence, story to story, trying to find the right words to make us real to ourselves, like the invisible man, donning clothes so that he can see his own shape in the mirror. To know that he is not just imagining himself.

Matt Cohen is among the most accomplished Canadian writers of his generation. He would be included in any selection of the top half dozen. Not singled out but included and that is a curse of sorts, arising out of his own creative vitality. His work elicits loyalty and enthusiasm from many readers, admiring appreciation from certain critics, from George Woodcock and the existentially compromised John Moss. But the curse of his genius is that whatever he writes, something about the writing suggests he is holding back. It is not that it is not fine work. No-one has published a novel of agrarian life to surpass *The Disinherited.* No-one has challenged the absurdity of death with such vital wit as he in *Last Seen.* But always there is the gnawing awareness as you read that, no matter how good this is, it is not quite enough. He is not surpassed by others but by himself, the implied writer who could have done more.

No-one, of course, achieves perfection by the measure of his own achievement. His most recent novel, *Elizabeth and After*, comes close. In a strange way, the heart and the soul at solemn play in this novel affirm the missing note in everything that went before. And why am I telling you this? You forget, you were never meant to be reading these words. I am writing to myself. You are listening in. It is only illusion that we are sharing the processes of thought, the dialectic of my existential quest. Yet I encourage you to read on. In exploring the mystery of Matt Cohen's imperfection, perhaps I will illuminate my own work or perhaps I will inadvertently cast light upon our mutual reality, or upon yours.

If you have not heard of Matt Cohen, you will likely think I am making him up. Let us consider the possibility. I could have reinvented someone I already know, brought him to life among words. The implications are awesome. Suddenly I see new proof of the dangers inherent in the creation of character. Not only does the procedure foster a neo-colonial gaze of superiority on the part of the predatory author, it also, I realize, empowers the writer with vision like superman's to penetrate selectively the personality of a living person and reduce him (in this case the male pronoun is apt) to a narrative cipher. This is essentialism at its most singular worst.

He does exist, of course. He rescued me from the Depot River. We drank rum together. We often ran side by side on the gravel roads past his place in the country.

Sometimes in the pouring rain, my crazy friend, sometimes laughing. I would never play him at tennis, I knew he was merciless, but, running, I could hold my own, sometimes running as hard as we both could run for an hour, then dropping him off and running another three miles home. Does this sound like someone I would make up?

Still, if you didn't know him, it is conceivable. Even if you know his work. Publication does not prove a particular author's existence. Someone else could have done the writing. But suppose I did invent him, it would have to be as an absence, a fiction to displace the friend still alive in my mind. Do you remember the brother's death in *Anna Karenin,* the imponderable absurdity of his dying? That is what happens in Matt's penultimate novel, *Last Seen,* a brother's death, inconceivable and absolute, is rendered absurd. Versions of the deceased keep appearing. The present and past intrude on each other. No matter how groteque the implications. The future becomes possible.

There is an imposter, perhaps, who inhabits the life of my fictional friend. This accounts for the unreality. He has been displaced but everything is as it was. He frets, this fictional friend, in an asylum in northern Ontario, protesting the larceny of his identity to a staff who have learned not to hear the chatter of their charges, listening instead for hidden messages like readers trained in the art of New Criticism. Meanwhile, the imposter lives with his children, sleeps with his wife, writes his books. If you find this offensive, remember *Last Seen,* the poignancy when nothing is real.

Perhaps it is a long lost cousin in his place, eager to re-establish his roots, a drug-dazed American draft-dodger who stumbled into nirvana, a blackmailer who extorts new epics from the lunatic in his northern sanctuary on threat of exposing his sanity, or an anti-Semite trapped in the life of a secular Jew, determined to exploit it for all it is worth. Perhaps it is me. That is the twist you have been anticipating, you who are conditioned by the workings of plot. You expect narrative complexities eventually to resolve with retroactive inevitability, as if life were coherent and death not the only resolution to our myriad confusions.

You might wonder that his wife and children could be taken in by an impostor but that is a writer's conceit, that each of us can be fooled by even those closest to our hearts, that until something goes radically wrong, we might not notice a beloved companion or husband or father has been gone for a long time and only an efficient replica remains in his place. The same could be true in a woman's life, but in this particular context I am talking of men. Matt Cohen and I were friends, and if I invented him he also invented me, that is what friends do.

Perhaps it is he who inhabits his life who was holding him back. Quite possibly I am wrong about this, and each of his works is the best it can be. That is no mean achievement. But whether I am in the Salem country of southeastern Ontario, among country people articulated with cunning familiarity, or in the cities, Toronto or Paris of the present, Toledo or Bologna, six centuries ago, in death camps or the tortured minds of pogrom and holocaust survivors, or in the minds of children, I have such a sense of the humanity behind the vision, I want more. I want more of the visionary. More of the man writing than what is written. He learned from the masters to write himself out of the text, refine himself out of existence. This is good for people who are less in their lives than the works they create. But Matt Cohen the man is alive like a flame in his writing and should declare himself real. In *Elizabeth and After* he comes closest to becoming the text; perhaps what I want is perfection, after all.

So much for that. You have no reason to trust me on

this, especially if you tend to the possibility that I am a character waiting to happen, resentful that he did not bring me to life. If that is true, then obviously I would suspect him of untapped genius, I have a vested interest. But read him yourself. Do you not, as you work your way through short stories that explode slowly in your mind and gothic romance and romantic comedy and sagas and confessions and angst-driven chronicles, do you not always suspect Matt Cohen knows more than he is telling? Sees more than he says? It isn't that he holds back. It is as if he cannot risk inflicting on you the true depth of his vision, the sheer breadth of his wit. What would he lose? Perhaps himself.

Readers who now, at the turn of the millennium, persist in demanding plot and character want the writer as well. It is not for nothing Matt Cohen is wary. And it is not by accident that I myself have abjured both, and write works that are uncompromisingly impersonal and constantly at odds with the linearity of syntax and print, with the sequential tyrannies of meaning and sense. If I cannot confound, how could I expect to keep my readers engaged? Not by personality. Not by transforming myself into words, the whole of me present in all that I write. It is enough that I offer access to language used in new ways; yet some readers want blood, literally, flesh and bones, a real person writing. I think of them, the modernist readers, as cannibals. It is not for nothing Matt Cohen is wary.

I am glad you are reading this, that you are my witness. If Matt Cohen held me somewhere in the illimitable reaches of his mind, among its infinite chambers and innumerable voices, I would have asked him to give me daughters whom I would love with touching simplicity, a life in the country that would unfold always with the awkward sweetness of Spring, memories to fill the present with dreaming, dreams to make the present worth keeping, and an honest personality, an admired sense of humour, boundless talent and sublime modesty. No, of course, I would not. I would be my own person. My daughters I would love with genuine complexity, I would leave the country to live in real time in a stone house on the edge of a town, and I would reinvent myself in the authentic world, a man utterly in love. Good-bye Matt Cohen. For now. Until we become fiction together.

Film Rights Pending

There was a woman who when she ventured from home always wore a hat with fresh panties folded out of sight on top of her head. In restaurants she kept the hat on, usually the only person to do so except for an occasional squad of pubescent boys wearing identical baseball caps with the peaks pulled down at the back to assert their individuality. The purpose of the panties was two-fold. She had an exquisitely shaped head; the sun-hats she favoured tended to rest low against her ears and so needed the added height afforded by lingerie which had just the right amount of lacework to catch in her hair without pulling. She also felt reassured by knowing she had a change of underwear, should she need it, especially during her periods, when she was confident enough of her purchasing power to throw a soiled garment away.

In the closing pages of *Coming through Slaughter,* Michael Ondaatje violates decorum. He cannot resist entering the fiction, perhaps because by then his rendering of Buddy Bolden's jazz-world, alien to Ondaatje's own experience, has been so successful that Bolden's reality is more authentic than his own. I can imagine Michael sitting in a corner of the barn at his summer place, the whitewashed walls absorbing shadows, space between the beams over his head shimmering with spider-webs draped into the diffuse natural light under the weight of chaff that has seeped through chinks in the boards from the hay mow above, flecked with the desiccated corpses of half-digested flies, not a calendar on the wall nor body marks of cattle that have rubbed against the cooling stone beneath earlier layers of whitewash for a hundred summers, thick stone warmed by their body heat through a hundred winters, not a book or article of clothing, nothing, an old Players Navy Cut tobacco can, dented, in the corner, empty, nothing else, the pressed-wood chair he sits on, and in front of him, across the elm desk retrieved from one of a thousand classrooms in southern Ontario with its two neat piles of paper, one blank and the other bearing hieroglyphs of type, above eye level is a small two-paned window that shows only the luxuriant green of grass-tips on an old manure mound and a triptych of dead elms etched against the sky, and looking to the light he can see a New Orleans that runs the length of his mind like an old film, and he can write himself into what he sees, flickering for a few frames, indistinct to anyone not paying attention, play a few notes, and withdraw, knowing his brief presence there has changed the world.

There was a woman who found it impossible to carry a tune. She could hear music in her head and had no trouble recognizing obscure instrumental pieces played on CBC fm. But as soon as she began to sing, the noise would set up such interference in her mind that all she heard was a pleasing dissonance, while others heard cacophony. She had an eclectic repertoire that she would vent in showers or driving alone as she usually did, or in solitary places she visited on holiday. Having failed to fulfill her aspirations for a musical career, she was shy about singing in public, although she had no idea she was off-key, had no rhythm, and rendered melody incomprehensible. Through some neurological quirk there was one exception in her repertoire which she sang perfectly. This was the theme song from the sixty's television sit-com, *Green Acres*. She could sing it like a sound-track, her voice rising for Eva Gabor, dipping for Eddie Albert, taking on a tremulous resonance when they sang together. She had never liked the show itself, and had always switched to *I Love Lucy* re-runs after the theme song ended.

She sometimes imagined herself an old woman with no-one to look after her, sitting in a chair outside her room in a home somewhere, staring at the floor. If anyone spoke to her, she would look up and sing in a quavering voice, "Farm living is the life for me...." When she died, her lips would be mouthing the words, "New York is where I'd rather to be...." She imagined being buried in the small cemetery beside the market garden where she grew up near Streetsville, now surrounded by office towers and parking lots. Sometimes she thought she would prefer to leave her remains in the tiny cemetery enclosed within the swirl of super-highways at the intersection of 401 and 427, which, however, has no entrance or exit, islanded as it is by arcs of asphalt and edged by a wrought iron fence without a gate.

The televised Academy Awards extravaganza that honoured *The English Patient* for its genius in obscuring the boundary between high art and common entertainment, and with every accolade admitted publicly the Academy's good taste, was curiously a celebration of the novel's author, the deep recesses of whose mind generated the narrative on which the film was based. No writer has been more applauded for the creation of a work leading to a screen adaptation than Michael Ondaatje on that night before an audience more vast than imagination can comprehend. He was not introduced but every award the film received brought an acknowledgment of his contribution. Even the woman who won for best costume design applauded Michael. Occasionally the television cameras would pan the front rows of the audience, or focus on a celebrated face, and Michael could be seen a row or two behind. His eyes were on fire. It was amazing the proceedings did not atrophy, while the vital juices of everyone attending were diverted to engulf his beatific diffidence, humility betrayed only by the fire in his eyes.

Beside him was a woman wearing a wide-brimmed

hat, with panties folded neatly under the crown to give her added height because she envisioned herself diminutive. On the other side, an older woman who every time the applause thundered mouthed words to songs no-one recognized from the way she moved her lips. Despite the celebrity, Michael appeared at times distracted, perhaps remembering countless airings of *Casablanca* at Blueroof Farm, each playing of the tape adding to the ones preceding like a serial in his mind, or perhaps plotting a visionary sequel to his celebrated English patient's borrowed life.

Actuality assimilated, then drawn from the writer's unconscious reservoir of experience, no longer belongs to its origin. It is not the function of imagination to sort out in the creative enterprise what is fact and what is invention; it would be impossible to discover the exact line between a metaphoric rose and a rose in a memory of gardens. If Ondaatje's mind is swarming with figures from popular and ancient mythology, Billy the Kid and Gilgamesh haunting each other in weird games in his skull, with great historical figures and the maimed and the nondescript and the briefly infamous on the margins, with musicians, magicians, and friends, it is not required that he stick to the facts in his grasp at the truth. Everything received by the mind becomes private; everything turned from the mind into art is open to public reception.

The woman who wore hats had a name, it was Estelle. The woman bursting with music was Harriet. There once was a man who knew both of them although they did not know each other. All three lived on the same street in the heart of Toronto, on Major St. in what is known as The Lower Annex. The man was not a science-fiction fan but he spent much of his time constructing alternative realities in his head, in search of the perfect conundrum, the ultimate koan, an absolute paradox, and the world around him yielded only varying degrees of irony and bathos.

One day he imagined cloning, where two people both looking exactly like Sigourney Weaver are born as adults, each with the exact neurological configuration of the deceased original so that they have precisely her memories, her reservoir of experience, emerging from their pods at precisely the same moment. For an instant, they are the same person. Then one of them speaks and the other listens. The words do not matter, but in their exchange the two women become forever different, their billions of neurons shifting to accommodate, in one, the generation of what was said, and in the other, its apprehension.

It is the same principle by which a tear alters the composition of the ocean, a poem the entirety of literature. It is not the same exactly, for there would have to be two tears falling in separate oceans which were otherwise identical, two poems added to parallel worlds of literature, each the exact replica of the other. Not exactly this, either, since you would have to think of one poem created out of a literature and the other imposed upon a literature, one tear lifted from an ocean, and the other dropped into another ocean. Not this, either. The man reached an impasse, as he always did in trying to explain his conundrums to himself. Until a new reality came into his head, he would be disconsolate. Estelle would bring him flowers. Harriet would sing to him and rock him in her arms. But nothing helped until, from somewhere deep within, another paradox or puzzle would be released to drift across the panoply of his conscious mind.

Michael must have loved the country. He spent every summer at the farm for fifteen years. Each late afternoon he would drive an old truck over the fields to the swimming hole, with kids and visitors loaded in the back. Across the river and beyond the trees Matt Cohen had a country place and he would walk the land for hours, in every season. Never did he encounter Michael walking on the land or on the country roads. Michael once walked

along the river bottom with his friend Stan Dragland and
made their adventure a poem and when they reached Bellrock prevailed upon the kindness of a neighbour who had
moved there from Toronto to lend them towels and drive
them home. He later dreamed of early timbermen driving
logs to Bellrock, and made that an opening image in his
novel, *In the Skin of a Lion,* fusing reverie and research to
create authentic fantasy.

The man on Major St., whose name is Philip, moved
to the country. He lives alone. He became a famous photographer, taking pictures of insects that lived in his
house. In the beginning, he photographed moths that came
to the bare bulb of the light on the table in the screened-in
porch through the broken screens. He replaced the bulb
with a coal-oil lamp and caught images of the moths flap-
ping against the chimney glass. When he removed the
chimney, he captured a variety of moths in dramatic
sequences of frozen motion flying against the brightness,
scorching their wings, fluttering to the darkness of the
table where by morning they would be expired. When he
discovered under his kitchen counter a colony of termite
ants, he chronicled their existence with a close-up lens so
precise it gave them personalities. House flies bouncing
against the window glass, when resting between bouts,
posed in threatening tranquillity. Mosquitoes drawing
blood from his arm engorged themselves ponderously and
unable to withdraw their proboscises from his flexed
muscles died soporific deaths, the moment of each passing captured in a colour print. A single daddy-long-legs
hidden among the pillars between the layers of a desiccated wedding cake brought down by Harriet while it was
still relatively fresh, unclaimed from the bakery she ran
on Harbord St., revealed itself when he probed at it with
a tarnished serving fork and got tangled in a spider web
where the drama of its death was caught in a sequence of
blurred precision. Maggots on unwashed plates in the sink

turned antiseptic in black and white photographs. Moth
larvae in a lanolin-laden wool wall-hanging created necro-
tic patterns which curiously complemented the weaver's
free-form design. Silverfish and beetles entertained his
lens, joined the others in the book of his adventures. His
genius was celebrated on *As It Happens,* the pictures
being described for the radio audience in image-laden
words.

Michael Ondaatje at readings is rude. He is sweet and
vulnerable. He is wary, he is amused. He is secretive and
confessional. He is polite and never condescending. He is
indifferent to praise and adores adulation. He is sullen. He
has the eyes of a predator, his eyes flash fire, he has the
eyes of a neglected child. There is something cruel about
his self-repose, something sad about his candour, something beautiful about the arrogance of his projected humility. He is a public recluse, a man-child, a trickster and
provocateur, an artist loving on the listener's behalf,
dying on the listener's behalf, a sort of Jesus manqué, a
martyr, no-man, singer enthralled with the voices of God.
At readings he is carelessly fastidious in his dress, a little
gone to flesh, each expression a disguise, and never condescending. In full command of an international vernacular, the raw particulars of any place made apprehensible
to all, he draws the listener into an embrace, their intimacy a wall against the fearsome world. Responding to
questions he is indifferent to pleasing, sometimes rude.

One summer before he left the farm and changed his
life he bought pigs. They were small and comical at first.
Visitors were taken to admire the piglets and watch them
chew on copies of *Animal Farm.* When they reached
human size, they were no longer cute. They looked like
fat naked torsos in the wallow. Their squeals were ob-
scenely evocative of Ned Beatty's humiliation in *Deliver-
ance.* By early autumn Michael had to prevail upon
Philip's generosity, the same good-hearted neighbour who

provided towels and beer the day he and Stan walked the river bottom all the way to Bellrock, to use his truck to get pig-feed at the Co-Op. Michael's own truck was unroadworthy and his car no longer big enough to accommodate the quantity needed as his charges rounded out to massive porkers. The day the slaughter-house picked them up was the last day of Michael's experiment in farming. Unlike Eva and Eddy, he preferred to observe country life from a distance that left amplitude for irony, or lyricism, or metaphor.

Michael Ondaatje is not an easy person to mythologize. There are stories but no plot. To make a movie of his life, as of most lives, it would be necessary to reinvent the nature of existence, assigning beginnings after the beginning, an end that would draw meaning from the episodes lifted out of context, closure where there is no closure. Yet he imagines the world in cinematic clips, creates scenes of static beauty, connects by inference. He describes the moment as a visceral phenomenon, arranges moments to surprise, delight, or horrify. With poetic vision and the vocabulary of a film-maker, he makes films on the page. It is sometimes, reading him, like the experience is not coming from the text but deep within the apprehending mind. His writing seems an affirmation of unconscious realities, as rote prayer affirms the soul. Fragments of perception, fractured revelations, figments of experience, orchestrated to haunt the reader; occupation of the intellect with rounds of common prayer; different as these may seem, both activities release the mind from consciousness to course the depths within.

One day Estelle brought Philip flowers in the country. They were greenhouse flowers from a city florist and he placed them in an antique milk bottle on the centre of the kitchen table, beside the vast bouquet of wildflowers and weeds he had arranged in a chipped porcelein coffee pot, so that the conversation between the two bouquets was almost audible. Beside them on the table was Harriet's abandoned wedding cake; it had been cleaned of spider webs and the daddy-long-legs bits caught up between the pillars. The sugar-icing had hardened to a dull lustre, like skin that has been submerged too long in soapy water. At this point Philip was no longer a photographer and was ashamed of his success. His walls were filled with souvenirs, as if his brain had been turned inside out and the remnants of his life placed on display. Estelle very carefully took off her hat and placed it on the seat of an outsized rocker which Philip explained was made by a cousin who had great talent but no sense of proportion. Seated at the table listening to the flowers, they took each other's hands, their four hands piled like a roadside sculpture. They were not lovers. They were friends.

Estelle told of how she had searched since adolescence for her mother. Estelle had been brought up by Anglican missionaries who forgave her for being a foundling and loved her, as they were fond of saying, as much as their real children. They released her to the world at eighteen with a small annuity in lieu of paying for a college education. She got a degree eventually, then took only jobs she liked, and only for as long as she wanted. Philip remembered that his friend Harriet told him just before he moved away from Major St., while she was rocking him in her arms and singing like Eva Gabor when he was depressed from trying to understand an anomaly of his own devising, that she had had a baby whose father was an itinerant blind musician, and because her own career as a singer was going nowhere she had left her baby girl in the doorway of a Tim Hortons just before opening time because she had always thought Tim Hortons had the kind of atmosphere she would like to emulate, if she ever had a bakery of her own, and they would look after everything. She had thought of Birks, but that seemed elitist, and of Eaton's, but they seemed unstable.

Tim Hortons was intimate, efficient, clean, warm, and caring. Philip told Estelle about Harriet and Estelle squeezed his hands and said that by coincidence she had been left at a Tim Hortons herself, and at the same location. They both remarked on this implicit endorsement of Tim Hortons as the epitome of decency and the Canadian way.

Michael had a dog with droopy ears called Wallace. He had a hound called Dashiel. After Wallace Stevens; after Dashiel Hammett. Wallace was a poet, he would stand on the harvest table beside birthday cakes, summer after summer, and encouraged by the family would howl to the tune of Happy Birthday. Even when Wallace got old and smelled he took place of honour on the table and sang in wobbling tones and hardly missed a beat. Dashiel ran. He ran everywhere. He ran in circles and along the edges of fields in great rectangles originally designed by land-grant settlers after the War of 1812. Michael loved his dogs and watched them furtively, with covert pride.

Philip's walls were covered with artifacts of his life as visual reminders of the period in his twenties when the world was imaginary, and he was blind. He had played the trombone then and travelled with a black group from the Mississippi Delta, although he was white from southern Ontario. Before cataracts enclosed him in darkness he had been a sideman with a CBC house band in Toronto. On a gig back in Toronto, at the Brass Rail, he met a woman who loved music and aspired to a career as a singer. She would sometimes sing to him the signature tunes of television shows and he was kind to her and said nothing about her lack of talent and wasted ambitions. When it was time to move on he went with his group and she never had an opportunity to tell him she was pregnant. Although their affair had been brief, he often thought of her, trying to reconcile the anomaly of her devotion to music with her ineptitude in its creation. After an opera-

tion restored his sight he gave up music and lived on a
disability pension on Major St., just down from Matt
Cohen's city house. He would sit on the small verandah
in all seasons, even in the dead of winter, and people
tended to avoid him, all except a woman with music
locked inside and a younger woman who wore panties
folded neatly under her hat whenever she went out, even
when she was wearing a tuque.

By coincidence both women were in California when
The English Patient was lauded with Academy benefi-
cence and it's author accorded celebrity as a literary
name. They were both outside the auditorium when
Michael entered early but neither of them knew who he
was, because of where they were, although they might
have, had they been in Hazelton Lanes, or having coffee
at Indigo or browsing through Chapters. As both were
dressed with particular style, Harriet like a minor movie
star left over from the fifties and Estelle looking otherworldly in her wide-brimmed hat, they were separately
plucked from the crowd to be seat fillers, their job to
occupy empty seats within camera range when motion
picture arts and science personnel were moving about to
give and get awards. Neither was asked to move through
the whole affair; neither talked to Michael, who was
seated between them; and only when they shuffled
towards the exit at the close and brushed against each
other did they speak, both saying excuse me, and smiling,
recognizing the other must also be Canadian.

Michael Ondaatje does not invent lives, he inhabits
them. He does not create alternative realities, he attunes
his reader to perceptions of the ineffable in their own. He
makes film in the reader's mind. His images unreel
between sprockets before a dazzling lantern, the radiance
of words. The authenticity of his vision is in the articulated absence of light, its substance a splendid illusion.

Estelle moved in with the lonely man in the country,

learned to rock herself to sleep in the outsized rocking chair, took to wearing underwear as nature intended. Harriet came to visit, bringing day-old chocolate croissants, and after Philip introduced them, the two women, neighbours on Major St. for years, recognized each other from the Academy Awards. They all became friends. When the three of them one day encountered Michael Ondaatje at the Bellrock intersection, researching the shape of the village where the river runs through it, neither of them recognized him, nor he them. No introductions were made and when he drove off he slipped from their minds before they had a chance to discuss who he was.

Harriet became a regular visitor and then her visits stopped abruptly. By the time Philip passed away, Estelle had become a country person, collected milkweed pods and branches of bittersweet berries and planted them in water in the chipped porcelain coffee pot on the kitchen table. Alone on her long walks she would sometimes find herself singing in two part harmony. Occasionally she would walk to the back edge of the old Ondaatje property but could see no signs of life. She still lives in Philip's house. When the tax bill came, it was addressed to her, and someone had arranged to transfer the utilities to her name. She now makes the occasional foray into Kingston. She is thinking of taking up photography. She will eventually move back to Toronto, to a house on Major St. left to her through the generosity of an anonymous benefactor. When she visited the house to take possession and arrange for tenants, she could smell the soft odours of a baking oven, even though the stove was off. She misses the evening walks that she and Philip and Harriet took together. Sometimes she goes to movies by herself in Kingston and wears a hat with fresh panties folded under the crown, but this is only in acknowledgment of her transitional condition. No matter how close she sits to the screen, she is always aware of herself watching a film, witness to an ulterior world. Never has she been surprised when it is over, as she has at the end of a book, to find herself who she is. Soon she will move from country to city, back and forth, whenever she wishes, and she will read a lot. She has always loved books, the way they get inside her mind and make connections she would never have dreamed possible.

A Romance for Barbara

Some novels declare at the outset that they were written by people different from you and I, writers we refer to as artists whose works we study in school. Other novels we read precisely because, in spite of inspired plot-lines and characterization, they seem to be written by people exactly like us, to be novels that we would write ourselves if we had the time and the talent. The genius of a writer like Samuel Beckett is that he makes the most commonplace experience absurdly exotic. Perhaps he does so through tactical deployment of language or perhaps through the militant ambiguities of narrative strategy, conflating humour with tragedy, irony with the ominous. He is strange and familiar. At the other extreme, the authors of popular romance make the most exotic of settings and circumstances reassuringly accessible. There is something in the polished transparency of their words that opens the most unlikely stories to the fickle sensibilities of readers who want entry into impossible worlds just like our own.

It is usually in the opening sentence that literary novels reveal their aspirations. For many readers, if I say the title you can supply the first lines of the text from memory: *A Tale of Two Cities, Anna Karenina, Pride and Prejudice.* You might have to think for a minute. If you need reminding, with a few cues it will all come flooding back, the best of times and the worst of times, the variability of unhappy families, the axiomatic necessity for a single man of good fortune to be in need of a wife. The rest follows effortlessly, as for hundreds of pages the authors elaborate on their initial prognostications—that is what such statements are, they foretell a future that has not yet been revealed. Novels written merely as diversions likewise declare themselves early, but usually through compelling syntactical simplicity and a felicity of language intending to engage without being provocative, to be pleasurable without disturbing, to charm not challenge. Some of the best novels close, equally as succinct. It is a far far better thing I do, I cannot go on, I will go on.

If I have only one novel to write, and I cannot imagine a person engaged with life having the inclination to write more than one, I would not want to squander my time or indulge my ego by writing an artistic novel. I would rather write to be read. With this in mind, I will proceed. I need to write; I have seen my spouse devour romances and I wish, just once, to stave off her hunger with a repast of my own devising. As an inspiration to carry me through my endeavour, I have a picture of Samuel Beckett that I clipped from a Toronto newspaper tacked to the wall behind and above my computer. My father told me that General Montgomery of El Alamein always kept a photograph of Field Marshall Rommel by his bed during the desert war, so that the last thing before sleep and the first thing on awakening he stared into the eyes of the enemy. Beckett is my enemy.

He is so, precisely because I covet his writing style and his chiseled face. I realize I can no more assume one as my own than the other, although it would be as enticing surgically to alter my appearance like Beckett as to write of despair with such wit. Beckett in the world is a snare and a delusion for a writer like me, setting out to create my first and only work. I must at all costs resist the desire to appear in my writing or person so opulently austere as my mentor and enemy. I am writing to my spouse, not posterity. I wish to be read, not admired. Life right now is game enough; posterity will look after itself. Veneration without sales is vanity.

My wife is a reader. She knows of the world through

books. She was thirty-seven before she discovered sex could be as real as breakfast, not something cleverly evoked through erotic evasions in a text. In another era she might have entered a convent in her teens and devoted her life to reading the same few passages in the same few books over and over, bewildered by her occasional nocturnal ecstasies in the height of prayer. Instead, she read her way through adolescence and a desultory career. While little happened of note in the theatre of her life, she had sinuous sensuous adventures offstage among words. When we met, we were both virgins and recognized this in each other as a defining characteristic long before it became a subject of negotiation. I was the same age as she, three months younger to be exact, and I was not a reader. I was a writer.

All my life I have been a writer. Not as you might expect. I have never written a novel before, nor anything of consequence. Nor am I a writer manqué, disporting myself as if I were Hemingway or Norman Mailer or a butch Margaret Atwood. Rather, I have always observed my own life from an authorial perspective. I have related my own story to myself, translating every conscious moment into the words of an ongoing narrative. In my head I am a third-person protagonist. His mother calls him to dinner. He swears under his breath, goes to the table. His father is absent again. He sits in his father's place. His mother looks frightened for an instant, then serves him his Jello. Dinner always begins with green Jello flecked with pineapple pieces and traces of parsley. He describes himself eating, words echoing through his head, the resonance of creating himself at times deafening. For respite he occasionally closes the world out, stares at nothing, wears silence like armour, but never for long. The world intrudes. He will finish dinner, then do his homework which at this age means practicing his capital C's. He has an itch. He will scratch it. He rolls into bed. He will sleep.

He sleeps.

It is not very complicated. Writing in my mind gives me an insulating distance from the vicissitudes of consciousness. While all about me flutters or rages and signifies nothing, deftly ensconced in my narrative I observe or ignore, contrive consolations, compensations, slip into lyrical flight, sensual delight, or immune from pain wrestle the most vexing conundrums to earth. You might see my life as an extended epistolary novel dictated in volume after volume which are shelved unread in the back of my mind. By thirty-seven years of age, I was beginning to lose track of the uncatalogued tomes gathering cobwebs and dust in my brain. Then I met Barbara and discovered a complementary psyche as obsessively bibliophallic as my own. Books for her were tangible entities, although the places they took her were no more real than my own contextualized autoerotic evasions. Within six months we were married and after another three spent on an extended honeymoon through western Europe our marriage was consummated in the darkness of a hotel room in Venice at midday, the velvet royal-blue curtains drawn close to keep out the light reflected from the Grand Canal and the eloquent blue sky above, and only the flicker of a single candle set against the marble hearth to break the absolute absence of illumination, without which we might both have envisioned the other a narrative device.

Since then we have conducted a normal sex life. For almost two decades we have been lovers when the mutual need arises. This tends to be on Saturday afternoons. I like to watch golf while she irons until four. There are no children to distract us. At five we go for a walk, regardless of the weather. Between four and five we sometimes retire to our bedroom and lower the blinds and pretend we are in Venice. Weekdays we are tired from work and Sundays we are enervated in anticipation of another week ahead. She has continued to read her romances and occasionally I read as well, usually a novel I have read before, a literary novel, nothing contemporary although my choices are eclectic. More often than not, I read newspapers. I take comfort in their portentous ephemerality. What is important one day, headlines emblazoned, the next day is gone, displaced by another and another and another, stories without beginnings or ends.

Lately I have come to realize how little I mean to Barbara. As a consequence I have become aware of how trite is my affection for her. She does not know how unimportant we are to each other. She does not know our marriage is about to expire. She reads her books, each one complete in itself; each provides her with a discrete reality beside which her actual experience of the world is pallid and flat. Although a few of her books such as Diana Gabaldon's Outlander series are connected, most have only the random contiguity her mind provides as she reads them. Together they form a bizarre jigsaw puzzle which is her life. The puzzle has no perimeters, it can expand indefinitely. The pieces do not collectively form a coherent picture, yet they relate to each other through common motifs and characters and plots, and the invisible presence of her own personality. The seams between the pieces, the weird interlocking cut of their edges, that is the world unread, the world we occupy together.

Samuel Beckett's nose is distracting. I cannot imagine him as a young man, before his eyebrows flowered like roadside weeds and brought his nose into reasonable proportion, although still it is stentorian, a nose to command respect. I stare at his nose in a newspaper photograph and try to remember his writing. Scenes from plays come to mind, comical distressing scenes, but no stories. There are no stories, only episodes. There are neither beginnings nor ends, only sequences of contemporaneous moments. I remember more intimate aspects of his novels and try to avoid myself in his texts. His nose forms a vertical axis to the horizontal axis of his piercing eyes. I look at my spouse, reading across from me on the sofa. I am in a wing-back chair by the fireplace. The fire is out. It is gas. I could turn it on. The room is cool. Instead I get up and find a sweater and settle back into my chair and stare at Barbara who is in the Scottish Highlands at the moment, gratefully in the embrace of a miserably handsome brute called Jamie, most likely.

Beckett's nose makes me think of Renny Whiteoak. Powerful. Aquiline. The nose of a romantic protagonist. There was a time when more people would have recognized Renny on the street than ever would have known the tall gaunt Irishman Beckett traipsing the boulevards of rain-soaked Paris. Despite being fiction, Renny Whiteoak was real to millions of readers enchanted with the saga of his family in the Jalna chronicles. He was a convincing alternative for a generation who saw humanity squandered in war and stifled by a great depression, more authentic than their own lives. Beckett, by contrast, reflects in his face the horrors of this century and radiates the strength it has taken to endure. Beckett's face is etched with tragedy, but there is comic wistfulness about the mouth, and when he smiles there is unutterable sadness in his eyes.

Barbara sometimes called me Renny after we first met. She had read all seventeen novels in the Whiteoak series several times over and could walk through the rooms of Jalna in any era from early Victorian to postwar suburban and describe the decor. She knew exactly which characters would inhabit each room at any given time and what they would say. She confessed to me once that she was so comfortable in Mazo de la Roche's romantic extrapolation of Ontario gentry that the only way out was provided by each novel's romantic conclusion. If she was not such a satisfying writer, said Barbara, bringing about closure in seventeen ways, I might have long ago made Jalna my home.

Of course, she added, I would spend much of my time in the family library reading romances, at least until the turn of the century when Renny came of age. Even then I might be content to read and observe, fearful that my affections engaged would disrupt the inevitable flow of events in the Jalna household. Looking at her now, across the living-room of our modest house, it does not seem difficult to imagine her elsewhere. She has not called me Renny since Venice. Before, not after, the consummation.

Venice for her was the closest she has ever come to living a piece of the puzzle. When the plane touched down in Rome she started calling me Renny and Rory and Lance. By the time we had driven to Florence, with a brief stop at San Gimignano to listen to open-air opera in a cordoned-off piazza among the medieval towers, she referred to me as her darling lover, never directly but to personnel at the small hotels where we stayed. We were in our third month of travel, plane-hopping from capital to capital, then driving around within the borders of each country as if they were not contiguous but had boundaries insuperable except by the magic of flight. Because we did not necessarily fly between adjoining countries but criss-crossed Europe in a random itinerary dictated by the novels Barbara was consuming with inordinate passion at the time, there was no sense to our travels of geographical or cultural coherence. Europe was proving to be a scattering of dissociated regions jigsawed haphazardly from an imponderable map. When we swept into Venice on a vaporetto from the parking place at the city's edge, then switched to a gondola off Piazza San Marco for a leisurely tour before arriving at our slightly decrepit hotel on the Grand Canal, a single rose in her hand that I had bought for her from a waterborne vendor, for the only time in her life, I believe, romance and reality merged.

Over the bed an etching of turtle doves, one dead and
one grieving, caught a blood-red shard of the westerly
sunlight through a crack in the velvet curtains. The candle
flickered in the hearth, pallid in comparison. By the time
the sun and our ardour both faded, Barbara had shifted
from the damp centre of the bed and recovered herself
sufficiently to take up a new novel by lamplight and drift
in the arms of a more handsome and accomplished young
lover atop the flotsam fragment of a shattered lifeboat to
an island where they would be marooned until the arrival
of a ship that would find her alone, her virtue restored by
the realization that her lover had been a wondrous figure
of her imagination, a spectre or ghost who mysteriously
secured her safety and well-being across the centuries that
separated their lives, he having been drowned in the exact
spot where her ship went down after being thrown over-
board by a splenetic captain who found out they were
rivals for the affection of the woman whose offspring
eleven generations later would be the woman he rescues.
It was a modern novel. Perhaps the marooned woman
would be pregnant.

I sat in our open casement overlooking the most
romantic canal in the world and dictated to myself the
narrative of the day's events. Especially regarding the
most recent situation, the third person voice seemed
appropriate. He had not discovered the sex act enthralling.
In fact, he found it quite awkward to arrange his body in
the peculiar positions such intimacy seemed to require.
He was embarrassed when sounds emerged from deep in
his throat that might have been coming from someone
else, but more so when his body exploded. He had not
been prepared for that. His wife seemed hardly to notice.
She was simultaneously so absorbed in what was happening to her that his presence was almost an intrusion, and
yet she was a great distance away, somewhere he could
never reach. Her imagination was filling in gaps and

ellipses in novels she had read between arousal and the
morning after. More contemporary novels had given her
details, of course, but without the accompanying sensa-
tions, while earlier novels did not so much ignore sex as
transliterate it into suppressed functions of sensibility.
Now and forever she had shared the ultimate experience
of women in romance, their ecstasies differing from hers
only in matters of degree.

He suspected, sitting in his casement, contemplating
his wife reading in the light of a glass-shaded Venetian
confection beside the bed, that they had made love well,
even though he had no basis for comparison. He also
recognized as his eyes strayed to the faux-marble fireplace with the burnt-out candle stub fixed to the bottom of
an inverted teacup that she would have no need for future
intimacies, having established in her nerve endings and
mind what love-making felt like. They would make love
again, they were married, it was expected, but he knew as
he watched her turning the pages, the bleach-white sheet
drawn taunt across her chest, that she would never be
present for him more than she was now. Staring at the
worn fabric of the machine-woven carpet, the tension
between the geometric precision of the knots and the
controlled chaos of the court design leading him for a
moment to consider other things, he grasped uncertainly
the sadness of their marriage, the inefficacy of affection
between them. His gaze wandered and then rested as he
looked upwards at the waves of light reflected from the
lantern of a passing gondola on the ceiling, softening the
sharp random lines in the plaster, casting wavering ridges
of shadow from the cracks. We will live like any other
couple, he wrote, etching the words deeply into the walls
of his mind. Between forbearance and despair.

After a late dinner in the open air on a small piazza
not far from the hotel, we returned to our room and read
ourselves to sleep. I was reading Cervantes in paperback

at the time and dreamed of myself as Don Quixote, writing his memoirs. While eating breakfast at water-level in the hotel restaurant, Barbara told me she had dreamed of Venice and then curiously added that it was a disappointment to awaken and find herself actually there. I told her I dreamed of myself as a knight in armour capable of doing great deeds. We walked for a couple of hours but by mid-morning the heat was oppressive and the canal waters smelled so we returned to our room and read for the rest of the day, having lunch sent up by room service. The next day we made the necessary arrangements and by nightfall we were on our way home, with a brief stop-over in Paris. Beckett lived there then. He would have been in his early seventies, a decade still from death. I thought of him as we passed through, thought of searching for him like I had years before as a student when I caught a glimpse of his gaunt figure in the autumn rain and followed him until he disappeared around a corner on the Rue Madeleine. But we spent the night at the Charles de Gaulle and by early morning were aloft, hovering among clouds, waiting for Toronto to spin into place beneath us. By night we were in our own small house off Davenport Avenue that we had bought with our savings before being married and Venice and Beckett were as absent as the expired images of yesterday's dreams.

As an Irish Catholic Beckett was gifted and doomed. Staring into those dark frightening eyes or frightened eyes in his pixillated newspaper image, I feel strangely connected to his power and weakness. Sitting across the room from Barbara, enthralled in the romance of the moment, reading with urgency to offset the dread of her eventual departure at the novel's close back into this world we share, I wonder at the strange confluence of lives and events that creates a vision like his. In another time he might have been an articulate grouch or a barbed-wit jester. To be who he was in the context of his times meant having God as an elusive oppressive antagonist, not an absence. It meant having the religion and state that he rejected as equally absurd forever casting light from behind so that no matter how nimble he danced it was always in the pool of his own shadow. I look to myself unmarked by ethnicity, indifferent to religion and the meaning of life, all my life merely living, to this moment unquestioning, ordinary, passively observed, and I think to myself in the first person singular, I will write. I will write a readerly novel, a romance for Barbara.

The long narrative of my existence is encoded in my skull like a convoluted labyrinth, this from a present perspective for it was recorded in sequence as it occurred but is remembered as a discontinuous maze of astounding complexity. As I prepare to write I find so much to draw upon from my meagre adventures in the everyday world, my existence excites me. It has taken Barbara to make me realize this. Existence excites me. It has taken a black and white picture of Samuel Beckett to make me see Barbara. She dwells among words and only emerges to do whatever she must to get by, so she can wander away in another romance and another, accumulating pieces in a puzzle that will never cohere because her life does not provide an over-all pattern or vision. Poor Barbara.

What I propose to do is write a popular novel, a romance. In this respect I recognize Beckett as my enemy for I cannot deny the desire he invokes within me to write the one book of my life as an artist, using the resources of language and literature to write a testimony to the astonishing strangeness of the most ordinary experience. But I must stay the course, my purpose is to enrapture Barbara. I will study the books she reads, and I will offer all the ingredients necessary to captivate her imagination. In the world I create she will approach utter contentment. But I will violate the conventions of genre. There will be no closure. No happy ending. No end at all. I will write the last pages so that they lead inexorably back to the beginning, and each time around the characters will invent themselves new to consummate their perfect union which will release them to travel back separately to begin again. There will be no need for Barbara to leave. She will remain there, always on the edge of fulfillment. I will not write another book. I might move to Paris and walk the rain-soaked streets for the rest of my life.

Kafkaesque

The names of some writers exceed in importance the achievement of their work. In my present state of distraction I find a search for examples unyielding. I can think of only one. Kafka. There must be others but Kafka is so appropriate to the moment the others seem unimportant enough to let the generalization collapse. I have no fondness for Kafka's writing, no sympathies, epiphanies, or revelations come to mind as I recall his texts. But the word Kafkaesque, that is another thing. The name of the writer evokes inescapable terrors, labyrinthine nightmares in the waking mind that seem the very essence of my own miserable condition.

I have not always been self-absorbed and wretched. I find self-pity contemptible. But there comes a time, or there has come a time for me, when every thought is an assault, and consciousness flays against the sensibility like strands of a whip against flagellated flesh. You may find this familiar ground. Stimuli of anxiety are everywhere and there are no alternatives or escapes. Life becomes so oppressively complex you wish desperately to expire, and the intolerable paradox is that it also becomes overwhelmingly simple, for there is nowhere to turn, only the rumble of the hours rolling under your feet as you forge ahead. When it is like this, you inhabit the word Kafkaesque, it fits like water around a submerged body.

There is strange relief in being able to put a word to my lamentable condition. In describing the experience of my present life as Kafkaesque, it becomes less so. That is testimony to the genius of language. If I could focus on the word 'Kafkaesque' and at the same time expunge the word 'my' from my vocabulary, I do believe the sun would one day shine again and the passage of time would no longer be a personal affront but rather a voyage I share with every living thing.

What Kafka did not understand is that true misery is based on happiness. If I did not remember awakening to the light of morning in my lover's arms, my anxiety would not be profound. I have been happy and now that my lover is gone I find myself utterly bereft of the desire to live, yet equally unwilling to embrace the absolute darkness of death. Had we not once been together, perhaps everything would not seem heightened, every touch more poignant, every smell and taste more potent, every sight more dazzling and every sound more penetrating. Perhaps, had we never been together, I would now be merely numb and relatively uninterested in anything.

I will explain in due course. You have a right to know the details. I will arrange pertinent information in ways that will enable you to make more sense out of my existence than I have found living it. Part of the necessary illusion of narrative is based on the assumption that coherence is possible, that what appear in a life to be random events do in fact connect. It can be infuriating to live amidst chaos; that is what makes plot so appealing. Perhaps in the process of resolving the story we will achieve catharsis, although mine will be invention and yours the purgation of imagined catastrophe.

What I am doing in the present discussion is establishing that narrative time is discontinuous, even when it seems inextricably linked to the syntax that carries you through from one sequence of words to another. The essence of narrative is the distortion of time, a conspiracy between writer and reader. While time outside the text may be a continuum, the fourth dimension of the universe, inside the text it is architectonic. In a Kafkaesque text, time is the walls of the maze and the course of the journey; it is the shape of oppression and the incentive to endure.

It is important to share with you my thoughts on time and narrative structure. You have suffered too, I know you have. You have been as wretched as I, and perhaps with even more reason. You have come through stronger than you could have imagined. Your pleasure in reading of my misery demands we both keep a safe distance from the actual events. You have no desire to renew your own suffering; I have no need to perpetuate despair. Yet something more than syntax drives us forward. You want to see reality arranged for revelation, you want to see my misery and by extension your own achieve meaning. In this we have a common purpose; to achieve this we must break free of the cumulative sequence of moments we imagine our lives to be, we must enter the optional reality of the text where time is spatial and language is linear.

Let me clarify. If I murdered my husband, long after we were divorced and in spite of finding my lover wholly satisfying, there is a sequence of causes and consequences, a history of the event, that will provide a context within which, retrospectively the deed will seem horrifyingly inevitable. You may be thrown off a bit at this point by my arbitrary revelation of a female persona. Does this mean you have to rethink everything that has passed between us? I hope not; gender has not been an issue. You made certain assumptions and you were mistaken. Accept with grace the error of your inference and we will proceed. Whether or not I murdered my husband is of more significance than confusion about gender.

Like all good stories, this one begins at the end—if the outcome were not already known, there would be no point in beginning. The ending I am going to suggest to begin with seems decisive enough at first. The handle of a large kitchen knife is protruding from the blood-soaked shirt stretched across my husband's stomach. Blood is dropping like a sheet of crimson foil to the floor and more blood is flowing down the handle, which is clutched in my hand. Soon my hand and the knife and the gaping shirt-front and his extruding innards are an amorphous mass of molten red. On the floor the foil ripples and spreads in an expanding pool around our feet. Soon, I am supporting his weight with the knife and the pressure makes the blade rise up through his diaphragm and lodge against his rib-cage. Involuntarily I release my grip and he slides down into his own pooled blood. I step outside the blood. The tops of my shoes are flecked with viscera. As I walk across the kitchen the soles leave prints on the floor that become progressively more obscure until I enter the hallway and they are only earth-coloured smudges on the runner that disappear into the ornate pattern before I reach the front door and step into the late afternoon sunlight.

The fascinating thing here is that you are relieved. After sidling about on the narrative margin, you are finally into the grisly details of a plot. This does not make you a moral monster, a ghoul in the garden of depravity. On the contrary, your mind makes emotional leaps driven by your innate sense of decency. Why has she done this? What happens next? You want motive and consequence. Meanwhile you suspend judgement. Deep in your skull you are haunted by the spectre of the author and Kafka in some sort of oppressive conspiracy. But blood drives your engagement with text; you need to connect on the level of experience. I have described an unpleasant incident in my life and you cannot resist being involved.

Let us suppose I loved my ex-husband. I had just arrived at Bertram's place from my job with an insurance conglomerate and walked into the kitchen. Bertram was standing by the sink with his back to me when I entered the room. He was hunched forward as if he had a muscle spasm in his lower intestines, the kind you get from running on a full stomach. When I touched his shoulder he straightened and turned around. His facial features had already collapsed into a death mask but deep in his eyes there was a flicker of something I could not interpret, for in the instant of his turning I became aware of the knife handle protruding at an awkward angle away from his corpulent body and was distracted as blood began to gather and seep through the material of his shirt as if my turning him had made it happen.

This was not a time for tentative gestures. I grasped the knife resolutely, but then lost all sense of what to do next. I tried to read his eyes but he was no longer there. I held on to the knife. It was as if to let go would break the strange bond his dying established between us, a kind of intimacy that is absolute, that only a person attending the death of another can understand. With the slightest shudder he became a dead weight and I could no longer support him; he slipped into the pool of blood at our feet. I stepped away from the blood and walked quickly out of the house into the bright sunlight of the late afternoon.

We had been divorced almost a decade before, after a marriage of twelve years. I was working for an escort service in Toronto when we met. Bertram was a farmer from central Manitoba. He had emigrated from Sweden as a casualty of war. Despite Sweden's neutrality his father had been killed by Nazis. Bertram spent his adolescence desperately in love with his mother. When she remarried he left for Canada and never again allowed thoughts of her to dwell in his mind. Bertram could be very resolute. He cleared the poplar forest on a neglected land grant and prospered in mixed farming. Despite his experience in animal husbandry, he had no knowledge of women and when he came to Toronto to find a wife who would help fulfill his dynastic ambitions he found our agency in the Yellow Pages and requested a virgin, whereupon I entered his life.

Nature's Bounty Escort Service catered to a wealthy

clientele and it was unique among such businesses in that it was not a front for prostitution. All the women, we called ourselves 'girls,' who worked for Bounty had to sign a document affirming that we would not consummate sexual relations with our clients. Some of the girls took this to mean they would not have an orgasm on the job. I had the advantage of actually being a virgin and found it surprisingly simple to convince the men I escorted that I wished my condition to endure. Most were incredibly excited by the opportunity to wine and dine an attractive celibate, somehow more flattered than challenged, and not one of them tried to use the leverage of money or power, both of which I understood well as an aspiring insurance adjuster, to relieve me of what one feisty septuagenarian banker described as the burden of my chastity

Bertram was different. Where the sophisticated businessmen placed a premium value on what they could not have, Bertram was only mildly appreciative when I gave him my salutary explanation of the terms of our engagement. My virginity was something he took as a given, one item in my mysterious arsenal of credentials. That's what I asked for, he said. Well, that's what you've got, I responded, unsure of his sincerity. Let's do the town, he said. He had read that expression somewhere, although where I'm not sure as he was not much of a reader. Not at the barber shop, since until I came along he cut his own hair. Possibly the dentist's. He didn't do his own fillings.

You have forgotten the grisly terms of his death. Admit it, you are more interested in the potential on that first date for sexual congress. And indeed, it happened. Bertram and I wound up in bed that night as naturally as in a fairy-tale romance for adults. He was handsome, then, and very intense. An oddly endearing lack of worldliness prevented him from knowing how foolish he was to fall for a call-girl, even one who sold innocence. I fell in love with his capacity for silence; I had never known anyone so apparently free of language. For our second date I called in sick to the agency. We had dinner at the Royal York. On the way back to Bertram's hotel, he raped me in the back seat of the cab. His wordless embrace gradually became an expression of control, his quietness a terrifying assertion of power. In a perverse affirmation of Newtonian physics, the harder he pinned me against the seat, the more I struggled. The quieter he was, the louder I protested. The taxi driver took it all in, accepting this as a brutal ritual of the strange city that circumstance had brought him to, half way around the world from his homeland. He opened the door for us at the hotel and looked at me with compassionate condescension as I adjusted my hair around a face which I knew showed little of the ordeal, my smudged makeup a mask of indecipherability.

Three days later, Bertram and I were married. Four days later, we were on the farm. Twelve years later we divorced. For the following decade I continued to love him, but more out of pity than affection. He followed me when I moved back to Toronto and the farm reverted to nature. Periodically I would visit him after work, spend an hour talking to him. No-one else did and he talked to no-one, including me. He was an emotional derelict, living on welfare, while I prospered. At the moment of his death, my love for him drained away like the blood that gushed from his wound.

I spent that evening in my lover's library, browsing for a book that would bring some light into my day. I was not grieving for Bertram but I was distracted by his death and the rapid shift of my own emotions. It was as if my love had been a kite string and after interminable buffeting in the wind the kite had broken free; and I was left with a weightless string fluttering to the ground in a sort of perpetual falling. First I went home, cleaned my shoes, had a long bath, put on comfortable clothes and then went to my lover's house even though I knew he was in Vancouver for the week on business. It was a large house in Rosedale with a well-stocked library. I had never seen my lover read a book. His former wife assembled the collection. Former is not the right word for my lover is a widower. Former implies the termination of a relationship, when in fact it was she who terminated. Former implies I had marital designs.

I pulled a volume bound in red from the shelves of my lover's dead wife's library; it was wedged among the shadows of matching black volumes, offering itself as an anomaly, at the same time reclusive, almost as if its ambivalence was a matter of volition. There was no identifying print on the spine or front cover. I opened to the title page. The author was Rebecca Arquette. That is my name. The title was *The Autobiography of a Suicide.* I have never written a book. I did not know the word suicide could be a proper noun; I thought of it as an act. I sat down in a wing-backed chair by the cold fireplace, circled in a pool of light by the murky crenellated depths of book-lined walls and turned to the first page.

'This is a work of fiction,' the book began. 'It would not be possible to be otherwise. Not because all stories are fiction or even because all lives perceived from a present perspective are fiction, but simply because you are re-creating in your reading mind my life from a verbal continuum of particulars and therefore constructing as fiction what for me has been reality.' The voice was familiar but it was not mine. There was a didactic edge to it. It seemed to be speaking to me, but not for me. I turned again to the title page. There, in bold italic print, was the pronouncement, this book is a posthumous publication. Well, of course it is, I thought. Otherwise, the title would be inaccurate. If you cannot trust words to mean what they say, then nothing has meaning at all.

I looked around me from my sphere of light into the shadows of the room. The walls shimmered in the semi-darkness with the souls of dead writers whose words were tremulous within their diverse texts, urging upon the sensibility of potential readers their desire to be released. It was like being in a cemetery in a raging storm that threatens to tear the dead from the earth and send them howling around you like banshees; like walking unseen within the circles of Hell while the keening dead call piteously for the company of a living soul to bear them witness.

It had not been a good day and seeking sanctuary, I continued to read. Since this book was an autobiography, the name of the main character would also be Rebecca Arquette. I was several pages into the lugubrious text before I realized the protagonist was male. Autobiography therefore was a fictional conceit. In trying to portray the resonance of a masculine voice, the author was dolefully verbose. Had she merely written with an open heart, she might have been more convincing. After several pages I discovered the protagonist's name was John. This sent through me a visceral chill; the name had significance I could not decipher. Then his last name: also a monosyllable, although closer to a stifled sneeze than the yawn of his first.

Having opened by situating himself as authorial voice somewhere between fact and fiction, John wrote as follows:

> Today a man I know at the University where I work died because his estranged wife had the affection of his children and they turned against him. He killed himself in a rage of despair and self-pity, both emotions familiar to me. He was not a close friend but I am in shock. I look to my own life, weigh his decision in the light of my own experience. His

children are very young. I did not know his wife or
the terms of their estrangement. But I know he died
for his children; we would, any of us, die for our
children.

I thought about this. Bertram and I had no children. I was
once pregnant by my lover, even though he was obsessively cautious. I did not tell him and I miscarried near the
end of the first trimester. We were only together for a
season. If I could have had my baby I would happily have
sacrificed my lover and Bertram both. Their lives meant
little by comparison, I could have snuffed them out like
candles, if the darkness would have yielded me a child. It
seems to me the men in my life have been impediments to
procreation.

Having introduced in such a macabre way his own
devotion to children, John began to recount his early
years, but interrupted his personal chronology to explicate
theories of narrative, concepts of time, emotional anxieties devoid of context. He was failing the first rule of
autobiography. Despite a scattering of trivial details from
his childhood, he had not given me reasons to read. There
were no radical time shifts to suggest eventual fame or
fortune, infamy or enlightenment, achievement or adventure, nothing of the future intruded on his past to make me
want to continue retrieving his life from among words.
After a while it was not enough to be carried forward by
syntax and the vague urgency I detected to have the reader validate him as a witness. I slipped the small repository
of his existence back among the ink-black shadows from
whence it came. So much for a life that was not even a
distraction.

I slept in my lover's bed that night and only went
home to change my clothes before going to the office. I
anticipated a visit from the police and wanted to be
prepared, which meant appropriate clothes and make-up

donned like a carapace to fend off the expected inquisi-
tion. It never came. The police must surely have known of
my existence. There were envelopes with my return address lying on Bertram's arborite kitchen table, some of
them splattered with blood. I know they were there
because when he was sliding away from the knife to the
floor I distinctly recall turning my head and seeing them,
and feeling a fleeting twinge of sadness that since I never
enclosed notes with my occasional cheques he had saved
the envelopes they came in.

Perhaps there was no incentive to find me; Bertram
dead was of no more significance than Bertram alive. But
what of my bloody footprints? The hallway runner was
threadbare. It might have been the work of loving hands
a century ago, a Kurdish bride's gift to her husband's
family, that had made its way through myriad stories and
successive markets to the thrift-shops of Toronto, and
now was so decrepit that blood-stains did not show to the
eye and no-one was sufficiently interested to send it away
for analysis. Perhaps the police had clumsily obscured my
footprints left on the linoleum with their own, or perhaps
there was so much fresh blood clinging to my shoes that
for my first few steps the smudged pools of my egress
obscured the prints, or perhaps Bertram's blood had
spread across the floor and engulfed my footprints, oblit-
erating them as it dried. I had thought of going back and
wiping them away and rolling up the carpet and throwing
it in the garbage. As it turned it, this was not necessary

After a few days I began to relax. My lover returned
from Vancouver and I stopped sleeping over at his place.
He preferred it that way and so did I. Not long after, we
parted. Then the terrors began, the asphyxiating despair.
It was not as if I had not been left before or left others.
But this was different. There was something between us
akin to a constant awareness of death, a bond that held me
together, although before we met I had seemed whole

enough, and when he went away I found myself fragmented, my interior world scattered like the shards of a
broken kaleidoscope.

In order to understand, you need to let me take you
back to when we met. I could have begun with this, we
would have reached the same conclusion. It would have
been the same story, really, plotted differently. And that
is the point. Story is not what narrative is all about. It is
plot that draws you in, then turns you out with something
new, an epiphany or view or vision. Anyone can tell a
story; you just start talking. Only a shaman or an artist or
the truly paranoid can surround you with a plot. So that is
why I have to take you back.

Our first meeting was in a kitchen at my girlfriend's
place. She was throwing a blind-date party; everyone was
to bring someone no-one else knew. It was her idea of
how to meet new people and it seemed safer than going to
clubs. I took a forgettable man from my office with a droll
sense of humour, whose company I enjoyed and in whom
I had absolutely no romantic interest. Considering the
number of people the party was surprisingly conversa-
tional. We all gathered in the living-room, many sitting on
the floor, and told stories about ourselves.

The bar was set up in the dining alcove, but I went
into the kitchen to freshen my drink with tap-water.
Standing with his back to me was a large man still in his
day-time suit. His posture suggested he was concentrating
on something. As I moved around him to get at the sink,
I could see he was leaning over a much smaller woman,
clutching the handle of a knife on which she was impaled
through the lower chest. She turned to look at me, seemed
almost to smile, then shut her eyes and her body weight
sank fully onto the knife which caught against her rib-
cage so that as her legs buckled she was suspended at
almost her full height.

The man ignored me and I was too shocked to scream

or run. My mind emptied and after an immeasurable delay I stepped forward and grasped the woman from the back and lifted her off the knife and laid her gently on the floor, not strong enough to move her away from the pool of blood that had gathered at their feet. I was now smeared with blood and when I placed my hand against her breast to feel for respiration I left an open hand-print on her blouse. The man dropped the knife which with preternatural reflexes I caught in mid-air, so that it would not puncture the corpse between us.

Suddenly I had the knife. In catching it I appeared to be brandishing it in his direction. Someone entering the room would have seen me as the killer, threatening a man who had come to the victim's aid, failed, and was being held at bay. Lock the door, I said. He looked at me, then pulled the partially open door that led to a fire-exit closed and locked it. The other door, I said. There was a bolt on the door separating the kitchen from the rest of the apartment. He slid it quietly across, then turned to see what I expected him to do next.

No, I said. Lock it loud, so they can hear. They'll give us privacy. They'll think we're having sex. There was tile on the floor. This had probably been a bathroom before the house was duplexed. Thus, the door-bolt. The tile made the floor easier to clean. We wrapped the woman in a shroud of garbage bags. I told him to take her down to his car, which he did. He returned to say he had to put her in the front seat as he drove a Miata and the trunk was not big enough for a body. We cleaned up meticulously, then shouted embarrassed good-byes and thank-yous through the door which we ostentatiously unlocked, and descended the fire escape.

We drove separately to Bertram's place, which was on the ground floor of a tenement in Moss Park. I distracted Bertram while my erstwhile accomplice carried the woman's body in the back door from the alley and down into the cellar which had a dirt floor. He buried her and left. I followed once I heard the Miata growl behind the house and fade. By morning Bertram would not remember I had been there.

A few days later our host called to say a woman who had slipped away from the party early had apparently disappeared but since she was having marital problems, according to the friend who brought her, everyone assumed she had simply escaped by going underground. As I expected, I soon received a phone call from a man who spoke with a familiar but muffled voice. He said, you may not remember me. We met at the blind-date party last week. Would you like to get together? I asked if he drove a Miata. He said yes. I suspect you will not be surprised that I then said yes, myself, agreeing to meet him that same evening. Having noticed an elegant insignia ring on his wedding-ring finger, a gesture I took to signify he was separated or divorced, covering the mark of an earlier ring or flaunting his freedom, and having noticed on the ring the letters RCYC, I suggested we rendezvous at the private Royal Canadian Yacht Club ferry terminal. Yes, he said. Dress accordingly.

Perhaps I should wait until he and I are alone in the shadows at the stern of the ferry, our voices swallowed by the noise of the turgid wake, leaning far over the rail to catch sight of the propeller slicing and grinding the water, to express my glee, despite my current misery, that you are with me. I am impressed. It seems you have either suspended disbelief because you are remarkably naive or, and this is more likely, because you are irrepressibly generous. You have accepted that I did not murder Bertram, that I married a man who raped me. You have allowed me without protest to help a perfect stranger— hardly perfect but a stranger nonetheless—to hide the corpse of a woman who died on the blade of a knife he was holding, and in my ex-husband's cellar. Now, on the ferry to the RCYC you observe what is either reckless stupidity on my part, or perhaps dreadless generosity of my own, and are still with me. Is it perhaps because we both have suffered?

We are caught up in a labyrinth of assumptions made somehow more horrific by my apparently cavalier attitude towards untimely death? You have been so good, suspending disbelief, abiding by the conventions of narrative, it is unfair to compromise your moral integrity further. We will address the problem, consider how you could have allowed yourself to become this deeply implicated, as lost among the improbabilities of my life as I am myself. Trust me, our experience of the same episode is very different. You have the advantage of common sense and imagination. I am bound by the facts.

Consider my marriage. You resolved the mystery of why I married a man who brutally assaulted me in the back of a taxi virtually in the instant you read of it. From the infinite capacity of your mind to constitute a coherent story out of the most elusive of details, you assembled the various possibilities in a critical pattern of explanation and then moved on. Perhaps I had been abused as a child, physically but not sexually, as I was a virgin, and believed I deserved to be a victim and found the violence perversely affirming; perhaps rough sex played to some pathology in me neither of us understand; possibly it was a fantasy sequence, retrospectively emblematic of my marriage to Bertram; possibly I was so morally depleted by his brutality, in a variation of the Stockholm Syndrome, I needed to bond with my persecutor. These explanations and innumerable others coalesced around my brief description of an unlikely event. In a heartbeat, you had come to terms with something that through decades of painful rumination I still find beyond all understanding.

As a reader you fill in between the words. You accepted from the conspiratorial disinterest of my tone that

apparently discontinuous events. Her absence in his story
suddenly produced a clarity I had not been looking for,
and did not want. I began to sweat beneath the sheets
despite the warmth in the air at the season's close

At the blind-date party each of them had been brought
by a friend of the host. To avoid awkwardness they did
not acknowledge their relationship but when they found
themselves alone in the kitchen, they quarrelled. You
know the rest. She could never have driven a blade so
deep; if she meant to hurt herself she would more likely
have sliced at an arm. As I grew increasingly feverish
under duress of these various explications, another image
from Bertram's death scene came forward. There were on
his arborite table two unopened forty-ounce bottles of
Crown Royal. Since I had not sent him money in some
time, he had another source. Bertram must have remembered more of the night we buried my lover's wife than I
had imagined. He had been indulging in blackmail,
having easily tracked down his victim through me.

I have not seen my lover since that night and I have
been overwhelmed by anxiety that verges sometimes on
despair. My whole life haunts me. I am not afraid of
anything that might happen, only of the past. I understand
my lover has moved to Vancouver. Despite everything I
miss him dreadfully. His casual familiarity with death cast
over my quite ordinary life a strange aura of what I can
only describe as authenticity. I was never more real and
alive than when I was with him, however distant he may
have sometimes seemed. I miss him desperately.

For endless hours I wander the night streets of the
city, so self-absorbed I seldom know where I am, and
eventually, each night, I end up outside my home just
south of Rosedale and look up at the windows which
because the lights are not on and the curtains are open
appear utterly blank. And I go in and change and go to
work. On the weekends, after prowling the anonymous

streets until dawn I spend the days sitting at one end of my big sofa, meandering in a waking nightmare through the intersecting passageways of my life, trying to imagine the overall structure from my vantage within. I do not know when I sleep. I must, but absent of dreams. Sometimes my mind seems empty as a crypt, oppressively filled with the presence of nothingness, and sometimes it is the opposite, filled with infinite shards of flashing light, like a maze of mirrors, and as I follow here and there, more and more frantically pursuing coherence, I repeatedly crash into myself.

It is likely that your understanding of my life by inference from my recent behavior and the ways I described it has led you to some kind of illumination—to which, due to the restrictive relationship between reader and writer, I cannot be privy. I hope it has. As for me, relating my story has not been cathartic. Nothing has been achieved to relieve the wretchedness into which I have fallen, trying to understand myself. In exploring the days of my life out of temporal sequence, I am thrust into the depths of confusion, the darkness of doubt. Like Kafka, I have learned that no matter how much you might draw on your life for a plot, it is impossible to make sense of the story.

James Joyce and the Emancipation of God

Religious intellectuals frighten me. On March 17, 1999, I listened to Patrick Grant, a visiting lecturer at the University of Ottawa from Belfast via Victoria, parse the intricate grammar of language and violence in Northern Ireland. At the conclusion of his talk, I suggested that he allowed sectarian violence a place on a moral spectrum, albeit at the extreme end, whereas it might better be examined in a pathology of its own. No, he said, if the moral spectrum can accommodate Satan it can deal with terrorist atrocities. And that, he thought, was an answer. And indeed, I thought, that is an Irish answer. While in Ireland for a year recently, in search of what inspired James Joyce to leave, I found that the Irish who condemned specific acts of terrorist brutality would invariably wind up their exhortation against the most heinous crime with an explanation of why it was, just so, in each particular case, accounting for the historic origins of the event. Thus, each act of destruction became retroactively inevitable. And I find it a terrible thing, to offer violence sanction. By including Satan in your estimation of human affairs you reduce the vilest aberration to a place in a mythic diorama that exonerates humans of ultimate responsibility.

I have never been anyone's grand passion. Perhaps that is surprising only to me, but I have felt all my life the capacity for profound love, and I have loved profoundly and been well loved in return. But no-one has ever starved for me until she has seen visions, pined for me in ecstasy, waiting for my love to enfold her, to breath into her renewed vitality and draw from her an opulence of desire. No-one has spurned another lover in deference to me, nor dropped on me the responsibility for sharing her virginity.

I have nearly married twice, but in neither instance could I supplant earlier loves, the first for a rogue and the second, a saint. Just as I could never be confident I had displaced the devil in one woman with my devotion, I lacked conviction with the other that I could occupy the ineffable void that filled her when her first love died.

I did not chose loneliness; it is an absence deep within that craves the affection my being in the world fails to generate. There was once in me a hunger of the soul that drove me to look into the eyes of every woman I met, young or old, beautiful or with her beauty hidden, in search of some connection that would replenish both of us and make us whole. It was a wistful longing, garnering no expectation of fulfillment. Aware of myself as a creation of conscious design, I did not have the depth of character to inspire passion. Still, where some men looked for physical attributes, vivacity, or signs of intellect or wealth, I searched within the eyes of women for a true reflection of my yearning to connect. When I turned fifty-six, an arbitrary age, and found myself as much alone as I had always been, I recognized my quest as vanity and resolved to make my solitude a sanctuary from the busy world.

Despite an enduring love for women, I have lived an ascetic life; I have devoted myself with the dedication of a medieval monk to the fading God of Christianity. Before He passes entirely from view I want to understand what He has been. In earliest childhood, when I scrutinized the ceiling at church and encountered the gaze of God, peering through the cracks at me, scrubbed and in my Sunday best, while outside I could hear the buzz of outboards and the liquid roar of powerful launches churning through the shallows into the locks that connect the Muskoka River with Lake Rosseau, I felt a proprietorial sympathy for His absence from the room. Beside me, my ancient grandmother sang in a powerful voice that made me proud, for I understood that while she was venerable by virtue of longevity, it was her enduring strength that invoked the congregation's capacity for sustained affection. She was beloved by the Presbyterian coterie of cottagers who gathered in the hilltop church above the river in Port Carling, and considered with something approaching awe by the local people in attendance whose grandparents and great-grandparents remembered her in her prime, although to me her prime was now.

I remember raising my eyes from watching her to stare into the eyes of God, who was curiously lodged among the rafters while His praises were spread upon the air as if He were a long way off, a bashful God or banished, I could not tell. All I could see were His eyes looking into mine, and it was then that we connected and from that point on that I would devote my life to our relationship. There was something preternatural about the way the adults all around me sang obsequies, who outside afterwards stood about the lawn and exchanged pleasantries as if nothing strange had happened. Only moments before they had declared voracious fealty to something even I could tell was fiction, a God among the rafters no more real or potent than a goblin or a sprite, both of which I also saw looking at me sometimes from the shadows or in the glare of sunlight among the beech and hemlock trees beside the cottage.

I was born with something absent in my heart. Even standing in the open sunlight after church clutching with affection at my grandmother's sleeve, wanting to share with her the wonder of the *Sagamo* steaming into the big locks, chock-a-block with Sunday tourists from Toronto dressed in white, this being in my memory the last summer before the onset of colours, I knew that belief and faith would always be, for me, elusive. Sometimes, over the years as I grew up and Muskoka changed and my grandmother died, I would try to accept or discover or invent the miracle of an unimagined deity, but it would not happen.

In middle age, I took a souvenir cruise of the lakes on the *Seguin,* the only one of the old steamships still in service, and as we passed through the Port Carling locks I looked up to see the gray board-and-batten Presbyterian church on the rocky crag in the heart of the village, and on the lawn from my vantage I could see the heads of people floating above the grass and though the trees, and I almost got off the boat to go up the hill and into the church, to share for a while the loneliness of God, perhaps descended from the rafters and seated in an empty pew.

Listening in Ottawa to the visiting speaker from Ireland by way of Victoria, a man with many degrees, I was stricken by the vanity of human desire. Working in a university environment, I am not unaccustomed to intel- lectual vanity. And I have known myself what might be called the vanities of flesh—the body's fickle appetites are apt reminders of our transient condition. Listening to Patrick Grant, recoiling at a world view from atop an edifice of spiritual conceit constructed to the most rigor- ous of standards upon the sands of superstition, I grieved for Ireland and by extension for the lot of us. It is vanity born of desperation deep within our dying cells that makes us yearn for eternal consciousness, and this that makes reasonable people adore a God Almighty who has not the dignity or power to save us from the Fall except through suffering.

My interest in James Joyce is of long standing. As a student I read everything but *Finnegan's Wake.* Like many other undergraduates in the arts, I bought a copy. I marvelled at the genius of the first few lines and thought, without humility but more with a practical sense of my own limitations, that eventually the whole book would open to me like a great tangled garden made entirely of words, but in the meantime I liked words to connect with the exterior and internal worlds beyond language and so enjoyed *Portrait of the Artist as a Young Man,* appreciated *Ulysses,* and found *Dubliners* exquisitely boring.

I read Joyce as a religious writer; perhaps at that age I read Hemingway and Faulkner as religious writers. It was not that I was on a quest for God in literature or I would have been immersed in Dante or Milton or even Blake. But I had a great desire to comprehend the religious sensibility, that capacity within the human psyche to subvert common sense and transform the mirroring world into a projection of human consciousness. Joyce more than others convincingly portrays reality as experience, the dimensions of which are determined by religion, community, class, and gender. There is nothing real that is not at the centre human. Hemingway and Faulkner are as solipsistic, but God seems an incidental attribute to their conceptions of His fallen world. In Joyce, God is everywhere. He is not a good God, but for Joyce's characters He is inseparable from the condition of their lives. Then, as it does now, this frightened me and held me in thrall—not religion, but a co-dependent God enduring the abuse of those He most abused.

On late night television not long after attending the talk by Patrick Grant, I observed a strange debate between a Christian fundamentalist and an Episcopalian bishop. It must have been an American show, since the bishop would have been an Anglican in Canada, and more circumspect. Or it could have been that I fell asleep on my sofa and dreamed an entire program, including commercials and the interlocutor's witty asides. The fundamentalist was a flamboyant celebrity with a short skirt and a way of popping her breasts forward as a rhetorical device. This disarmed the bishop and made me suspect their discourse was dream, a suspicion undermined by the presence of a Manhattan Buddhist dressed in white and a nervous Jewish journalist in the casual attire of a television regular. I could not have divined such a panel on my own. The bishop wore gray with a purple bib offset by a modest cross in gold, the absence of the hanged god a declaration of neo-Catholic decorum. The host was wearing a sweater with a thin gold chain that flashed at the neckline as their discourse on the nature of God progressed, dominated by the fundamentalist who spoke on God's behalf and the bishop who addressed an unseen but innumerable congregation.

How different from the hell-fire battering of Stephen Dedalus, to hear enlightened discourse about the meaning of God on a television talk-show. Ignorant of the boiling point of liquid sulphur, the conversation circled amiably around notions of guilt and original sin, responsibility and atonement, while the brimstone lake of Revelations cooled. James Joyce could not set a reader's guts to quivering with scenarios of damnation in a world like this, so reconciled to the fall from Eden that only irony defines our fears. It was perhaps in Auschwitz we discovered nothing of God's hell could be worse than what we inflict upon ourselves. A generation later, not prepared to abandon God so trivialized by human action, we chat about His stifled power and the perils of free will between commercial breaks for panty liners and antacid pills.

I often fall asleep in front of the television and since the advent of cable and all-night programming I sometimes do not awaken until the cheery decibels of morning shows penetrate my slumber. Then I get up and go to bed, where I doze until my alarm goes off. Later, at work, I sometimes have recollections float into consciousness of things that never happened and I cannot be sure whether I am in the presence of dreams or playing out bits of television that might have infiltrated my mind as I squirmed to find comfort on the sofa through the night. Students sitting across my desk from me, awaiting advice on how to upgrade their essays, are sometimes confused by my distractibility, but most assume I am a visionary, because

I smile solemnly when I recover, as if I had been working out their salvation on another plane, and I make a note to myself when they leave to raise them with a Calvinist flourish from the dead heap of mediocrity to a better grade, whether they deserve it or not. The really good students and the really bad seldom bother to cross the threshhold of my office door.

Bishop John Shelby Spong, the author of *Rescuing the Bible from Fundamentalism* and *Why Christianity Must Change or Die,* is well known for his outspoken desire to make religion relevant by secularizing the supernatural, rendering God an insentient presence, something to be found within each of us that he calls the Ground of Being. Jesus of Nazareth, the Hebrew evangelist catapulted by historical circumstance on a bewildering trajectory through history to become a superannuated relic, he demeans with the approbrium, Spirit Person, as if Jesus were a New Age avatar. The fundamentalist of depthless bodacity seemed oddly more convincing in my dream or memory when she dismissed the bishop's intellectual revisionism with a giggle and asserted the necessity of narrative. God gave us an appetite for stories and the stories to satisfy our appetite. The truth of *Genesis,* disparaged by the bishop, she held inviolable. It does not matter what science says or reason dictates, if the word of God is otherwise. Eden and the Ark, she declared, are facts beyond the limits of human understanding. Through faith we know a lot of things we do not know, she said. The bishop smiled.

Listening to Patrick Grant speak of Ireland and violence, language and religion, I thought myself in the presence of a man who believes what he may not believe, has faith in what he knows to be the limits of understanding. If I were to have asked him, did he actually believe in Satan he might have answered with a theologian's explanation: Satan is necessary in order to explain ourselves to

God. If I had said, do you believe in God, he might have answered, God does not need my faith; and as to whether God believes in me, my presence in the world affirms that He does. In an upper room of the university Arts building, overlooking parking lots and Parliament and the Gatineau Hills in the distance, the visiting speaker evoked a dialogue in my head that would never take place. It is unlikely he could imagine the absence of God, as it would be for the bishop to conceive of His absolute presence.

I could not listen without thinking of Joyce. The Church has been shaped by the needs of Man as God has been shaped by the Church. From Paul's earliest forays into explanations for his own ecstasy as he transformed the mortal Jesus, born of woman, into the inspired conduit for God to reach the fallen human heart, to Bishop Spong, with equal solipsism reifying God to salve the wounded spirit of the present age as a sort of internalized Star Wars 'Force,' an ointment to be released from deep within the human psyche by the power of love, theology has served the deep desire of theologians to be more than who they are. Joyce in *Portrait of the Artist as a Young Man* wrote with valiant passion to redeem himself through Stephen from the Church and sent his protagonist from Ireland in the end to find his own humanity, to become what he had always been. In trying to make us more, the Church from Paul to Bishop Spong has made us less, illusory creatures in an imaginary world. It was Joyce, the counter-theologian, who tried to set the balance, to explain us to ourselves and make us real. If he had attended to the emancipation of God, not of the world *from* God, he might himself have died in Ireland a happy man.

There was only a brief period in literary history when it was both feasible and desirable to write a portrait of the artist. Joyce seized on the prospect that the maturing self was not informed by a higher power but determined entirely in the middle world. Most versions since Joyce's seem derivative, many intentionally paying homage to the genius of the prototype. A few articulate the relationship between mind and imagination, sensibility and soul, as if Joyce had never happened. But it is no longer reasonable to write such fiction. Freudian notions of the psyche have dissipated with the death of the unconscious, the Künstlerroman, as academics call this short-lived genre, seems quaint. The brain, demythologized—we understand ourselves as simpler and more complex than philosophy and religion and the quasi-science of psychoanalysis could comprehend. At a time when the words 'mind' and 'imagination,' 'soul' and 'sensibility,' evade definition utterly, how naive it seems to account for the rage and inspiration of artistic genius through literary explication of the artist's limited realities. Joyce wrote during that brief time in our evolution when it seemed possible to explain everything.

I know exactly when I first conceived of God as an absence. It was following the time I observed a terrible fire in my early teens. Until then, I accepted God as inhabiting a realm of potential knowledge that I expected would come to me when I matured. Although we had an intimate relationship, I regarded Him as an unwieldy consortium of particulars with the same mixture of fear and esteem I had for my father, just as I accepted Jesus with devotion comparable to what I allowed my righteous and loving mother. I grew to puberty a secular Christian, familiar with the trappings of church ritual. I had been to a wedding and several funerals, all Anglican. From my Presbyterian grandmother I had learned the importance of kindness and sin. After that Sunday in Port Carling when I discovered myself in the gaze of the hidden God, He had been a secret presence in my life. He was not the subject of faith or object of belief, nor was He an old man with a beard, nor an illuminated dove on the shoulder of Jesus. He was simply there. Then quite suddenly everything changed. He became, in my last winter before entering high school, a terrible and lamented void.

Trudging through the sidewalk snow one day on my way home from the library, I encountered a great commotion. A fire was consuming a tenement house on the Lakeshore Road; there was much screaming as firemen worked methodically to control the blaze. There were children inside and a brave fireman was trying to penetrate the smoke billowing through the smashed front door. A woman beside me was prostrate on the snow, praying for her child to be spared. The fireman disappeared and time stopped and he reappeared with a child in his arms, wrapped in a smouldering blanket, alive. It was the praying woman's child. Four other children died in the flames and their bodies were consumed. Stunned, I listened to a murmur through the crowd, thankful the child was spared. All that night I lay awake, addressing myself to the God of the fire, and by morning there was nothing left of Him but the odour of smoke that lingered in my clothes from standing close to the conflagration and witnessing the ghastly cost of His love.

For the rest of the week I stayed in bed, indulged by parents who thought I was traumatized by the fire. It would never have occurred to them my problem was God. My father, who seldom talked to me directly, brought me a model fighter plane to work on as a distraction, not knowing I had outgrown making planes two years earlier. My mother set up the radio so I could listen to Arthur Godfrey and "Our Gal Sunday," her favourite programs. But alone in the room with the lights out, the blinds pulled down and the curtains drawn, through the middle of the day I could lie in relative darkness and imagine myself dead. My only regret was that I had never had sex, otherwise death was horrifically enticing. In this way, embraced in the arms of oblivion, I identified with the children who died and contemplated the absence of God.

As time progressed, outrage gave way to an infinite

loneliness and this in turn gave way to a sense of relief. Suddenly, following the third day of my confinement, as if I had passed through a long tunnel of darkness into the dazzling clarity of absolute light, I rose from my bed with the conviction that God was absurd. He was not my adversary as I at first supposed. Deep within my heart, the world transformed; it was as if I had been born again, free at last from the terrible burden of having to account for my cultural heritage, the God of my ancestors, as if He were more than a word. I could think about that, examine stories surrounding Him in holy texts and history books, as constructs of language, projections of consciousness on an unconscious world.

Freed from the oppression of faith, yet with the deep longing for transcendence born of our human capacity to comprehend time, I mourned the passing of God. I abhorred what we had done to Him, making Him the ineffable projection of corporeal desire, capitalizing His several names, assigning Him a gendered pronoun, subjecting Him to stories born of fear and vanity. As I made my way through my teens, I found myself passionately committed to sharing the purity of His absence. Others found me strange, but I was committed to revelation. The only girlfriend I had was a born-again Christian who mistook my quest for religious devotion, and initiated me into ecstatic celebrations of the human body as temples of the Lord, although we always stopped short of violating the building code against simultaneous consummation. In university my relationship with God, as I struggled through my studies to comprehend the holy nature of His absence, led me into a protracted affair with a Catholic woman a year ahead of me. She dealt with my metaphysical obsession as punishment—she would writhe in guilt as we made love, weep afterwards about the ephemerality of carnal pleasure, and after suitable atonement, finding me unrepentant and unscathed, would seize depravation once again to plumb the depths of my apparent innocence. I have the capacity to love profoundly. Through graduate school and before I reached the age of passive androgyny, that age when the single man is assumed to be a celibate, indifferent to sex or content with masturbation, I had several romantic relationships with beautiful women —someone the object of love is invariably beautiful. Two, in particular, I might have married. But the devotion of one to the devil-made-flesh, really an ordinary fellow with immoral predilections on a petty scale, and of the other to a saint whose moral disposition affirmed celestial connections, whose beatification was affirmed by his untimely death, were distractions in my quest. As a man committed to the amoral construction of my own being in the world, choosing to be good by choice, to avoid corruption as a matter of conscience, I would have been compromised by marriage. Despite my grand passion for both these women, neither was prepared to risk her venerable past on a man so apparently distracted by God.

Loneliness was the cost of my impious obsession. Sometimes I feel oppressed by my convictions, but nothing in life has made me rescind my adolescent relief in discovering I was no longer responsible for God on Earth. He is my heritage from days of ancient superstition, when my culture was tribal, to the present sophistries of Bishop Spong which embed Him in the human heart as if such enclosure would honour the Lord of all creation, to be bound by viscera and time. I want to understand this. Not where He originates in fear of death or the plenitude of dreams, not how we have turned anxiety into desire, responsibility into righteousness and guilt, ignorance to obeisance, the reassurance of ritual into the rule of law, principles of love into the politics of religious bigotry. These things can be explained by theological apologists, anthropologists, psychologists, historians, philologists, and philosophers. I want to comprehend

God's identity, not a supernatural phenomenon, mystical emblem, force, or being; God who fills the places empty in my heart with His absence, the God I would set free to float with sound waves of my dying voice toward the distant corners of an endless universe.

Last year I went to Ireland on sabbatical. I needed to read James Joyce while surrounded by the people who shaped his life like the occupation force of an invading army that has been so long on alien territory it seems like home. No-one is truly at home in Ireland, for the Irish have separated place from time, and live on the surface of history while the land beneath their feet perpetually falls away as a context of previous lives more real than their own. It is only by going abroad, as Joyce did, that they can wipe the past from their eyes, look over the mounded depths and into the present. Not the future. It is enough to see what is here without succumbing to visions of what might better be.

As the world that Joyce confused with memory recedes into the pages of his books, as the fears that consumed him and the fires that set him free turn with time to literary artifacts, it becomes evident a secular world is born, and Ireland shall one day celebrate the heretic—how I wish it were true, that Ireland would cease to be the reservoir of Christianity. It is certain, hell-fire no longer burns, sexuality is riven from guilt, and God has been largely emancipated from His captivity in the nave. But still, the Irish love religion. Even Irish atheists believe that it is God Himself who is dead; they have faith that left to our own devices we will endure the Fall, which they seem to accept as a given. They have exchanged one religion for another, and follow the absence of God as if He were God. You do not have to believe in Satan for Satan to be real, nor God, for God to provide the perameters for mortal experience, the perimeters of being.

I think it was in the small gray church on the rocky

bluff in the heart of Port Carling, with the sound of my grandmother's voice sending shivers of pride through my small body, when I first understood that God is language, and words can make you see what is not there. It did not seem a special occasion at the time, except that everything with my grandmother was special. But in retrospect, I believe I was touched with the gift of tongues that day, not to speak but rather to hear. All living things have languages. The leaf unfurling into sunlight reads the signs of its survival. The hawk rides wind on muscles tuned to read equations of gravity and speed while the fieldmouse reads a predatory shadow and skitters out of sight. The human child reads annoyance in a parent's eyes and turns away. All things alive respond to signs, interpret symbols, process information and conduct their lives accordingly. Language is God. For all my life I have listened to its voices.

When I turned fifty-six and discovered no-one loved me, I felt strangely relieved. That was when my elderly parents died within days of each other following a car crash in which their passenger, a visitor from Ireland, was mercifully spared. I have no friends, although I have acquaintances at the university—if I were to be leaving on a trip with no return, there is no-one to whom I would need to say good-bye. I still sometimes feel embarrassed for my species, for supplanting curiosity and fear that come from being creatures of verbal consciousness with notions of the supernatural. I have long since lost the need to share the beauty of my vision and feel comfortable observing folly without comment. I am not unhappy, I think of God, and all my work goes well. I avoid religious intellectuals like Bishop Spong and Patrick Grant when I can. I am pleased to have the capacity for dread, and I regret that I will die. In four billion years on this planet, however, I would like to think that we have learned, everything that begins will end but nothing ends forever.

The Reconstruction of Forgotten Dreams

Hugh Garner once told me he usually started short stories with a title. That was back in the days when he was still writing excellent stories, when he was as old as I am now. The market was diminishing by then and the older he got the longer it took to squeeze from the implications of a title a narrative of sufficient complexity to charm the changing world. He knew the world was changing, he understood that younger writers were writing to a taste informed by television, not movies, wars, and ideology. He kept writing as he had always done, so that a recent story and an early story could not be chronologically determined without composition dates attached. A writer was a writer and the notion that a writer would improve over time simply meant he was not trying hard enough in the beginning. Or she. He recognized that women write, that sometimes, like Alice Munro, they write well, but he thought of writing as a masculine activity. He once told me Alice Munro's astonishing beauty was an aberration. He died from alcohol when he ran out of things to say. Many writers of his generation died of tobacco and alcohol. That was before drugs.

Most writers I know have done drugs, but invariably before we met. Writers like to cast an aura of iniquity across their past like a coloured strobe light, so that what you see is dazzlingly elusive. Most writers I know live clean and ordinary lives. Most of them title their fiction after writing it. Like tying a ribbon on a parcel, the title is part of the packaging. As a writer, I approach a story the same way Garner did, I start with a title. Our stories are not the same, however. His are well-shaped and treat the unities of time, place, action, and voice as the four wheels of a delivery vehicle. I think of a story as a gyroscope, all the parts whirring every which-way to make the whole thing stay absolutely still. It is stillness in narrative that excites me, not the flurries of movement. In a moving world it is wonderfully subversive to be still.

Garner did not realize my sex until I appeared in Toronto at the door of his apartment on Erskine Avenue, after extended correspondence to set up an interview. Jjan, he said? He slurred my name as if it were French. I said no, Jean—as in genetic and blue. That quip seemed to break through the inherent mistrust of an inveterate flirt towards anything female, and he invited me in. I stood in the middle of the living room waiting to be seated. So you're a woman, he said, as if I needed assurance. By the time we arranged ourselves at the kitchen table, I was absolved of subterfuge, and as we became friends over the next few years he moved from forgiving me for being a woman to forgetting my sex entirely. By the time he died, he thought of me as an honourary male, and would have thought of that as a compliment.

My own writing is esoteric. Only small-circulation magazines subsidized by provincial arts council grants would consider the stories I write for publication, and then only if I seed them with regional references. My chosen genre is the literary horror story and it is as easy to set a gothic haunting in an abandoned Manitoba farmhouse or a deserted fish cannery near Vancouver as in the Scottish highlands or American deep south. I should perhaps have said the literary horror genre chose me. I decide on setting, character, and point of view, but the scary parts come unbidden. I write literature; I use the resources of language and tradition to fuse aesthetic with thematic effects. But the loathsome dread that dominates my work rises from a darkness deep within, beyond my comprehension. I write to a small readership by choice.

You realize, of course, if I were a man it would have been taken for granted—that I was a man. You think not, you think I am whining. Consider this—no, chances are, if you are unable to understand what I mean, you would have stopped reading already. I like being a woman on my own. It allows me to write as I do. Horror stories are seldom born from domestic convention. Not the kind I write, which draw their lifeblood from the living dead.

I began this story with the title "5-5-7- J." That was my first telephone number. Unlike Garner I am not bound to arbitrary procedures. I feel free to rename my stories as they unfold, sometimes several times as they reveal unexpected twists of plot or implication. "5-5-7-J" was our number back in the days of my earliest memories, immediately after the War, when a small girl in the village of Blair could pick up the telephone and ask Central for her grandmother and the operator would make the connection to the Clare house in the town of Preston a few miles away and ask for Mrs. Clare. I told Hugh about that the first time we met. He had invited me to interview him at his home in Toronto, after I had requested a previously unpublished story for a literary journal I was editing. I was halfway through my second tumbler of rye. He was not drinking. He would not be drinking until he finished the murder mystery he was writing. When it was done he would get drunk. He would go on a bender and then dry out at Homewood and then start another novel. The short story market had pretty well dried up. We paid only $100 for a story then, this was 1972. I was not a drinker, and my questions in the second half of my recorded interview transcribed as gibberish, although Hugh's responses were cunning and precise.

I said that I prize stillness in a story. That does not mean nothing happens. It would be difficult to generate terror without flourishes of narrative movement. It is the ominous stillness of death that truly horrifies, not banshees screaming or erupting crypts. From the beginning of my stories to the end death dominates—they are metaphors for life in the Heideggarian sense. Not that I am a philosopher. I have never actually read Heidegger. I am a poet. Writers of fiction who are not poets write the kind of stories Hugh Garner wrote. Many of his are fine stories. But they do not have the visceral depth of a story informed by dread. They do not confound common sense the way a good horror story does. Edgar Allan Poe was a poet and lived his whole life suffering from the imprecations of his own mortality, a burden he shared with his readers. The best comic writers are poets. From Leacock to Richler, you are aware always that levity implies its opposite, that satire exposes what it seems to hide and humour is a diversion from death. Poets see hell where heaven applies, and if hell is their game they see angels as players who have fallen askew.

Everything connects and nothing makes sense. Poets know this. In a world where stillness pervades at the edge of the mind, for the incessant deterioration of cells in the brain will never let us forget we are hurtling towards death, the only certainty is oblivion. As matter and energy we are fleeting equations, but no more nor less in sum than we have been forever. It is the limits of consciousness that worry us, and this that I explore in my stories of horror, that I capture in elaborate contraptions of stasis and motion. I accept that not everyone wants to read stories like mine, to discover the absurdity of death in the twist of an image or episode, the poised shape of imminence. I am not a popular writer. I earn enough from horror to make a living, nothing more.

Even before we met I admired the ingenuous honesty of Garner's stories. Hugh was old-fashioned. There are no subtexts in his stories, no subliminal messages. Any meaning beyond the obvious, which is often arresting, is attached like a moral in italics at the end of a fable. His stories make you think and make you feel, but thoughts and feelings are never in conflict. Hugh was not an artist; he was a craftsman. He understood exactly how to hold the chisel, how to shift his rock upon the wheel. He did not write about writing. He was not interested in trying to explain how thoughts leapt from his mind to become real on the page. He told stories because it did not occur to him not to; he told them well because he could.

There was a directness to Hugh Garner that I cherished when he was sober, and found in his writing, even the pot-boilers he ground out between binges. He would say what he meant. When he was drunk, this made him mean. Sometimes it just made him stupid. He walked through a plate glass door in an Ottawa hotel because he was preoccupied with a temporary lapse between language and consciousness, he was upright and moving but had nothing to say. He was rude to a woman in the corridor of a community college in Hamilton once—she cried because he was offended when she asked for an autograph. He declared no-one had the right to such a literal emblem of his identity unless to endorse a cheque made out in his name, which he suggested she do for extraordinary services he would render if she had sufficient stamina and elasticity. I had to drag him off to the bar. The next day I pointed the woman out to him and he was ashamed and apologized profusely and flirted with her; she was older than he was and had blue hair. I am sure she left feeling she had had a tragic encounter with literature, and was happier for it.

Hugh did not flirt with me, drunk or sober. I think he was afraid. Not the way most men of his generation were afraid of women, fearful of their own ignorance about female sexuality and the power of the unknown. He was afraid of my beauty—do not think because I have chosen to be alone I am unattractive. The presence of beauty undermined his confidence. He would never have connected the effect I seemed to have on him with nervous depletion brought on by the sublimation of sexual desire, which in turn made him wary, yet pleased to be in my company. For all his worldliness, he was too innocent for that. So innocent, in fact, that he thought of me not as a woman but as a friend. I have never actually been beautiful, but there was a time when both men and women noticed me and I have aged well .

Sometimes drifting to sleep I come upon a small house, a cabin in the woods, and when I go in it seems to have endless rooms; other times I see a grand mansion across a manicured lawn and when I enter it the door locks behind me and I am in a small room with no windows and no other exits. These are not dreams but visions. They come to me while I am aware of my surroundings in this world and yet cannot awaken. Dreaming, I am not always myself; sometimes I am a point of view and at other times a persona, sometimes identifiable as the dreamer unaware she is dreaming and sometimes someone I have only conjured for the moment. In this state between wakefulness and sleep, I am a visionary. What I see I understand and my emotional response is consistent with the experience perceived. If something startles me, the walls of the expansive cabin or the stifling mansion shatter, and I am instantly in this other world. If sleep comes, memories of the cabin and the mansion linger when I rise. Unlike dreams, they do not slip away but haunt me through the day. The feelings they aroused colour everything that happens. There is no meaning attached to these memories. Either I am trapped and claustrophobic or lost among indeterminent possibilities for refuge.

"5-5-7-J." Hugh would have liked that as a title, but before actually writing he would have worked out what the story was going to be about. Literally, the story would be plotted, the plot arising from the implications of the title playing in his mind. I told him once that writing for me is like the reconstruction of forgotten dreams. A sentence begins and does not know where it will end. It unfolds in accordance with the principles of grammar and resonates with all the meanings and allusions eliminated by this particular arrangement of these words. If it is right it seems immediately familiar, like encountering in the fragment of a day the memory of another life. As sentences accumulate an unruly variety of voices swirl like the souls of the dead in torment or ecstasy upon the page. And if the story is good, the reader fills with heaven's held breath, or hell's, when the story is done.

That is a lot to expect from a literary horror story. Perhaps only a woman can be as extravagant in her ambitions. No man could understand the complexity of pain required to write affectionately of terror. Men are not subtle. Men envision unrelenting conflict between opposing forces, heaven and hell, good and evil, right and wrong. Men endure within a Manichean universe, their cosmology composed of an endless struggle to survive between extremes. As a woman I am caught up in the only quarrel that really matters, between life and death. Those others are distractions, antinomies born from the desire to impose order upon the arbitrary world of our experience. The tension between pairings throws restraining cables across the prostrate body of humanity; from my perspective it would be better to live by what best nurtures life, to embrace disorder, and with subtlety prepare to die.

Hugh and I once argued this. It was the only time we really had a falling out. Since we cannot evade death ever, we should pursue the quarrel against it with grace. Hell no, he said. Death invades the living world through evil, the suppression of right and good, and must be vanquished at every turn or it will overwhelm us. Through the atrocities of the Holocaust when Death reigned rampant, it was evil that extinguished human decency, and grace was absent utterly. I have taken refuge, he continued, among mangled corpses in the mud of Spain and sailed with dead sailors retrieved from the North Atlantic sea, I know death and evil are inseparable companions. For heaven's sake, I said, with self-conscious irony, the pain we cause comes out of our capacity to endure, as does the pain we suffer. Evil is a grotesque evasion of responsibility. Death is not the adversary but the outcome. Men cannot seem to comprehend the subtleties of being mortal. Men cannot understand the complexities of pain.

This is a stylized version of our conversation, of course. More explicit and more enigmatic. But in the vernacular of the moment Hugh expressed blunt expletives of outrage, that a man who had seen so much could know less of life than a woman. Stumbling upon his own acknowledgment that I am a woman silenced him. Like all men, he suspected I knew things men could only guess at. It has to do with the mysteries of menstruation and birth. We live closer to the process of creation than men, the function of our bodies an incessant reminder of our mortal condition. I am not saying this is true, I am saying this is how men perceive the female experience and it frightens them. They simplify human existence with the invention of evil, and the conception of death as the antithesis of life instead of its consequence. He finally muttered, no wonder you write those horrible stories. Horror stories, he said, correcting himself or withdrawing the insult. You should write about childhood. Everyone does who thinks writing is art. Or about degenerate genealogies or migrant workers.

The interesting thing about a mid-century telephone number, it was a code. Push button dialing, as we now call it in a lovely conflation of eras, has lulled us into believing that numbers have meaning. But in those times before dialing we encrypted ourselves in digits symbolically, and when dial phones came in, for a few years we used generic metaphors like EMpire 3, and OLive 6. We knew these sequences stood for something else. They were not alternative modes of identity the way numbers are now, the way our social insurance numbers, our SINs, have become. They were code, and if you deciphered them right and used them correctly, they connected you to other people in secret ways that only listeners on your party line would know.

The thing about a party line is you could listen in to other people's lives. You were not supposed to. You could, but it was against the rules. That is why, at seven years old, I was surprised to pick up the receiver and hear a voice that was not the operator's, and to find myself listening. The thing about being seven is that you surprise yourself often, sometimes doing what you are not supposed to do, and if you are not caught you are distracted from guilt with surprising ease. You expect the voice I heard was going to make a declaration on which to hang a plot, a confession of murder, an expression of inappropriate affection, something threatening that would send me running to a disbelieving mother—no, I would not run to my mother, I could never admit I had been eavesdropping, even if it meant my entire family were in mortal jeopardy.

At this point in my narrative, I can hear Garner growl and demand I get on with the story. Why hide behind words, whatever happened to imagination? Make it up, he would say. I am, I would say. We never had a telephone when I was small. Until we moved to the city when I was twelve, I had never heard a human voice that did not directly issue from a human mouth. I grew up in the wilderness. My father was an insect scientist and we lived in a remote cabin in northern Quebec. He would travel south to give his lectures but my mother and I were left behind. He was an extremist devotee of Dr. Spock and I was his experiment and she cooperated. They wanted to see how I would cope, not being introduced to the civilized world until puberty. I went to Leaside High School and became a heroine as the best marksman in the Army Cadet Corps, where I had to dress as a boy because girls were not allowed to pretend to be soldiers. At university I learned to ski in High Park and switched to biathlon. I only failed to make the Olympic team because my interest flagged from having to shoot blanks within the city limits. In my final year I took up writing. The serial number on the binder I bought to keep my fiction fragments in the order of their composition began with the number-letter combination "5-5-7-J."

I cannot reconstruct what the voices on the party line were saying. What fascinated me at the time was the surprise acquisition of power. Through the mere act of lifting a receiver carefully from its cradle, I placed the lives of other people within my control. By breathing noisily I could invoke anxiety or anger or patient forbearance. With a word or two I could provoke terror, evoke laughter, arouse exasperation. I knew this intuitively from the way the voices spoke as if for my sole benefit and yet were entirely unaware of my presence. This small epiphany, I think, was my first intimation of an artistic sensibility. In retrospect, it offered a perfect paradigm for the function of language in the creative relationship between writer and written. At the time it seemed magic.

Never again did I intrude on the telephone. When the neighbour's twin spaniels destroyed the primitive architecture of my rabbit hutches and slaughtered my eleven rabbits, I thought briefly as I pieced together the shredded cadavers that perhaps this was retribution for having eavesdropped. It seemed a gruesome price to pay for the revelation that language is power. Coming home from school that same year I stopped by the cemetery fence and watched silently as a lowered casket was raised and opened for belated viewing of the corpse by late arrivals to the funeral, who commented how peaceful he looked and thanked Mr. Moyes and departed, after which the casket was lowered again and earth shovelled into the hole above it. That night I imagined the body awakened and talked on a telephone to other bodies buried in the cemetery. I imagined conversations in the night among the dead. I discovered, lying very still in my darkened room, I could listen in.

I Know Who You Are, Jane Austen

When the world is too much with me, I escape into words. At my most oppressed, I turned to Jane Austen. You can read Jane Austen and know every detail of her intimate world, every nuance of clothing and furniture and social atmosphere, you can know her characters, their affections, afflictions, and affectations, you can know everything but Jane. Only the most vaporous hint, the most insubstantial suggestion, of an individual personality comes through. You know more of a potter, seeing a thumbprint embedded on the base of a vase. When I read her novels I lose myself among their splendid particulars, the sheen of lamplight on velvet, the sensitive gestures and subtle virtues, the follies, the small consolations, the carriages and triumphs, and for a while I am no-where in the world where real pain occurs.

But there came a time when I could no longer forget myself over tea at the Pump Room in Bath. I took to writing myself into fiction. Part of me says, you are a wretched man, you have caused the earth to shift on its axis, the oceans to rage, the Balkans to fester and erupt, potholes in the street to open. Then I want death; not suicide but the cessation of responsibility, a closing down of the terrible awareness of all that I've done. Part of me says, you are not so important, you are only one person among six billion flung by the force of our hurtling through space against the surface of this tiny sphere. Parts of me say these things, and the saying, itself, sets me free. What writing does is to allow the illusion that I am language, not human; that I am syntax and diction brought under control by the power of invention; that I can be as finite and infinite as words. Nothing can be imagined that

183

cannot be said, nor said that cannot be imagined—I, like Jane Austen, can choose to do both and be neither.

My beloved and I sat in the Pump Room at Bath, eating scones with thick dollops of cream, smeared with highlights of strawberry jam. It was off-season and the central pavilion was packed with Japanese tourists, only the waiters were English. Jane Austen presided. Victoria was not yet a Queen and Princess Diana, still alive at the time, seemed equally remote, as the liveried staff served us to the sounds of chamber music from the wings. We looked at each other and delighted in our own ephemerality, that this contrived version of the past was more authentic, for a brief time, than the present.

After tea, we took a tour of the baths and marvelled at the ingenuity of the Romans. When my beloved and I were in Rome we kept being confronted by our own incredulity that such buildings were built, such sewers were laid, such laws and diversions and statues were made. The Romans must have been perpetually astonished for the good fortune that befell them, due to their being where they were when they were. In Bath, beneath the Pump Room, we were intensely aware that over our heads was Jane Austen's world, and beyond that were the instruments of late twentieth century commerce, the change rooms and cash registers that sustained the illusion.

This was before the measure set in of what I had done and what it would mean for the rest of my life. It was before I had begun to write, before I took up reading in desperation. In the evenings, in those days, after work we would browse through magazines together, or read novels, my beloved on one end of the blue sofa and I on the other, my legs stretched out along its length and hers curled up beneath her, and the warmth of my toes against her thigh was not a distraction. We read through our first winter together, sharing good passages, unusual figures of speech, enthusiasm or dismay for the turn of events in our separate texts. She was more prone to re-telling entire narratives than I, and I would attend even if I had read the book already, for the sounds of her voice and the light in her eyes as she talked. I was more apt to drop word clusters, deft or inept turns of phrase, into the lovely silence that held us enthralled all through that cold season. That was still when reading was the wondrous unending maze we wandered together, not yet a prison or sanctuary or portal of escape from the world.

In those days of our innocence my beloved and I read ourselves into other worlds for the companionship one discovers in travel. Sharing the intensity of perception encountered in unfamiliar places and among new people, all made accessible by the generosity of the texts, brought us closer. Not in terms of affection, for our love was absolute, but on a more practical plane. Since we had not known each other until well into the depths of our lives, me closer to closure than she by a decade, we did not have a background of common experience. She had lived a rich life, as you might have suspected. Mine has been emotionally diverse and not without drama. But we did not know each other before a few years ago. Our lives at times ran parallel, for we moved in much the same circles, but they never converged. Geometric anomalies aside, after we came together we needed to invent a history, to contrive a context, construct a common reality.

We went to Italy, we went to England, we went to Australia. We swam among elegant schools of fish and fabulous columns of coral at the Great Barrier Reef. We window-shopped on the Ginza in Japan and admired a melon for sale at two hundred dollars. We back-packed to the Barnes Icefield on Baffin Island. We read Jane Austen and dozens of others. We read detective stories, murder mysteries, science-fiction, great books in translation. We bought a house and redecorated it to suit both our tastes. We talked to each other about our jobs as adventures, our work as the source of anecdotes and wry observations on human nature. It would be hard to imagine new lovers at our stage of life being more resourceful. We were infinitely happy.

At what point reading became an obsession, I am uncertain. Worlds collided and I cannot even say when. The actual timing is lost in the details. That may be difficult to imagine, for you would think the moment of impact would stay in the mind. Sometimes in the aftermath of a great conflagration, only awareness that things have gone wrong leads you to realize you must have been too shocked at the time to inscribe it in memory. Try to envision the galaxy of our own divination, my beloved and I, being slowly imploded, pressed from outside by the force of a gigantic black hole that gradually collapses what we have created into an absolute mass. Yet the black hole is a worm hole and we hurtle through, one world passing right through another, colliding only from an observer's perspective. We go on, much the same as before. The black hole remains behind us, an absolute vacuum.

That all must seem pretty obscure. Such explanations come of too much reading, then writing as if it were therapy. The point is, an insidious force from outside our enchanted union pushed and pushed against me, which in turn threatened the integrity of our relationship, if only by proving a profound distraction, and I turned increasingly to books for escape. As I suggested above, no writer served the purpose more effectively than Jane Austen. Too much oppressed to be an adequate partner in the real world, with Jane I could lose myself in the diffusion of our two souls into the general atmosphere of her texts.

Then, part way through *Pride and Prejudice* I lost the incentive to go on. There on the blue sofa, with my beloved close by, I suddenly caught sight of myself with Jane, the two of us peering at a very small world from around the edge of a hedge, the entry to a labyrinth in which I knew every turn as well as I knew my own heart. There was no point in proceeding, since there was nowhere to go where I would not already be waiting. That is when I turned language around and took up writing. I first tried to write autobiography, to write myself into a narrative reality in which I could more easily get lost among words. This was not wise. Nor was it practical. It led to debasement of genuine feelings in over-wrought imagery and convoluted expression. The harder I tried to capture my recalcitrant life, to contain it in prose explication, the more elusive it became, the more ephemeral its signal events. Rather than expelling or quelling my pain I made it a spectacle, I proffered my despair as diversion.

Fiction was the inevitable alternative. I quickly discovered what is not said in fiction has more narrative presence than what is; it is not the same with autobiography, where revelation is plot, confession is character, and the reader's vicarious pleasure is the purpose for being. Fiction is about hiding and misdirection; drawing readers into an epiphany inseparable from their own personalities and their experience of the text. This insight came obliquely, while I was trying to conjure devices that would make murder seem reasonable. How do I deploy aesthetics to create a narrative in which redemption has occurred before the crime takes place, and I, as the hidden narrator, disguised within the text behind a facade of syntax and diction, am the implied person redeemed?

My beloved, whom I feel it inappropriate to name at this time, is more objective than I. She understands how fiction absolves the reader of all responsibility for what occurs in the text. She could explain, perhaps, how I found in fiction the sanction I craved to release me from the oppression she knew I endured. But she is now so immersed in reading, herself, that interrogation would be futile.

Still, she visits me regularly in this awkward place.

She arrives each morning and stays through the day. She brings lunch and we picnic on a small gingham tablecloth that belonged to her mother, who died before we met, whom from the haunting eyes and solemn smile of my beloved I know was a woman who took love seriously, as does her daughter. Sometimes, without conspiring, I know we are both imagining us sitting in the Pump Room at Bath or swimming among coral in crystal clear water. We sip diet colas and nibble on sandwiches, prolonging the fantasy as long as we can, aided by the genteel procedures of a leisurely meal. Sooner or later, bolts in a door slam against steel, or someone at another table swears or bursts into tears. My beloved is patient and we both wait for the return of illusions. When she leaves I resume writing, she goes home to her books.

My first efforts in a creative mode were fantasy adventures. I tried to write myself into fictions already written. I would cast a persona with whom I could identify, usually someone quite unlike myself on the surface, into familiar narratives from my recent travels through literature. I envisioned myself a young woman, a virgin caught up in the company of Sancho Panza and Don Quixote, who each felt it his duty to save me from the lascivious appetites of the other, but so successful were they in their quarrel that I quickly tired of unchallenged virtue, and stealing Rocinante I rode off the pages in search of excitement; once beyond their enchanted milieu I fell into a profound sadness and, still a virgin, expired. I imagined myself shipwrecked on Robinson Crusoe's island, after he had been rescued, waking each morning in his absurd little garrison, praying no-one would arrive to take me away. I imagined myself the coachman driving with the head of Julien Sorel on the seat, the divine woman of his dreams having left it behind in her hurry to begin a new life. I wrote myself into a crazy-quilt pattern of remnants from Dickens, Sidney Carton's bereaved friend and Estella's mysterious lover and David Copper-field's benefactor, and many others, besides. I wrote my-self into a Borges story, but, once there, found I was a character trying to write myself out again, back into the real world. These procedures were amusing, but amuse-ment was not enough. I needed more compelling diver-sion.

I decided to write a murder. There was no point turning to American writing for a prototype, for Ameri-cans kill off other Americans with narrative impunity. I wanted my readers to be sympathetic to the murderer, but not indifferent to the moral complexity of taking a life. British fiction provided no better model. I needed my killing to be more than an expression of eccentricity, carried to a dire extreme. This murder was to be Cana-dian. That does not mean it was intended as an expression of post-colonial venality. I had no desire to fling blood-soaked garments of our discontent across the abyss of crumbled Empire back upon the silks and brocades ware-housed in the metropolitan centre. No, nor intended as a challenge to the lust for carnage and carnality to the south, a subversion of constitutional rectitude. My desire was to write a simple murder in which my readers would forgive me the killing, even love me for having to bear the travail that would drive me to such an extreme, and would take me to their hearts for having to endure the moral responsi-bility for my action.

It would be necessary to invest my protagonist with a life of his own, for myself to fuse with the fiction-like Jane Austen, to be there, yet impossible to find. I decided his best disguise would be to make him exactly like me—in magic that is known as ironic distraction. I would have to create an unsympathetic victim. It would be a woman and that posed the biggest challenge, for the reader's inclination is to side with the woman as surely as the blame in a spousal dispute goes to the man. It would take fine writing skills, perhaps more than I had, to reverse the equation.

The subtext: I left a marriage of long duration because I was unhappy. I am a widower now, of course. In the last few years before it ended, I would awaken in the mornings disappointed at being alive. I felt a stranger in the most familiar places. I was often apologetic, sometimes afraid, and I had no power. I was not good at quarrelling as I always envisioned a time when it would end and therefore measured the cost of continuing, which is the sure road to being overruled. I was not good with money. She was no better, but found my weakness an excuse for her own. The pattern of rage and submission, contrition and reconciliation, was eventually as worn and banal as linoleum. When I left, I thought she would be relieved.

Instead, she was devastated, which translated into sustaining hatred of such enormity I could not escape its virulent reach. I found my beloved, I had met her briefly before I left home and perhaps in her eyes saw something reflected that I had thought inaccessible, and when I went to her I found unequivocal love. The possibility was there in the first flash of excitement at finding each other, and then in the passionate calm that engulfed us it came into the open. But the inspired ferocity of my estranged wife, who blocked the divorce or a settlement—even lawyers were amazed at her facility for turning legal procedures into an arsenal—infected my love, not my love but my capacity to give myself wholly to loving.

For three years, the happiest in my life, and the most distressing, I tried to make peace. My lawyer's bills mounted. I changed lawyers but made little progress. I offered her everything but myself, all properties, investments, family heirlooms, everything of worth, but always she wanted more money. My beloved and I travelled and read. We worked and in the evenings we sat on the blue sofa with our books or sometimes, in each other's arms, we watched television. We visited libraries and galleries in Italy and England, mountains and coastal escarpments in Australia, restaurants and bookstores in Japan. Always in the background, a sinister subtext, the twists in the plot, shifts in agreement, lost documents, refusals, evasions.

Grasping to comprehend and override the onslaught of anger, I recognized an echo emerging of innumerable quarrels from the past. But in this, more awesome than the rest put together, I was refusing to submit, refusing to collapse on the floor, sobbing forgiveness for causing her rage. She was getting on with her life; she had a better job than I; a new man, not long after I left, moved into the house I had built on the land I had cleared; our son was established in a medical practice so esoteric I used to keep the name on a card in my wallet, and he loved his mother more than ever because he thought I had eviscerated his childhood, deconstructed the past we had shared. But until I was utterly vanquished there would be no end. And how could this happen? Perhaps if I was forsaken by my beloved, went bankrupt, had an emotional collapse, lost my job, got cancer. Then, perhaps, the lawyers would agree I had offered enough and it would be over.

My son grew to despise me. Tolerance of what you abhor breeds contempt. On December 11, a year ago now, he called me to say that enough was enough. I was to give in, to confess, to submit. But how, and to what, he could not say. Only that my being in the world as I was was unconscionable, that being who I was was corrupt. In an attempt to be fair, he charged that his mother and I are both stubborn people, and I felt I was drowning, strug-gling to surface, while another as stubbornly was holding me under. This boy now a man as he spoke, the warmth of his newborn breath I could feel against my neck, the fresh smells of winter in his hair as a child I could catch on the edge of his voice, his strength of body and will as a teenager, skiing cross-country loppets with fierce grace

I adored, I could envision as clearly as the walls of the empty room where I listened, said my claim to being only human was selfish, that I was cruel, a sneak and a liar. I did not know what to do, so I wept.

That night I began to think murder. For the next two months, unable to deal with my life, I re-invented myself as a writer, caught up in resolving the problems of text. That put me at several removes from reality, and having abandoned Jane Austen in a search for Canadian models of authorial absence I was almost happy again. Perhaps what pushed me over the narrative edge was the futility of my quest. Certainly my beloved never wavered in her devotion, remaining as passionately serene as the fantasy lover I dreamed from the times of first dreaming. But as I ranged through Canadian novels in my mind, searching through their familiar particulars, I could find none where the author was not on open or covert display, none who acceded to the admonition by Joyce to write well from your life, then pass out the other side. The twentieth century has seen the authorial voice merge with the voice of the author, sometimes naively, sometimes for won-drous ironic effect.

This is true in Canada more than most places. It was certainly true for me. But I had learned from my times with Jane Austen, when my beloved and I would read her together and, later, as I submitted more and more to oppression and read on my own, it is possible so wholly to transform yourself into text that you are nowhere to be found; you are neither within it, nor, except to your intimates, outside. I know you, Jane Austen. I know you in the same way I know myself. I inhabit my life from one extremity to the other, the way you inhabit your novels. My son may read me in an episode, or divine me in the character I animate at a particular time; but it is not me, no more than the people and events you created are you. To insist on understanding me through the interpretation of another is like trusting a critic's opinion instead of the novel itself. If I am to be judged, let it be by my life, not through self-righteous presumption.

Having said that, I realize my pride is a facade. I was driven to fiction by the implosion of love. When righteousness erupted last winter, there was a familiarity to the emotional pattern, and it was all I could do to resist. I did not ask my grown child's forgiveness for having forced him to judgment. I retreated into my writing and schemed murder, and such is my beloved that she loved me no less for my absence. I suspect what happened next, my son took as proof of my moral corruption, and perhaps his contempt will help assuage grief. I do not remember exactly how it occurred. I thought I was working through the details of a novel, and everything was falling into place, the right words, setting the scene, the characters interacting, the weapon, the argument, the event, and the aftermath. Only the blood was real. The blood and the overwhelming sense of release.

I am still trying to finish the novel. I no longer anticipate being understood by my son. I yearn for redemption. I have decided not to care. My beloved is patient, our love is passionate and serene. I am reading Jane Austen again; we both are. Before long, we will have tea together in the Pump Room at Bath. There is much we will talk about, my beloved, Jane Austen, and I.

Waves Break Stone

I first became aware of a Manitoba conspiracy late in October of 1970, while living in Fredericton, New Brunswick. There, under the commodious shadow of David Arnason, both of us new to the justly famous graduate program in Canadian literature, myself feeling a little in everyone's way and David as genially loquacious as a Prairie sunrise, I learned that Gimli is the axis of the world, if not Earth, and Winnipeg is the cultural capital of Canada. The progress of my awareness may have begun decades earlier, for as a toddler I passed through Winnipeg by train with my mother and brother on the way from Waterloo County to Rivers, Manitoba, where my Dad was stationed with the RCAF; and as a student I stopped over in Winnipeg on my way to Jasper Park Lodge where I was to drive a tour bus for the summer, long enough to stand at Portage and Main and remark to myself that I was standing at the most famous intersection in the Dominion. In retrospect, I may have had premonitions of the sinister importance Manitoba was eventually to assume in my life, but it was not until one evening at a party in 1970, sitting in the Arnason livingroom in Nashwaaksis and listening to David share with a makeshift symposium of conspiring academics the pleasures of his home province, that I realized, what I am absorbing is beyond my control to resist. Here in greater Fredericton, the most beautiful small city anywhere, I am falling dangerously in love with Manitoba.

My dissociative affection for a part of Canada I hardly know came to mind recently, owing to the strange convergence in my life of a discarded newspaper and a nasty bit of bad weather. A North Atlantic storm combined with mechanical difficulties in the aircraft I was on forced an unscheduled landing in Iceland. Stranded at Keflavik International Airport, preoccupied by the inconvenience and desiring distraction, I picked up a newspaper that had apparently been thrown at random upon the bench I now occupied. I do not read Icelandic but, since it shares a common alphabet with those languages I know, I began working my way through the unintelligible sequence of letters laid out with seductive precision, looking for recognizable combinations. My flight was delayed indefinitely; transportation into Rekjavik was impossible. The terminal was a world on its own, and being there as I was, I had no other purpose than to endure the passage of time.

Reading Icelandic struck me as an act of redemption for time otherwise squandered. Before my attention had begun to flag, midway through column four on the first page, the whole of which was arranged to accommodate a shadowy photograph of two men and two women, suddenly I encountered the words, 'Martin Heidegger.' Here was a configuration of letters I knew. Almost immediately, my eye scrolled down and then over to alight on 'David Arnason,' in the fifth column. Four words on a page of indecipherability around which a narrative could be constructed that might take in my whole life, or so it seemed at the moment, in this place so completely severed from anything familiar. Four words to fill the time, the undifferentiated hours until take-off, and to endow with mystery this gaunt structure, the sole purpose of which is to process people, pass them through from one place to another, like the portals of Heaven or Hell.

I could not immediately discern the relationship between Arnason and Heidegger. I knew that David knew the philosopher, although not as Martin, or so at this point I assumed. The resistance of text to the yielding of meaning meant their true relationship was tantalizingly inaccessible. Yet I could not help being drawn into the unfathomable plot of their coincident representation. Driven by the prospect of intrigue and looking for something I could comprehend, I turned from the encoded Icelandic text to consider the photograph that divided the columns in which the four known words now shone from their enigmatic field of alphabetic obscurity like beacons of absolute light.

What you have to realize about David, who as you know is a writer, is his genius for writing his reader into the text. If he loves Manitoba, then you love Manitoba. If Manitoba provides the cultural apparel which David wears like a mantle of justified privilege, then you are bereft for having Manitoba as an absence in your own past, you are naked without his memories of place, haunted by the presence of emptiness. In his livingroom across the broad surge of the St. John River from Fredericton, in 1970, a strange province far away was invoked deep in the crenellated passages of my brain, as if it had always been there, awaiting discovery, and I was homesick for someone else's world. As in conversation, so too, that is the way with his writing. You cannot separate David's words in your mind from what they describe.

I often remember a dog called Skrag, for instance, especially when I am trapped in a secure place—like I was at Keflavik. I have never actually known a dog called Skrag, but David Arnason has; he wrote the Skrag poems. The poems do not argue his affection for Skrag, do not articulate passion. You read about Skrag and love him yourself, the way you love anything that speaks to you from within, even though you may fear it or loathe it, which you do not, in Skrag's case. Skrag transcends language, is alive in your mind. When he lopes away from the imponderable awkwardness of conflicting emotions and over the farm bridge, it is because he has things to do in the south pasture, he has things to do. Between words and what they describe there falls no shadow, there is no mediation. I would rather have written David Arnason's few stanzas about an old dog than all the love poetry of Elizabeth Barrett Browning or of Shakespeare, himself, for those writers are driven to metaphor, and I can admire their tropes, even borrow them on occasion, but Skrag, who is only a dog, inhabits my life, is affirmation of my being in the world. Metaphor reduces everything to meaning, and Skrag and I, we simply are.

David the writer, that might have explained his name encoded in a newspaper among words of his ancient lineage—Icelandic to him being an impenetrable mystery and familiar as blood. It is strange to have something as intrinsic to your genetic design as the language in which your forebears dwelled inaccessible except in translation. As I contemplated the extent to which this profound dissociation conditions the experience of most Canadians, myself included, immigrants in a settler society, I observed with a slow awakening of surprise that the photograph was not a picture of David. Yet if it was meant to illuminate the article, one must assume it related to his prodigious canon as a poet, storyteller, playwright, and critic. If so, whatever it might reveal of his accomplishment was obscured by a swarming of letters that refused to coalesce. Just as he appears in his own writing, David among Icelandic words in the newspaper was an astonishing revelation, and utterly elusive. Elusive, but intriguing. Inviting complicity. But complicity in what? If I were to commit sufficiently to his story, as I felt compelled to do, I recognized there was a risk of being caught up in something beyond my control, the very contemplation of which summoned tremors of anxiety from deep within.

The uncaptioned photograph, the gloom of the emergency lighting in the terminal lounge, the scratched lenses of my reading glasses, combined with my uneasiness at being stranded in a place without sufficient comfort for a traveller plucked out of the air from a determined trajectory, all this conspired...but why would a picture be deliberately blurred? It could be archival, I thought. Yet the people in the photograph wore contemporary dress. It could be an aesthetic phenomenon, the prioritizing of medium over message. But it was singularly uninspired in design. It could be a mistake. Icelandic editors, however, are no more prone to technical error than others, I thought, in this age of desk-top publication, when even the most esoteric ephemera appear correct and substantial. Finally, the blurring could have been intentional, done for me alone—solipsism was sanctuary in a setting that seemed eerily otherworldly. What might appear paranoid in fact allowed solace. The blurred photograph: for a soul disembodied by the ephemerality of its present surroundings, palpable affirmation in the possibility that the picture was printed just so, for my sole benefit; left, just so, for my discovery.

If this fourth and final explanation was true, then my strange solitude was part of some larger plot. I was not stranded as I had supposed, but positioned. A piece in a game, perhaps virtual chess. Not knowing my own value, whether pawn or bishop or king, or even for sure if the game was chess, I could not anticipate my next move nor deduct from preceding events what moves led to my presence here, now. Should I look to the last few hours or days for the pattern that would allow me to anticipate what lay ahead? Since I could divine neither the game-master nor the scale of the game, perhaps I should look for a larger design—but given that time from a human perspective is two-dimensional, could I as a piece on a game-board comprehend the relative movements of myself and the pieces around me: can a pawn only know the movement of pawns, and a king of kings?

With mounting anxiety, I contemplated the paradoxical notion that almost any conclusion the mind can seize upon is retroactively prophetic; ends anticipate the pro-

cess by which they are achieved, although the beginning
and the end of things from my present perspective within
an arrested continuum were both incomprehensible. In
need of definition, compelled to align myself with the
familiar, I returned my attention to the blurry photograph,
looking for Arnason. I held the newspaper at arm's
length. I squinted to throw everything out of focus except
that portion of the picture under assessment. I examined
each face in turn, the two men and two women. I did this
repeatedly until my arm was tired and my eyes watered
from the effort. On the final survey, the last of my looking, I suddenly realized in looking for Arnason I had
missed the indistinct but undeniable image of Martin
Heidegger on the extreme right. It was knowledge preceding experience that allowed for what amounted to revelation. In looking for Arnason I had nearly missed the point
of the photograph.

There was Heidegger, standing in front of the Manitoba legislature. The building itself was in focus, as if the
photographer had purposely hidden the figures not behind
but in front of an architectural form that would be generi-
cally familiar to any viewer of the Western world, and
thus a distraction from the foregrounded subject. An impulse to narrative took hold, generated by a clamour of
questions. Who were the other three people; why were
they apparently indifferent to the man on their left, who
was of course on the right from the viewer's perspective,
unless the photograph was reversed? From the way shadows fell in a thin bar across the snow to the right of the
figures I surmised it was evening; the sun in the west, on
their left, meant the picture was printed correctly: I could
tell this because I happen to know the legislature faces
northwest. It is a key element in the Manitoba geography
I carry within me, which I long for with the irrational nostalgia of a lover for his imaginary beloved. I can see it all.
Winnipeg straddles the fiftieth parallel and thus in winter

the sun rises from the southeast. If it were a morning shot, the sun would throw shadows in front of the figures, casting their silhouettes forward across the snow and the legislature would itself be shrouded in residual night, as would the figures being photographed.

Who were these people, posed with such deliberation, like permanent tourists? Why was their photograph taken, what event does it record; or obscure? Why was it printed on the front page of an Icelandic newspaper? Was it printed on every copy of the edition, perhaps indifferent to the bewilderment of Icelandic readers, or only on this one copy, left here for me to find by someone who anticipated the bad weather and my condition as a castaway surrounded in a pool of dim light by the sounds of terminal emptiness? Where was David in all of this?

But even as I asked the question, I knew—Arnason was the photographer. Once realized, it was obvious. This was a photograph of David Arnason, he was there, within the shadows and textures and contours and depths, as surely as if someone at that moment had taken a candid shot of the photographer photographing. It was a portrait, not unlike those trompe d'loeil compositions which at a distance seem to be of James Dean but up close reveal scenes of motorcycles and Porches and fifties paraphernalia. Looking around me to confirm my relative solitude, I then said aloud, this photograph is not what it seems! My voice echoed with such resonance I peered into the dismal reaches of the terminal to see if there was someone mimicking my words, mirroring my presence. Finding no-one, I subsided into contemplative trepidation, and nurturing my fears dozed for a few moments while sitting absolutely upright as I always do in public places.

I may have dreamed Icelandic sagas. I remembered nothing on awakening. Yet I felt an affinity with the location of my estrangement that only a subconscious rehearsal of the stories first told to me by David over beer in Fredericton could account for. Possibly I had dreamed the *Islendingasögur* or perhaps in that infinite moment of suspended time between waking and sleep I had actually lived the entire narrative as if it were my own story—and then in the jarring journey back into consciousness and time, it had escaped. In any case, while I fell asleep as a Canadian I awoke robust with imagination. Perhaps I was Icelandic at last, my ancestral affinity for Manitoba, no longer neurotic divination.

Being a diagnosed narcoleptic I have a vested interest in dreams. I cannot always distinguish between wakefulness and sleep, nor do I always have the urge to try. The two states of mind are not mutually exclusive: asleep, I sometimes dream I am awake, and awake I often suspect myself to be sleeping. Normally, the elision of boundaries between one mode of consciousness and the other is not problematic. Many of my university colleagues seem to share the same condition. But sometimes it can be disconcerting, not knowing whether the Cartesian notion of *cogito ergo sum* affirms the solidity of my foothold in the waking world or is proof that in dreams the reality of thought is as absolute as it is ephemeral.

If I were now Icelandic, I reasoned, it was because I was either still asleep and dreaming wakefulness or I was awake but someone other than the person I had thought myself to be. To test this new sense of myself I picked up the newspaper again and began to read. The words tumbled by, nearly making sense, their unintelligibility no longer an affront. If I was not Icelandic, then why, while I sub-articulated the Icelandic text, was the letter 'r' rolling against the back of my mouth, as I had so often heard it in David Arnason's own peculiar accented vernacular?

Newly centred by my unremembered dream, I shrunk away from the surrounding gloom that seemed to reach towards me like strange dismembered limbs out of the architectural twilight. Finding myself Icelandic after a

lifetime of being Canadian, you might have thought there
would be great comfort in being marooned at Keflavik.
You might think I had inadvertently discovered relief
from the lack of definition by which I have been haunted
all my life. Instead, I felt afraid. If an interlocutor had
asked at that moment, what is the farthest place in the
world from here, I would instantly have replied, Manitoba! That is where in imagination I am most secure, and
where the world is most sure. But I was centred, now, in
mounting terror. Despite myself, my pride in being emotionally self-reliant and a rational anarchist, impervious to
the conflicting implications of intellectual apperceptions,
I was transfixed within the singularity of my present
experience in Keflavik airport. This, I reasoned, must be
what it is like to know you are dying.

What you have to realize about David Arnason is that
in October of 1970 he was the most imposing man in
Canada. His scowling grin, voluptuous beard, fearsome
girth, the shambling authority of his movements, the precision of his articulation that seemed to envelop him in a
luminous carapace of words, the tremors of earnest enthusiasm in his voice, the thundering resonance of his convictions and his sweetness of disposition, all this, once
met, became the measure of what a fully authentic person
could be. He carried Iceland in his blood, although at that
time he had never been to Iceland. He could play any
musical instrument, after watching it shape sound for only
moments. One simply expected he would do well, and he
always did. Whatever my own mark in a graduate-school
essay or project, Dave always got one mark better. It was
the way professors like Fred Cogswell and Tony Boxhill
acceded to and sustained the natural order of things.

David was an accomplished story-teller even then. He
spun out sagas where the truths of his own life were indistinct from wry and wondrous fictions. You knew his dog
Skrag would become a book one day. And as with all

good story-tellers, the better he got, the more inseparable he was from the telling. When, some two decades later, he came to publish a novel, *The Pagan Wall,* it was inevitable that I would look for him there, in its cadence and vocabulary, and in the lives of his characters. And of course he is there. It is and is not his own story. But do you know who else is there? By name. Martin Heidegger. David disguises his own presence in exquisitely controlled misdirection, turning confessional into narrative strategy, but the old Nazi philosopher he draws into public display, neat as a pin. There he is, Heidegger, among words.

That, in itself, should not be surprising. There is a connection between Heidegger and residual colonialism coursing the veins of most Canadians, invisible and deadly as a low white cell count. For Heidegger death is the key to being; we must each accommodate the knowledge of our inevitable end, live knowing we are incomplete and that on completion we no longer exist. So it is with Canadians of a certain age, alive with the burden of being on the edge of being British; and for younger Canadians, being not-American. Much as we may fidget on the outside looking in, that is our perpetual condition. If Canadians were at the centre, we would experience perfect annihilation—to be British, or American, would mean we cease being Canadian. We live in a state of becoming, our ongoing anxiety a constant reminder of who we are not. We hover, never truly ourselves.

That is the Manitoba conspiracy in a nut-shell. In a world where we are what we are not, there is an insistent reminder coming from the province at our dead centre— that phrase, I use fully aware of its implications: it is not Manitoba that is dead but the absence it signifies for the rest of us deep within our collective psyche, nurtured by the knowledge that there is at our centre a place that for most of us is accessible only in imagination, a place so special we long for it with a kind of misbegotten longing that is for some of us very much like grieving. The insistence by Manitobans that the measure of Manitoba is Manitoba itself is a profoundly Heideggerian notion in our collective Canadian cosmology. In my own private dislocation, not unlike unrequited love, which is a sort of grieving if you think about it, David Arnason is the prime mover. In his conversation, in his writing, even in *The Pagan Wall*, which is set entirely in Europe but informed with uncompromising fidelity to authentic experience by a Manitoban sensibility, I am continually reminded that such authenticity as some of us can only imagine, others can actually live.

At this point in my ruminations, I promised myself that I would re-read David's novel, if ever I escaped the dreary confines of this terminus, the ominous theatre of my isolation and conjecture. In the dismal light I seemed to be making a pact, let me escape, move onwards in my journey, and I will explore once again the confluence of an Arnasonian protagonist and Martin Heidegger in a context more coherent, less disturbing, than the present situation allowed. I am not sure whether the pact was with God or the Devil, and it was not important since I believe in neither, although I am frightened by both. Perhaps it was with David, who had been conjured by the letters of his name, so that he seemed to be there, standing just back from my field of vision whichever way I turned to peer into the murky gloom, or perhaps the pact was with Heidegger, an old old man in *The Pagan Wall* who was now middle-aged and standing with an air of expectation in front of the Manitoba legislature, insisting I resolve the puzzle of his appearance there as a perfect example of the living dead, for while I knew he had expired on May 26, 1976, he had clearly posed for this picture in the 1990s and, while not entirely in focus did not seem the worse for wear?

I did not start this; David, as well, has him alive after death. Arnason's contextualized Heidegger animates a vision of moral decadence in Europe that is offset by the loves of a man and a woman from Manitoba who are caught up in its machinations, yet as innocents abroad are able to resist its power. Heidegger as the living dead seems less an intellectual vampire haunting the shadows of a post-war continent and more the sly superannuated attendant of inexplicable Being.

David can talk to fish. That is one of the strange things about him. To mermaids, yes, but given their imagined being, that is not surprising—accomplished mermaids can appear wholly human if they wish, and will listen to almost anyone. But David talks to fish. I have seen him, drink in hand, sitting eighteen inches from a tank of tropical fish, engaged in esoteric discourse, as if his reflection in the glass were responding point counterpoint to his argument, and the fish meanwhile were scurrying in phalanxes of meaning, careening as rhetorical signifiers across the front of the tank.

The terminal now appeared to be empty, save one despairing soul, myself. If my dread and insubstantiality seem intemperate, consider: I was alone in the gloom of emergency lighting, caught up in the purgatorial limbo of waiting, waiting for nothing but time, for time to resolve, as if time were suspended and I had no choice but to endure until it resumed its normal function as a context of consciousness, into which I might rediscover myself thrown, like clay on a wheel, spinning beneath the hands of an unknown potter, shaped by an imagination beyond my control. Where the others in the terminal might have gone, who had been swarming as apparitions at the very edges of my awareness, flight personnel, security people, passengers in transit caught like myself between departure and arrival, I could not tell. There was no evidence of egress, yet if others had been there they were now absent.

Fighting panic I clutched at the newspaper as the only familiar object at hand. In my agitation, I ripped the front page lengthwise from top to bottom.

Offended by what seemed my incontrovertible cowardice, I flung the paper's several pieces against the dismal air. Two parts of the torn page caught an edge of atmosphere; swirling upward, they looped and fluttered to my feet. Between the written Arnason and the written Heidegger a shard of marbleized floor obtruded like caesura in a sonnet; in the torn photograph of the Manitoba legislature a neatly severed Heidegger now stood apart from the other figures as if observing them from across an insuperable abyss. The precision of this apparent accident, far from making me wonder at the meaning to be drawn from chance action, served rather to affirm my suspicion that not only was the photograph tampered with, to make it tear just so, but my every action was being monitored and manipulated by an unseen witness.

It stood to reason, there must be a purpose to all of this. Someone must be in control. I immediately suspected it was David. Somehow I had found myself in an Arnasonian plot. I had become a character in an Arnason narrative. Even more disconcerting, perhaps it was only my awareness that was new, this epiphany representing a shift in my perception, not my condition. Perhaps I have always been a figure in the narrative design of David Arnason. That would explain my sense of Manitoba as a home-place, although I have never lived there. That would explain my present discovery of myself as Icelandic, for I had long since acquiesced to the probability that, just as the heart of the Canadian nation lies in Manitoba, Manitoba itself is transcendently informed by its heritage of Icelanders, including the Arnasons, who fled from the conflagrations of fire and ice in the nineteenth century to settle of the shores of Lake Winnipeg.

Here is the problem. At what point did Arnason and

Heidegger come together in my mind? In terms of philosophical verities, they converge only at the vanishing point, where each might be abandoned to the other from the inquisitor's perspective, although this is an illusion fostered by post-Cartesian valorization of the viewer's eye, the witness reconfiguring the witnessed, seeing perception as reality. Here is the problem. David is and is not Heideggerian. Of course he is, for how could a thinking being not be. But he is not, for how can the spirit resist imagination. David, in his fine morose and whimsical, diffident and erudite, generous and solipsistic renderings of himself as fiction, constructs a personality where soul and imagination are undifferentiated, imagination being the spontaneous presence of the self, and soul, the accumulation of these myriad selves through time. David is a pretertextual phenomenon. Heidegger lies soulless among words, never quite lifting himself from the pages of an endless text.

Heidegger does not understand irony: to do so demands awareness within language but also beyond it. Incapable of irony, he could not comprehend the unnatural nature of Nazi atrocity. Unable to distinguish between living-with-death as a set of mind and a social condition, Heidegger committed himself to the latter, to death as the measure of society's authenticity and hence of his own. Oh David, I murmured, my words penetrating into the dismal air of the terminal lounge. How did you ever get involved with such a man, you of the powerful bones and immeasurable capacity for being alive?

I slept again and thought I heard Umberto Eco speaking. It was October in my dream. I was in a large room with a gaunt cathedral ceiling, like a holy place abandoned to ordinariness. There was a big crowd. He spoke in English. He said that some things cannot be improved upon: he named the spoon. He named several other things but in the dream I did not agree with him on anything except the spoon. The bicycle was one of the other things; but the bicycle has been manifestly improved upon over years and may be infinitely refined. The spoon is what it does. A good spoon has perfect shape and balance. Some spoons are better than others for one purpose or another, but once found the perfect spoon retains perfection. Eco named other things but they have slipped from my mind, all except the book. He named the book, and it too is what it does and does so with perfection. I agreed with him on books. On spoons and books.

It is October 6, 1998. Umberto Eco invites his listeners to think. A number of people get up and walk out, not angrily but not awkwardly; more as if they suddenly remember they have appointments elsewhere at precisely the moment of their departure and of necessity walk headlong through his words and into the adjoining corridors. He says dictionaries are systems; the dictionary is a limited cachement of words but its contents offer infinite possibilities, possibilities of infinite meanings. He says that in a democracy hypertext can be dangerous, offering as it does a kind of intellectual anarchy, but in an authoritarian state its refusal of authority can signify freedom. Freedom signified, he says, is revolution. The alphabet, he says, is so small it takes the breath away, and it is infinite in disposition.

I listen to Umberto Eco. He offers an overhead projection of plus signs and minus signs, and using this he explains permutations of the relationship between text and hypertext, books and the net. Unfortunately, as he does so, he moves in and out of microphone range. Much of his explication is lost, but he seems happy. Most of us share his happiness. When he stops talking there is much applause, after which I awaken.

Looking around me in the shadows of the terminal for alterity, for assurance that I was no longer sleeping, my gaze included a long window overlooking the runway, then projected through the glare of the glass into the murky atmosphere outside, then fixed upon a fuselage at some distance across the tarmac, on which I read 'nada' which I assumed to be Canada encrypted by my line of vision into an ominous abbreviated cipher. Had I created Umberto Eco? Stunned at such power, I did not immediately recognize the corollary as equally possible. From nada, ça nada, had I made him happen, written his books, spoken his words? I knew we must have a vocabulary in common or I could not have read his books, never mind written them. Had he ever been to Canada? If so, if I could prove he had been there, would that establish that I had not created him? But then of course it could open the possibility that he created me.

This latter seemed unlikely since I had already arrived at the possibility that I was a peripheral figure in a David Arnason fiction and could not very well also be an Italian persona. In any case, I felt Icelandic; I was marooned in Iceland, estranged from Manitoba, and had a personal history, or so I believed or was allowed to believe, rooted in Waterloo County, in southwestern Ontario. I was Italian only in that dim connected way the whole of Western civilization is Italian.

No sooner had Waterloo County appeared in my mind, superimposed over the vision of an Air Canada fuselage in the streaming fog, than I grasped a terrifying connection which brought the significance of my present situation into sharp relief. Erb Electric! The manufacturers of wire conduit used on Canadian airliners; the company is a family affair. I possess an original Erb birth certificate, Johannes Erb, born in Lancaster County, Pennsylvania, 1754. Fled the American revolution. His son, Christian, married a Mohawk woman from the Grand River valley. One line of their progeny begat the founders of Erb Electric, another begat the line that begat me.

In consequence of having been borne here on the

grounded wings of Canadian technology and at this precise moment having become aware of convergent narratives, my own and that of the manufacturers of a critical
component in the aircraft's function as a vessel of safe
passage from this tedious place, an involuntary shudder
reverberated throughout my system as if someone had
desecrated my grave. Such convergence forced me to the
realization that my presence here might be part of an
unresolved narrative equation, the working out of which
was inseparable from my own end. That might seem to
verge on the psychotic, but consider the ineluctable irony:
if someone else was in charge of my story, how could he
or she resist bringing me down as the absolute and arbitrary consequence of Christian's birth in a small cabin on
the edge of a Mohawk village where the Speed meets the
Grand, two hundred years previous. If my story was in the
ironic mode, would resistance be possible?

My affection for Manitoba led me on this venture in
the first place. I was on my way to give a lecture at a congress in Strasbourg on Manitoba writers. These included
such Icelandic-Canadians as W.D. Valgardson, Laura
Salverson, Kristjana Gunnars, and David Arnason, and
here I was, suspended from the normal progressions of
time in an Iceland that swirled with elemental fury beyond
these walls, this impossible labyrinth of my own mind and
destiny. Being a man of my age, however, I was able to
look at death square on. The imminence of death was not
absolute. The trick was to anticipate it and find alternatives. The convergence of forking paths that in retrospect
would provide my survivors with an overweening sense
of synchronicity could be avoided. Everything that has
happened had to happen just so, to bring me here, waiting
to board a plane in which a faulty strand of wire would
cause the plane to explode in mid-air, its residue to fall
plummeting through layers of weather and crash piece-
meal into Arctic seas. The past could not be changed but

its implications could be denied. Of this I was relatively certain.

I looked once again at Arnason's photograph, now lying on the floor. The Manitoba legislature adorned with a golden icon—that, I realized, was the very fulcrum of my own peculiar cosmology. If there was a visceral heart to my visionary sense of myself in the world, this was it, in black and white. Somewhere along the way, I had come to understand Manitoba as the vital throbbing heart at the centre of the dying organism that was all I could ever hope to be—the conspiracy was to make me accept this. Such sentiments could not have been self-induced, for who would knowingly accept such morbid dislocation, even in an immigrant society such as ours.

Feeling arbitrary, utterly, I almost gave up at this point, nearly submitted to the inevitable. To dwell in meaninglessness, that is nothing—to be conceived, to conceive oneself, as arbitrary, that is more than mortality can bear. I looked to Heidegger, then across the abyss to the other three. They were not couples, but stolidly individuated, despite the pixillated blur of the newsprint. They occupied their severed rectilinearity on the torn page like gladiators in ordinary modern dress, each turned in upon his or her own private darkness, each turned out to face the dying light. Why was Heidegger here like this, just now, just so? Precisely, it occurred to me, because there was no reason, no explanation.

In accepting the arbitrariness of Heidegger within language beyond my comprehension, in a photograph of my own dislocated psyche, the meaning of the other three leapt immediately to mind. Heidegger, separated, was spectral; presence without substance. The second man was a configuration of impotent lechery. The two women —a lesbian, and a nymphomaniac. The four of them were David's joke, borrowed perhaps from Jean Paul Sartre. The conspiracy, to make me submit. It was through David that I now perceived them in this fashion. The story was his. In a story by someone else, or by David stranded elsewhere in time, in Fredericton, perhaps, in 1970, instead of his beloved Winnipeg to which he returned after graduate school, the same four figures could be something else again, a troupe of dead-pan mimes, four strangers, swans in human form.

Caught between Heidegger and Sartre, as it were, trapped in a discontinuous world, I could embrace meaninglessness as justification for submission to text and my fate, or I could seize my own being, turn from the unholy foursome and embrace freedom, instead. Believing David was providing me the option, that this entire situation was somehow his doing, and that as a figure in his narrative I could choose to be free, I realized it was up to me to create my own future. That meant, of course, I must avoid getting on the plane which, if I were aboard, was destined to crash in an extravagant and gruesome display of ironic inevitability.

With self-preservation in mind, I rose from the bench and strode to a door at the end of a short hallway in front of me, stepping as I did so on the torn newspaper, grinding it to cryptic fragments. The door opened into a windowless room that was empty but for a single chair beneath an overhead light, a bare bulb that swayed on its corded wire in the still air. No-one could find me here. The flight would proceed in due course and the threat of my presence would be eliminated. I turned the lock on the outside of the door, stepped in, pulled the door shut behind me. There was no escape, no turning back. Sooner or later someone would come, open the door, and set me free. Meanwhile, beyond a world of meaning and control, beyond even Arnason's reach, I would endure with grace and with the conviction that an entire universe was unfolding as I wished.

In locking myself in, however, I now realize I have

committed an unpardonable narrative offence; what is, in effect, a mortal error. In this empty room, there is no longer the possibility of a witness to my life, no-one to relate the closure by which this, as all human stories, must come to an end. Out there, someone would surely have emerged from the shadows to provide dimension to my isolation; but here, whether or not I am even alive is of no consequence. I have placed myself in an untenable position. While I can negotiate how the story is to be told, the story itself is beyond me. I have anticipated the disaster of the plane plummeting into the sea as an inexorable consequence of my own genetic destiny. I have evaded the fate that would have left me, bits of flesh dissipating on estranged currents of the mind as the chess-master gathers himself or herself into separate consciousness, awakening, perhaps, into a separate dream.

But where to, from here? If, perhaps, my existence is unreal, if Descartes is wrong, must I remain in this room forever? If so, then time is meaningless. In a world without meaning, all meanings are possible. If that is the case, then all stories that are possible will occur as equally authentic. In at least some of them I will be Icelandic, I will be the protagonist, in some the witness, in some an omniscient narrator so inaccessible in semantics and syntax, a truly absent presence in the text, that language itself will seem to be saying whatever is said. In at least one of these stories I will know what the future holds for the man locked in a room in the terminal who anticipates closure, believing time merely a projection on the infinite moment of his tenuous life. If all stories are possible, in one of the possible stories the reality will be that only one story is possible. In one story, only the future will be known, while the present will be virtually indecipherable.

In this story, I am sitting on an uncomfortable chair under a naked light bulb, immobilized by the certainty of my impending death. There is no other reality accessible into which I might insert myself, driven by my desperation to alter the inexorable. This, of course, is not a matter of preordination, since while the future is known the present is not—such is the knowledge that separates us from animals and angels, alike. I am sitting, immobilized, in reckless contemplation. Then with a crash the silence falls. My mind goes still. The end is about to begin.

They will find these notes among the debris. This collapsed corner of the building will have given way to structural fatigue at the precise moment that I finish writing. I had not even been aware I was writing. From the outset I thought I was recollecting all this from some indeterminate safe vantage at my eventual destination. The notes will be close to my outstretched hand, as if I had let them slip away carelessly. In order to extricate my body from the rubble, they will have to bring in power-jacks to hoist the imponderable weight of a steel girder from my chest. On the twisted side of the girder will be a single word, printed as the construction company's logo, repeated in a sans-seraph font from one end to the other. Arnason, it will say. Arnason, Arnason, Arnason. At one point in the line of words the letters will appear stretched to indecipherability. That is where the bend will occur, the break in load-bearing equipoise which caused the collapse.

In the unalterable course of this particular story, these notes which I now realize I have been making from the beginning as a means of coping with the emptiness of time between arrival and departure, and of constructing a perspective from which to observe myself as my own witness, these notes will be forwarded to my daughter, Laura, in Winnipeg where in this version she is a colleague of David Arnason at the University of Manitoba. At my family's request, my remains will be rendered into ashes in Iceland and my ashes will be delivered for scattering to Waterloo County. The notes will be examined by David who will marvel at the ironies of my demise and explain to my daughter that his cousin's construction company had never before had a problem, and that it was an earth tremor, Odin's whim, an act of God, and not a faulty girder, that imposed an end to my story.

Once alone, David will light a cigar in his office sanctuary and with the same match he will set ablaze the original print of the newspaper photograph. As they burn, the four figures will briefly share their common plight, like four gates to a beleaguered city, four heads to an immolated beast: for a moment in the contorted paper Heidegger smiles; in a twist from the flame the other man's face leaps with sudden passion, before shrinking into the heat; the two women turn intimately towards each other, then fall away into the fire's embrace. The Manitoba legislature crumbles. David will see all this. It is dangerous to write as he does, where meaning is in the service of being. He will not take notes. He dreams, perhaps, of Gimli or maybe of Fredericton, and of how much he loves Manitoba—so much, in imagination there is nothing he cannot do.

Writing Aritha

Let me put my own turn on an invidious comparative strategy. I would rather have written *Places Far from Ellesmere* than *The Alexandria Quartet*. For one thing that would mean I am alive. Lawrence Durrell died in 1990. It might be worth being dead to be Jane Austen. I would willingly sacrifice myself for *MacBeth* or maybe *The Sound and the Fury*—if personal annihilation were the determining factor in whether or not they got written. Otherwise, while I am not proposing an exchange of my life for Aritha van Herk's, I would like to have created her brilliant conflation of earth and the world more than almost anything else.

I am a creative writer, I have never completed a literary project. I decided to become a writer last year when the inchoate particulars of my life threatened to gather, through the extended darkness of winter, into a distinct personality. Despite my familiarity with the loose arrangement of physical characteristics that are reflected from my mirror as an occupied entity, who answers to my name, wears my clothes and animates my expressions, I am not used to thinking of myself as a definable presence. The conjunction of oppressive weather and the pernicious sensation of time rachetting moment by moment towards my inevitable death forced me into a confrontation with myself as a singularity, something I would prefer not to be. An evasive strategy that might allow me to stay unresolved, I decided, was writing.

It has not been as easy as I had supposed to get behind print after being in front of it all these years, to push words ahead like the wind pushing leaves of a book lying open on a picnic table in an ancient wood. Do not misunderstand. I have been writing as long as I have been able to read, but always as an outsider, a visitor to language, looking in. Words have been walls, I have read them and covered them over with words of my own. It never occurred to me before to enter the rooms they obscure.

Before becoming a writer, I produced several academic manuscripts. These do not count as real writing since they deploy words as a delivery system, not for the generation of an alternative reality. My indifference to the ultimate disposition of these works cast an aura of excellence over their esoteric ruminations such that they found their way into publication and onto the shelves of university libraries in sufficient number to make them useful as bibliographic referents but not enough to earn royalties. The point is, I know how to construct sentences that perfectly obscure the authority on which their assumptions are based. You would not know from my scholarly work my sex or my race, my age or my class. Last winter, however, it slowly became clear that being ephemeral was no longer enough. I took up writing not merely as an escape from morbidity but in quest of the ultimate disguise. From being nobody, I needed to be somebody else.

I do not want to give the impression that my death is imminent. So far as I know it is not, but I prefer to keep an indeterminate buffer zone between me and my eventual demise. Having entered middle age inadvertently, I wish to extend it as long as possible and to leave it equally unaware of the transition to whatever lies ahead. Writing promised to be a suitable distraction. You need to know, however, that mine is a passive vocation. Think of a contemplative cleric, abjuring the world for the seductive anonymity of the cloister. It is not numinosity or transcendence I seek, but only to be dissipated among words—renunciation in pursuit of the ineffable. Self-effacement or self-abasement are to be avoided as solipsism, the monastic celebration of the self who endures. I wish to avoid any semblance of activist euphoria.

My reticence is not a recent phenomenon. My early years loom over the present as an indistinct shadow. I hardly remember my parents. I groped about in the confined space of childhood and eventually I became aware of time. When I entered puberty, time opened around me like an amphitheatre. The clock on the wall began to tick louder and louder and I was overwhelmed in anticipation of silence, the dazzling white glare of my inevitable death. The only thing to do was slow time down. I could not make it stop, but I could make it linger interminably. Since time drags when you are bored, I determined to show no interest in anything for the duration of my life. It might not take longer to reach the end, but it would seem that way.

Before I read *Places Far from Ellesmere,* my favourite literature was a few lines from Dylan Thomas. Not, as you might have imagined, "Do not go gentle into that good night," for I could not comprehend such an admonition of rage, knowing that passion would be a distraction and the end would sneak up on its victim all the more quickly. No, it was the sentence about Tinker, "the aunt-faced pom," asleep by the burnt-out fire. That subtle display of the perfectibility of words is on the opening page of *Adventures in the Skin Trade.* I mention it, not to diminish Aritha van Herk's work by placing it in context with Thomas's astonishing trope; but rather as a laurel to indicate the extent of my admiration for her achievement.

Not that my taste and judgement are relevant. Aritha van Herk is the authorial entity under scrutiny, not myself. Before we proceed, however, let us consider this awkward but necessary use of the word 'entity.' The problem is, there is no word for what we really mean in a situation like this. I do not mean author, for it is not the person, who having written her book has long since gone on to other things, whom I wish to invoke. The author lives in Calgary and might, as we discuss a book she wrote some years ago, be in Germany right now, or in Spain, visiting friends. I certainly do not mean authorial persona, for that is a literary device, a character within the narrative. Nor do I mean the authorial voice or authorial vision, neither of which is separable from the text except through critical abstraction. What I mean, I suppose, is not quite the personification of the text, its human co-equivalent. If I say, I like Shakespeare, I abhor Virginia Woolf, I love Atwood or Alice Munro, I am obviously not talking about people and relationships. Nor am I talking about books. I am talking about the content of books, but then, not as text; rather, as the text has been assimilated into my experience. There is no word in the critical vocabulary for this. It has to do with communication between levels of consciousnesss, the invocation of an authorial entity allowing access from the intellectual surface to the hidden recesses of our complex responses and memories as readers.

This definition of authorial entity lacks authority, of course, since it relies on an unlikely commonalty of textual experience. If you have not read *Places Far from Ellesmere,* a book which changed my life, and we have both read van Herk's first novel, *Judith,* which you thought brilliant and I took to be promising but flawed, then what do we understand of each other by inserting the phrase 'Aritha van Herk' into our discourse. What if you have never heard of her, and I am her friend? Then what? I say, van Herk writes the north into Canada, transforms words into the place of our being. You have no idea what I am talking about. Or what if you are her friend, and Aritha and I had not met in Calgary in 1978, just before *Judith* won a publication prize of $50,000, more than most writers in Canada earn altogether, and suppose I had only discovered *Places Far from Ellesmere* after travelling fifteen times to the Arctic myself, then I would be in

awe of your vicarious attachment and you would have no
idea why I am staring at you across an empty room,
unable to speak for fear of dispelling your borrowed
luminescence.

Before I took up writing I was an Arctic explorer.
Now that I have a new diversion, I no longer have anything to write about. That is untrue, of course. I have
never done anything of interest. I have never been to Calgary or Edmonton. Imagine me as a blank slate, or written
with erasable chalk. In all my years of reading, I easily
remained an observer from the narrative sidelines. I came
to regard myself as the ideal reader. Nothing of my own
life interfered with the text. When I decided to take up
literary writing I assumed the ephemerality of my life
would be an advantage. But I could not progress beyond
language. Every time I tried to say something creative in
print, I ended up talking about words as things in themselves, grammar as a matter of relationships, language as
the extent of conscious reality.

My turn away from the deployment of facts in a
rhetorical design in favour of writing as an act of creative
evasion was not enhanced by my limited range of experience (something that proved a god-send in scholarly
work). Furthermore, I was occasionally disconcerted by
the intense visceral pleasure of dispersing myself among
words—I would almost say sexual pleasure, but I have
resisted confrontation with sexuality all of my life and
therefore cannot be certain how apt the analogy might be.
This led to my recognition of a desire I had previously,
perhaps, quashed, to engage with my own corporality, to
write my body into the convolutions of language within
which I had thought to hide.

To get away from the world and myself, I needed to
get deeper into both: I needed more of life to have less,
the opposite of Thoreau who chose less, to have more.
One day I left my small room off Jarvis Street near

Gerrard, and went over to Yonge Street and bought myself a chocolate milkshake. I drank it, sitting on the curb, watching tires roll by carrying slab-sided cars north. I was on the east side, facing west. I observed myself, the observor observed, and I wanted to reconstruct this moment in my mind as something dramatic, tremulous with thematic potential. Instead, I thought about why writers spell out the word Street in narrative, as if we fear the reader will sight-read the sound and miss the cadence of our prose. You can see why my progress as a writer has been slow.

I took to standing outside Alfred Britnell's Bookshop, north of Bloor, where I thought interesting things might happen. One day, out of the depths of the store came a nondescript man, clutching a book in his left hand. When he saw me leaning against the light standard looking in his direction, he suddenly tossed the book to the pavement as if in appeasement and scurried away. So integral was I to the scene, he must have taken me for a store detective doing exterior surveillance. Startled to be thought as sinister as he, I hurried off in the opposite direction, but not before picking up the discarded book and tucking it under my arm.

It was, of course, Aritha van Herk's *Places Far from Ellesmere.* Back in my room, under the bare light-bulb strung from the centre of the ceiling to a hook over my bed, I read it in one sitting. My own creative efforts at this point consisted of sentence fragments on a few scraps of paper, failed postmodern experiments in the extinction of narrative voice. Imagine my astonishment, then, that writing could do this, that words could be what they named, her childhood described could be the reader's experience, her Edmonton years as immediate as memory, and the Arctic so real on the page that it filled the mind, flooded my mind with boulders and flowers and streams. If she could write Ellesmere, transform words into place with

such utter conviction, then perhaps out of my small
knowledge of the world in conjunction with the greatness
of language I too could write.

Places Far from Ellesmere is not a big book. What I
like most, it is a book caught up in the process of becoming. This is how a book should be. Never finished. It implies forms uninvented, genres whose conventions refuse
to coalesce; it offers people who resist being characters
but are alive to the writer and therefore yourself, and no
plot, apart from the narrative convolutions of syntactical
elegance. It turns the reader dyslectic, its words swim in
the mind, restless, evading coherence first one way, then
another. You can read it over and over, and it will never
end.

I have not been north of Highway 401, but I am aware
that above me lies all that makes my country a nation,
while the space I inhabit is a nexus of commerce and culture that exists only in a brief flurry of the historical
present. From reading van Herk I know what is north. I
have read others who write of the Arctic, but either their
feats of adventure exclude me, to garner applause, or they
treat it as a concept of the critical mind. But Aritha van
Herk, writing about Ellesmere, makes of her words an
Arctic I discover within, conjuring from her vital images
that have assimilated as part of my knowledge of myself
a vision and memory of a real place that contains me. In
our Ellesmere is the time before humans, is the eons-long
epic of weather and seasons as the Earth resolved into our
awareness of its prior existence. These extremities of
place and of time that have coallesced into the territorial
extent of our imaginings as a people, these are the conditions of being Canadian.

One evening I talked to the man from the room across
the hall. Although we share a bathroom and a refrigerator
in the hallway, we seldom speak. No-one does in a place
like this. It is safer, less complex. He is Inuit, an Inuk. He

told me a story that has no beginning and no end, except the arbitrary insertion of his voice into silence and its eventual cessation; it has no character or plot. It is a story of his people and I record it for Aritha van Herk. Listen to the man's words, they are beautiful. He is speaking Canadian, dividing the year, alive within time. There is Qaummugiaq, the beginning of daylight. There is Qangattauqsi, when the bear dens are secure; Avrunniit, time of the frozen seal pups; Nattiaqaliqtanga, time for the seal pups that live. There is Tupiqtuut, time for the tents. There is Qiqsuqqaqtuut, when there is a crust on the ice, and Iksuut, when there is flooding. There is Saggaruut, when there is new fur on the caribou, and Akulliruut, the time of waiting, and Aminaijaut, when velvet falls from the caribou antlers. There is Tusaqtuut, the new season. There is Tauvigjuaq, the dark time. There is one other, we give it no name. That was the end of his story.

I live in time that is parsed by the naming of gods and emperors. I subsist on a small disability pension. When it became necessary in high school to decide on career goals, I had just read Melville's "Bartleby the Scrivener," so to every option suggested by teachers and counsellors I responded, "I would prefer not to." In university I fell by default into a general arts program. Because I got every assignment in on time and kept such a low profile none of my professors knew who I was, I was given high grades. As I never took the initiative to register for graduation and kept taking English courses because I spoke English and read a lot to keep me distracted from university life, I was eventually admitted to graduate school, my file having been submitted by a departmental secretary who could find no more courses in which to enroll me at the undergraduate level.

I adapted well to the graduate program, in my first months perfecting a kind of insolent inscrutabilty. I would speak only when spoken to, but then retort with splenetic

ambiguity that suggested a superiority of intellect sufficient to pass me quickly through a Master's degree and
into doctoral studies at a better university. My Ph.D. years
were the best in my life. I found my capacity for boredom, my appetite for mind-numbing subversions of the
temporal continuum, utterly appropriate to the tasks associated with academic excellence. At the end of the maximum period allowed for completion of degree requirements, my dissertation project was deemed complete,
although I felt I could have sustained it indefinitely.

As I had no interest in a career, rather than see their
reputation at risk through my indolence, which was taken
for brilliance, my university arranged for a post-doctoral
fellowship at Harvard. I had never been out of Ontario
before. I arrived in April and the magnolias were in full
blossom. With a score of universities, the Boston area was
ideally distracting. I could wander from campus to campus, like a chameleon switching from sweatshirt to sweater to jacket and tie as required, and never be noticed. I did
not talk to anyone. I met no-one at Harvard. A year after
arriving, I discovered myself in receipt of accolades for
work it was assumed I was doing. These took the form of
a letter, a copy of a which I found in my mailbox, which
I only visited after hours so as not to attract attention. It
was addressed to the Chair of the Department of English
at the University of Toronto, praising my post-doctoral
work and urging my employment, which Harvard of
course would take as a compliment.

After six weeks on the U of T faculty, I was given an
indefinite leave of absence and placed on a long-term
disability pension. It was awkward for the university, I
was told, that my lectures were so boring the students
demanded my dismissal. Auditors confirmed that the
students were, if anything, generous in their appraisal, but
since I was lecturing in good faith, sharing the fruits of
my desultory academic labours with what seemed to me

was ennervating candour, I could not be fired. In fact, after five years I was informed by mail that I had been given tenure and, after two more, an associateship. I am expecting the rank of full professor within the next year, and nomination to a fellowship in the Royal Society of Canada, which I will not resist, since refusal would demand a coherence of personality I would prefer not to endure. Considering my academic status it is surprising my pension is not more generous.

Which brings us by a commodius route of circumlocution back to Aritha van Herk. As I had never engaged with the landscape in which I lived, knowing from childhood that the bond between people and place was a principal source of self-conscious identity, it was disconcerting to read in her book the visceral presence of land in the text, as if words could be wind and water and stone, and the mind of the reader, with the mind of the writer, could be merged with the earth. This was language unlike anything I had known. Words did not express a narrator's feelings about flowers, Arctic poppies and purple saxifrage, words became poppies and saxifrage, but what was more astonishing, words felt the experience of flowers. The words had what critics call agency. They felt. And they invited the reader to feel what they felt, to share their delight in being flowers.

I use the past tense to describe my discovery. The text could, of course, be more accurately described in the ongoing present, for what language and landscape do with each other in van Herk's visionary fusion, they continue to do. However, it is my own recognition I wish to record, the moment of my epiphany in the past, not protracted as textual analysis but isolated in the context of personal history. I was a writer unable to write, caught up as I was in evasions of self, and here was writing that collapsed the boundaries between writer and reader, the perceived and perception, between words and what the words named.

Places Far from Ellesmere was an event, the occasion of my entry into the parallel world of words as a narrative entity, utterly anonymous and wholly authentic. If I could be simultaneously present and absent, substance and essence, in van Herk's visionary aesthetic, I could be so in my own. Whether or not I would ever write such a work for myself, she had made it seem possible.

I became a writer in earnest. When the Inuk across the hall asked what I do, I told him I was writing a novel. He told me he is a hunter. He is old and nearly blind and has an unspecified illness; that is why he lives in the south. Other tenants are transient but he and I have both lived here for over a decade. I have not been in his room nor he in mine. We talk in the hall. From my point of view, being unfriendly would require a greater concentration of character than congeniality does, so I am pleasant. From his, I suspect he would prefer minimal intrusion on the dream world he inhabits, the landscape within, where the wind blows snow-laden against tumultuous hills and the caribou dig for fodder under opulent skies. He still hunts in his sleep, and more and more while awake. I see him trudging down Yonge Street, hunting for polar bears, or sitting on a bench on the University Avenue boulevard, waiting for seals.

My writing is getting better, I think. Reading *Places Far from Ellesmere* made me realize what writing can do, in terms of creating an optional reality for an ulterior self. It showed me the potential for critical fiction to construct a new mode of literary discourse, using conventions of narrative and aesthetic contrivance in the place of analysis to illuminate a text or a writer's intentions. In her interrogations of Tolstoy and her passionate subversion of the contraints in Anna Karenin's Russia that killed her, Aritha van Herk liberates the critical imagination, sets it free among the saxifrage and poppies of Ellesmere, where thinking and being are not offered as mutually exclusive, where language and landscape are equally substantial, where the author is not refined out of her text but inextricably a presence within it.

As I continue to write, with van Herk as my model and unknowing mentor, I find myself less inclined to obscurity. I have not absolved myself of my life, nor resolved into someone else in my text. I translate time from one medium to another, one mind to another as I write. I am beginning to enjoy writing as much as being written. Tomorrow I may ask my Inuk friend to join me for dinner. I will keep on writing, but not from boredom or despair. I might even travel someday to Ellesmere myself.

The Juxtaposition of Alice

When you think of Alice, who are you thinking about? Probably when Alice Munro peers into the looking glass, if she is thinking about Alices, she is thinking about Tenniel's Alice, having never recovered from her earliest study of the prepubescent eroticism that flirts through his illustrations of Lewis Carroll's imaginings. Perhaps not, perhaps she has other Alices in mind. Possibly she is humming along with Arlo Guthrie. Or reconstructing brownie recipes with Gertrude Stein. Perhaps she is thinking of herself, of the Alices she has been, of how these girls and women have found their ways into fiction, more real now, captured in the amber or aspic of print, than her own handsome reflection.

After a certain age, my mother began every sentence with "Do you remember?" I loved her for the urgency of her quest and she loved me in her memories. Sometimes her refusal to live in the present could be demoralizing, for this was not an involuntary surrender to the past, she was sharp to the end. And this made her dying more poignant. Only after she was gone, as I grew ancient myself, did I understand the extent of her sorrow over the larcenies of time, her displeasure at the indignities of aging.

My grandmother lived to one-hundred and two. Mother died relatively young, in her eighties. When I was eleven she read me *Alice in Wonderland*. When I was twelve I read *Through the Looking Glass* out loud to her. We lived alone but we always had books. She received only a small pension for my father who died in Flanders. She preferred to buy books when we could. She said they were my dowry. Still, we made regular forays to the library to supplement our habit. The man I married was not much of a reader. It happens that way, you marry your opposite. He died during the Second World War. In a car accident, so there was no pension. I moved back in with mother, I had hardly moved out, and I have lived here ever since, in this house where I was born a century ago, where she was born, in the same room, before me.

From the sidewalk on Queen Street you can see, through the fringe of ancient lilacs and beyond the big elm, the Victorian bow-window of the bedroom where we both entered our lives. It is upstairs over the front parlor which had a bow-window of its own, the room where I was married and where mother was laid out for the viewing after she died. Something I wish to avoid myself. Being laid out. For myself, my friends are all gone, I have no family to speak of, I do not want strangers gawking, nobody saying how life-like she looks. Fold me up, stuff me in a sack, haul it off to the dump, bulldoze me into the earth. After a good long winter, I'll come up dandelions and bring a little beauty to the bulging terrain—sometimes aesthetics, ecology, and eschatology are inseparable.

My choice here as a writer is difficult. Eschatology pushed me over the edge. We have an implicit contract, you reading my words as if they were tumbling spontaneously out of our mutual purpose, me writing to keep up the pretense that we have an autochthonous reality in common—before you look it up, it means the right thing, that the world of the text we are sharing will seem to have generated itself. We are as much its creations as it is ours. We both have moral obligations, you to evaluate illusions of authenticity, and me to enforce the efficacy of illusion. Moral, I say, because ours is an earnest business, reading and writing, and the implications are profound.

In taking you into my confidence, I made a critical decision. Even though you were willing to suspend disbelief, I am uncomfortable trying to be someone I'm not.

That's what writing has always been, of course, for when you fix words on the page you step out of time, you observe yourself writing, and the voice, no matter how much it echoes your own, is the subject of invention. But changes in fiction have changed the writers who write it. In my lifetime we've gone from Thomas Wolfe, transforming himself into art in a sort of Joycean metamorphosis from flesh into fiction, to Tom Wolfe, strutting through the real world like a character in his novels, and writing as if each of his characters were a bizarre variation of his own personality. We no longer write under the dispensation of Stanislavski and the Actors' Studio; writing is no longer cathartic. We write now to play many parts. Lewis Carroll could project the strange diversions of his elegant mind into print, with illustrations by Tenniel; we, now, those of us sensitive to the moment, dress narratives in our diverse emotions, let characters stand in for our innermost selves. I do not become them, they become me.

This is all, of course, hypothetical. I am a writer. You are reading what I have written as if I am writing it now. But I am not a real writer, I am too much aware of myself writing in a present tense of my own. There is too much between us, too much self-consciousness. Perhaps it all comes down to the problem of voice. You expect the narrative voice to be mine but you also want it to belong to the story. This works for Alice Munro. Whether she is writing in first person or third, she is writing to you. This is her story, you and Alice achieve conditional fusion in the consciousness of her character; her character is Alice, you know that for certain, and her character becomes you for the duration of your reading. This makes Alice Munro delightful to read and impossible to write about. That may be overstating the case but you see what I mean: her fictions are a delight in the way of Hironymous Bosch, extravagantly detailing the joyous and morbid, the ordinary, the unusual, the loathsome, all equally essential to the over-all composition. But try writing about her achievement; critics make fools of themselves, confusing her fictions with mirrors, confusing the image in the glass with Alice, and simultaneously seeing it as a reflection of themselves looking in.

You expect all the Alices, all to be me. This instability of identity you see as a virtue, my strength as a writer. But I am not a real writer. You deserve better. I have been mining my own life, but it is shallow, an open-pit mine. Some of what I told you is truth. What I said about mother is true. And my grandmother, Isabelle Cameron, did live to be over a hundred. I am Alice Munro's age, myself, in my late sixties, and have never been married. If you had to place me on one side or another of the gender divide, I am male. It is true I have lived in the same house from birth, I never left home. I did a correspondence degree in literature and psychology, a deadly mixture of unrealities. Sustained by a small legacy from our nineteenth-century forbears, who were in manufacturing, I have never had to work. And so on; the facts are only a story. What interests me is the subtext.

It has been my hobby to read books. I would not say it is a passion, it is an interest, books of all sorts, mostly novels. I have very little imagination, and so I have bought and borrowed the imagination of others. This was the way of my mother all her life, and perhaps of my father, although he left when I was seven. He went out to walk the dog one night, my mother said, and never came back. It was not until my mid-thirties that I thought to ask about the dog. My mother said, what dog, we never had a dog? Some years later, I asked her to explain, and she said my father was allergic to dogs. It occurred to me that walking the dog was a euphemism. After she died two years ago, I recall sitting in the darkness by her casket in the parlour, the part about the parlour is true, and suddenly wondering what walking the dog was a euphemism for. But whatever had happened, it was too late to ask. Without turning on lights I went upstairs and crawled into my mother's bed and fell asleep, wrapped tightly in sheets still smelling faintly of lavender and the mild acrid odour of her castaway cells.

The first year after her passing, I read nothing but Alice Munro. The lovely thing about short stories is that you can read them again and again, and if you change the sequence in which you read them, this gives them a different context and they seem as fresh as they did the first time through. On each visit to my doctor, I borrowed old copies of *The New Yorker,* which I eventually returned by mail, and I read a number of her stories among cartoons and exotic advertisements, stories that were also in books I already owned. There were enough *New Yorkers* that I estimated I could read Alice Munro stories this way for almost a decade if my health remained constant. After a year, however, I stopped reading Munro; I stopped my visits to the doctor. Everything changed.

In another version of my life, I was married for thirty years. We lived in mother's house. She died a month after we moved in. A week later we took over the front bedroom. We had the red Victorian brick painted a light gray after our second child was born, and the shutters removed. I supplemented my modest legacy by working in the town library for twenty-five years, shelving books. After our children left home, I stopped work and devoted myself to reading. I was deserted the next year for a travelling ventriloquist who performed in the marble alcove in front of the old Park Cinema which closed twenty years ago. I now live on my own, spend long nights sitting in the small library off the parlour wondering what to read next. In this version I can never decide whether I am a man and my wife ran off with my evil twin who was stolen from the hospital at birth, or I am a woman and the ventriloquist was an age-stricken stripper. The children never call, they have lives of their own.

The truth is, I have never had many friends, in fact none. When I was little, before my father went away, I used to play on my own in the root cellar. Our house is one of the oldest in our part of town, built for my mother's parents late last century. It has both a root cellar and a coal cellar with a wooden chute leading in from outside, although our heating was converted to oil before I was born. The rest of the basement has a poured concrete floor but the root and coal cellars are dirt. I was not allowed in the coal cellar because of the filth; anyway, the root cellar without windows was my preferred sanctuary. Sometimes I would play; I would dig small cavities in the dark earth and surprise myself months later by digging up whatever it was I forgot I had buried. And sometimes I would sit for hours, under a bare lightbulb so ancient it had a curl at the end of the glass as if it were melting, and when it warmed the atmosphere I would savour the fetid odours, trying to separate scents of long-gone apples, potatoes, turnips, onions, beets, the sour smell of leaked preserves, the dry smell of old funeral bouquets that mother retrieved from our church and could never bring herself to discard. Sometimes, there, I would try to make up a friend. My regular visits downstairs ended after my father left. Occasionally, over the years, I would be drawn back to the root cellar for an hour or two, longer since mother died. Sometimes I sit on the cool earth with the light out and after a while I do not know where I am, not until the natural functioning of my body leads me upstairs again to the kitchen or bathroom as the case may be.

The truth is, before mother went, I would sometimes pretend to be a literary critic. I had no interest in putting my thoughts on paper but I enjoyed observing myself having them. This required sustained effort because my natural inclination is to suspend sense for sensibility, as a good reader must, and read with an open mind. Drawing my responses together on a cerebral plane, to the exclusion of everything else, gave me unexpected options to contemplate, access to narrative worlds I could not have imagined. Reading in a critical mode, I created parallel realities that had little to do with what I was reading. If I were to have written my responses down, they would not have converged with the original text except by arbitrary design. As it is, this set of mind gave me something to talk about with mother in addition to our shared past, which had been notably uneventful.

At the end of a year reading Alice Munro, caught up in the exquisite density of her short stories, each with the intricacy of fine lace, the complexity of well-cellared claret, I reached a point of nervous exhaustion, and, strangely enough, what I can only ascribe to a limit of transparency. Imagine me, like Tenniel's Alice, dashing this way and that through the backroads of southern Ontario, backwards and forwards though resonant episodes in the lives of mothers and daughters, like flipping through flash-cards of time. It was all so much more real and frenetic than my own experience had ever been. With each story, I moved a little closer to seeing my own life like a sheet of clear clean glass. Not a mirror, a transparent mass. If I assumed the critical mode, the glass shattered and there was nothing. Only the story. And since I was nowhere else to be found, it seemed reasonable to think of the story as me, all of the stories as my own.

It was a nice conceit, but it was just that, conceit. I am a man of modest pretension, but I am a human being, I exist in the same world as books and their authors. Notice, I say books, not their content. Finding myself to have become a composite of Munro characters in my own mind, and therefore an extension of Alice, herself—for as I said, each of her characters, no matter how different from one another, you are certain is her—this made me unutterably sad. The day I realized I had abandoned the exterior world, that having stepped through the looking glass and plunged down the rabbit hole I had given up hope of returning to the surface, was perhaps the emptiest of my entire life. I sat up in the parlour all night, that night, which is a room seldom used except to mark signal events, and I cried a little as dawn broke through the big bow window.

Another version of my story would have me, as my mother's daughter and only child, returning home to care for her after my father walked out of a thirty-year marriage. This one I conjured with for several days: I like being a woman, I would have been a university professor, an expert in Donne, one is an expert *in* something, not *on* something, in my university. I have come home on compassionate leave; my father was too uncomplicated to be much of a presence in my growing up and my mother suffered from narcissistic personality syndrome which made her enthralling. It seemed the right thing to do. I do not have children; it would be beyond my imagination to conceive.

You can see where I was going as a writer. I wanted to do something about mothers and daughters, and about time. I made various attempts. I settled on the past as a haunting, it seemed right; and to make myself a hundred years old seemed appropriate. I named the street Queen Street and put an old elm in front of the house. This was to be Canadian, but not self-consciously Canadian. That is why I decided against a maple. The long winter and dandelions in spring, coupled with the allusions to royalty and ancient lilacs, to wars fought far away, to our local library, our local church, all this was to be unmistakably matter-of-factly Canadian, the way Alice Munro does it. My problem now is, this is all born one way or another from my own small life, except for my sex and my age, both of which seem unimportant. I wanted to create not a mirror but the images within; however, I can't believe anything I could make up would be of much interest. Transparent in an invisible world, it is all I can do to envision the surface of things. Draw from your own experience to give my story whatever texture and composition you can imagine. The whole idea of story seems arbitrary, now; I am sure you can tell one better than I, given the background details we have conspired into being.

Two things I have left out. One is a description of my reading over this past year, after I abandoned Munro. The other is that I murdered my mother and no-one knows except you. It was not euthanasia, or youth-in-Asia as I often think when I say the word in my mind. I was bored by my life. Murder was something out of the ordinary for both of us. Mother, I said one night, I am leaving. I am going to go away and leave you alone. I do not know why I said this but I did. I needed a change in my life. I needed narrative. She looked up from her book, then back at the page and within seconds was immersed once again in the text. I was not going to shock her to death. Mother, I said, would you like a nice pot of tea? No, she said, I had one at four. It would keep us awake. Without tea, and mother not in the habit of eating before bed, arsenic seemed not an immediate option. Violence was unappealing as I loved her and had no desire to inflict pain. She fell asleep in her chair, her book fell to the floor. I took a down-filled cushion and placed it gently against her face. Without stirring, she expired, and I carried her up to her room, which would soon become mine. I laid her out on the top of the bed-covers, and called the doctor, who dropped in to sign papers and contact the funeral home for me, who took her away, prepared her for viewing, and returned her to the parlour in a plain oak casket exactly like the one I had picked out in their full-colour brochure.

Ours is a small town and neither mother nor I ever wanted to attract undue attention. That is why I disguised myself in my story as a centenarian and sometimes a daughter. It is why, in the two years following mother's passing, I read even more than usual. I wanted to be the same person I had always been, only more so. Munro's stories confirmed the reality of my world, made it more tangible than my living in it could, for no-one writes of small town life and the intersecting layers of consciousness of the people who live there so well. That is what she set herself as a task in the closing pages of *Lives of Girls and Women;* young Del Jordan on her author's behalf declares the writer's primary purpose to be the detailed recording of place through time, inscription on the nerveends of the reader's mind the exact way it was, whatever it was, and is now, whatever remains.

At first I found it affirming, exclusively reading Munro. But I began to miss my own life, banal as it was. Mother was gone, I began to suspect my own departure had occurred as well but no-one had noticed, least of all, me. I took to checking in mirrors to see that I was still there. The day I looked in the front hall mirror as I was ascending the stairs and perhaps due to the odd angle in the way it was hung, perhaps the weight of its heavy gold frame having pulled the nail askew in the plaster, I saw only the opposite wall where my reflected image should have been, that was the day I stopped trying to lose myself in the perfection of Alice Munro.

I took up writing on my own. I wanted to recreate myself as an actress or perhaps a librarian, something exciting. Sometimes I would sit for hours, wearing mother's dresses. Women are intrinsically more dramatic than men, who have to go out and do things to make their adventures worth recording. That much I had learned from Alice Munro, who turns the ordinary particulars of a woman's life into small gothic splendours. Of course, I did not wear her underthings. I had already folded them neatly and put them away. It was inspiration I wanted, not arousal. Anyway, as I have implied, it would take more than that.

If I have done this right, you will be wondering what I did over the last twelve months besides making up stories. I took in a boarder. She was very beautiful. We had children who grew up and left home. We never married, so when she decided to leave it was uncomplicated, she departed and I never heard from her again, nor from our children. I grew old, fond of memories that would never quite coalesce into objective co-relatives of what I was feeling. On my deathbed, I imagined my children returned to congratulate me on a good life. Then it was over. I have not yet decided where I was buried. Perhaps beside mother. Perhaps on my own.

What I actually did was read books. My response to transparency: after a night of painful reflection, I set out to read other Canadian writers. Mother was descended through eight generations from the original Mennonite settlers in our area west of Toronto. Had I managed a life of my own, that would have made me the ninth, and my children the tenth. As it was, I always assumed that our line terminated with mother; I was confirmation somehow of its end. When I was a child, after my father vanished, I learned to recite all the names of each generation preceding from mother to the third degree of kinship; offspring, siblings and their spouses, first cousins and their spouses, second cousins. Although I had never been out of Waterloo County, except once to attend a public lecture in Hamilton—I do not remember the subject, but Hamilton was all that I had expected—I regarded myself as a native Canadian. Not because my ancestor, Margaret Wallace, was Mohawk, but because I was not anything else. Munro gave detail and drama to my ancestral present. This was not erasure, since I had little in the way of details or drama on my own. It was a matter of displacement. So I decided, after a year with Alice Munro, after a lifetime of reading American and British writers and a smattering of Canadians with names not unlike my own, to explore Canada as others conceived it to be.

I had been ordering books through the mail since mother passed on, so I was a little surprised when the woman behind the desk at the library called me by name when I checked out Rohinton Mistry's *A Fine Balance.* This novel won The Giller Prize for Canadian Fiction so I had no doubt it would help me to a renewed vision of Canada, give me the illusion of remembered experience the way Munro's short stories do, and yet, more, I could tell from the dust-jacket blurbs, it would take me beyond the familiar.

And so it did. I read the novel from cover to cover in a single sitting, not counting bathroom breaks, that lasted from Thursday night to Sunday afternoon. I did not sleep, I did not eat except on Friday evening when pizza arrived at the door as it always does. Pizza was our one engagement with ethnicity, mother's and mine; we had a standing order for a large 'all-dressed' to mark the beginning of each week-end—which otherwise was no different from the rest of the week, although on Saturday afternoons the library was closed and on Sundays the church bells rang awkward intrusions through the day. I thought it a wonderful novel, a delight to read. Briefly, I felt moved to resume the critical mode, but decided the novel deserved better.

What puzzled me, however, was the absence of Canada. Mistry, I read, resided in Toronto and had done so for decades. The experience has had no impact on him, as far as I could tell. The novel is set in Bombay. It is about people in Bombay, it transforms aspects of Bombay into narrative reality of such voluminous vivacity the rest of the world seems vague in comparison. Perhaps it reflects an expatriate sensibility, perhaps the writer had to reconstruct Bombay from elsewhere to capture just the right ratio between nostalgia and ironic detachment. But it could as easily have been written in Melbourne or Auckland or perhaps Singapore. Not the United States or Britain, either of which might have imposed on his sensibility the way England has on Salmon Rushdie, America on Bharati Mukerjee. Much as I wanted it, there is nothing of Canada in Rohinton Mistry's excellent book.

Another version: I was young, and after my parents died I married a woman from Ireland who came to our town to unearth her emigrant ancestry. She was very proud and spoke to me only in Donegal Gaelic. I tried my best to understand but I speak no Irish. She was very beautiful and became more beautiful as we aged. She spoke fluent English to others and when we had children she spoke to them in both languages. Our old brick house resonated with talking and laughter for two decades. Our children grew to adults perfectly bilingual and never noticed which language was used. When they left home, she went away, back to Ireland I imagine, although I did not understand her farewell good-bye. The house is quiet now, and I am not lonely except when I dream.

Well, I thought, after my Bombay immersion, as I drifted off to sleep for the first time since the previous Wednesday, perhaps this is what it is to be Canadian, to be invisible, as transparent as I had become in the fictions of Alice Munro. I slept right through Monday, but Tuesday morning I went back to the library and took out a half dozen more novels, each by an author from elsewhere. Some, like Michael Ondaatje's *The English Patient,* was as Canadian as Hemingway's Africa is Michigan. It is in the voice, in the values, in the lovely blend of the lyrical and the grotesque that only a Canadian, perhaps only a Canadian from Sri Lanka via England, could muster. Then I turned to M.G. Vassanji's *The Book of Secrets.* This won The Giller Prize for 1994. Alice Munro was on the panel of judges. She has been both winner and juror in the Giller competition, and not, as you might hope, in that order. There is nothing of Canada in Vassanji's novel, not in its vision, not in its language, not in its characters, plotlines, settings, or moral significations. I read Shayam Selvadurai's *Funny Boy* but did not connect. I read Austin Clarke—now this is a Canadian writer. He is also a Barbadian writer. I read Brian Moore, I had read him in the past but since he had just died a few days before, I took home a couple of his novels. One, set in Canada, was authentically Canadian; and the one set in Belfast was authentically Irish.

For exactly a year I read novels by Canadian writers who came to Canada as adults, who came here out of desperation or by choice, and stayed out of affection, or necessity, or carelessness. I discovered myself the object of anger, of fear, of contempt. Never before had I achieved such definition. I discovered as I read that both the eloquent extravagant landscape of this country and its clarion history, gathering itself into being, rising awkwardly out of a confusion of commerce and exploitation, fortitude and forbearance, were both erased, no longer of interest. The proud flawed troubling resilient culture that shaped mother and me, who we were to each other and to ourselves, was no longer valid. The old nation was dying. In the novels I read, there was no past except shame. There was no present worth knowing. No future, except as a consortium bound together by weather, and bitching ingratitude or condescending neglect. There was no new nation rising.

Suddenly, after a year of this, I wanted to write back, to speak for the landscape, to speak from the past. As soon as I began, though, I realized there were going to be problems. If Canada is defined by Bombay, to the exclusion of Baffin, Belleville, and Batoche, if guilt over settlement of lands that were home to native people prevents the possibility of our affection for their present descendants, of whom I am one, as much Mohawk as I am Men-nonite, and much else besides, if cultural mosaic means a haphazard pattern of superficial insignias, if sensibility is separable from place and the fullness of historical time, then I can have nothing to say, nothing at all. My life has been ordinary. Alice Munro wrote about it, made it too real to endure. I am the end of my line.

Tomorrow is my birthday. I shall take mother's ashes from the library and descend into the root cellar through the mirrored door in the back hall, step carefully so as not to plunge headlong into the darkness, and under the beam where the bare light dangles like an anachronism I shall deposit the ashes. Then I shall hang myself above them with a burning rope; it will smoulder and break and my body will drop into the pit I have prepared, having opened the dirt floor to expose my father's bones. I have always known he was there. If we are lucky, no-one will find us. Our remains will fuse, and as the foundation crumbles around us we will become one with the mouldering earth.

Eleanor Wachtel Has Read Everything

Everyone knows Eleanor Wachtel. Everyone whom I can imagine caring about in Canada listens to the CBC; each therefore knows Eleanor Wachtel as the voice of cultural authority, interviewing writers of all sorts with the astonishing confidence of an interlocutor who has actually read their innumerable books. Everyone outside Canada knows Eleanor Wachtel, everyone I can imagine. I have not travelled much and find myself indifferent to foreigners, except those who have written books that might be of interest from a Canadian perspective. If they have, then she has interviewed them. If I seem edgy, it is from a lifetime of being Canadian.

I do not read much, myself. I am an unsuccessful writer. My writing is very good but no-one reads it. Book after book comes out under the imprint of one small publisher after another who allow aesthetic appreciation to override economic discretion. I have never made enough money from my books to cover the cost of publication. Still, I keep on writing, so long as there is a publisher sufficient to the enterprise. I do not live in fantasy but I envision someday being interviewed by Eleanor Wachtel. Not because I want to be interviewed. I am a writer. If I were a conversationalist, I would read more. I would travel. Perhaps I would interview writers.

I live alone. I construct alternative personalities. These are not fictions but parallel beings, sometimes like myself and sometimes radically different. They are people I might have been. When I am writing I become the people I write about. You notice I do not call them characters. They are real. What the imagination conceives can be more authentic than actual experience. That is ironic. It is a mystery and the genius of our species. Eleanor Wachtel would under-

243

stand.

Many of the lives I imagine are occupied by unsuccessful writers but occasionally I come up with a protagonist of
astonishing accomplishment. There is less satisfaction in
this than you might think. Sitting with my feet on my desk,
my laptop poised on my legs, its faint whirring sending
subliminal erotic codes into my quadreceps, I observe
words that appear almost of their own accord on the screen,
there being a synaptic discontinuity between the mind
moving fingertips on the keyboard and the imaginal world
that seems to emerge from somewhere behind the screen.

When I was small I thought that was how movies
work, that the dancing light beams illuminated what was
already there, and when I learned in my teens about the
oscilloscope I immediately understood that television was
not a reflected but a projected medium. At the movie
theatre I am still drawn out of myself, it is I who am the
projection, I suspend self-awareness, extinguish my own
personality, live for the duration between close-ups and
long-shots in the human dimension on screen. With the
same movie experienced on video at home I am me watching television. Writing on the computer is like going to the
movies. When I used to write on a typewriter or by hand,
it was me doing the writing, the creator creating; now on
my computer it is the creator created, like the Escher sketch
of a hand sketching a hand, I am immersed in what appears
on the screen as the subject of my own writing, transformed into unexpected personalities, a few of them far
more successful than me, all of them indifferent to my
existence as the precondition to their own.

This is quite complicated, really, and suffers from
explanation. When I was eight years old I used to read big-
little books. On the right hand pages were cartoon drawings
of Andy Panda and Charlie Chicken caught in a sequence
of tableaux and on each left hand page was the text of their
adventure without which the pictures appeared an arbitrary
arrangement—unlike panels in a comic book, they did not

constitute a story in themselves, they were black and white illustrations, not narrative. I had a gift subscription to *Looney Tunes and Merry Melodies* at the time, an annual birthday present from a pair of elderly aunts who had no idea they were giving me comics and not what they assumed were nursery rhymes in monthly increments. I had been reading comics since before I could read and I was familiar with the migration of souls from page to provisional experience, talking animals insinuating their ways into my head. But the big-little books were a shift in the reading paradigm, text and language superceded the pictorial, and a strange thing happened. Andy and Charlie were not just in my head, enacting adventure, they were inseparable from consciousness, part of my remembered world, my experience of self. Even now in memory they are as real as Russell Haunisch and Dick Livington and the Fielders, or Miss Moore and Mrs. E. Sue King, our teachers.

At this point he sat back and pondered. He had been writing first person narrative and that seemed appropriate since he was drawing directly from his own life story. He wanted to insinuate in his reader's mind the impression that an authentic personality had strayed into a fictional context. The problem was, the fiction was not convincing, time and place were insubstantial, and the narrator, therefore, was ephemeral. An experienced reader like Eleanor Wachtel would see through his first person disguise for what he is, an evasion of authorial responsibility. He unfolded from his normal writing posture, which placed him on the very edge of plausibility, his powerbook poised so precariously across his outstretched legs it seemed only gravity's ineptitude that kept it from plummetting to the floor, and with the computer as counterweight gone, him from plunging as well into an elongated pratfall across the carpet, he being very tall and not at all graceful.

He was not an unpleasant man, he was not a very good writer, he had a great deal of success and counted Eleanor

Wachtel as one of his friends. They seldom talked, however, because she was always busy reading. Whenever he had a new book come out, she would interview him for broadcast and later he would listen, lying in the darkness on the cool linoleum of his kitchen floor in the Annex, that part of Toronto where writers live, and invariably he would be astonished by her insight into what he had been trying to do and ashamed for not having done it and gratified at her generosity for making it appear that he had. There is something uncanny about her insights, he would think.

From where he was lying on the floor he would reach over and pull out the radio plug and in the dark silence imagine himself a hitchhiker after Eleanour Wachtel had dropped him off, alone in a featureless landscape. She would vanish into the ether and he could not get his bearings, the horizon blended with the sky so that he seemed to be inside an illimitable sphere, there was no-where for his next ride to come from, and then he would cry. Gently at first, then his whole body would shudder and he would sob against the dark until the wet linoleum on his cheek would rouse him into self-consciousness and he would get up and turn on the light and begin to think about his next writing project as he prepared a snack of cider and wholewheat sandwiches.

I took William Faulkner with me when I went south. Coming from Canada, I understood our destination to be less a direction than a set of conditions. I know the Turks and Caicos Islands are a long way from Jefferson, Mississippi, but it seemed to me that once we boarded the plane at Lester Pearson, there would be no egress until palpable sunlight and tumescent flowers were set to embrace us. I might better have chosen Katherine Anne Porter, since we were about to embark for a week upon a small ship and she knows all about the characters one encounters at sea. But I wanted someone who would write me out of the north, without the leaps in imagination that Derek Walcott or Austin Clarke might require. Or Wilson Harris. I love

Wilson Harris, but I wanted diversion emanating from a sensibility conditioned by factors both exotic and familiar, and Harris, who writes English as sinuous as Faulkner, writes of a visionary's Guyana that is discontinuously south of my own world, connecting only through our common humanity.

As it turned out, I never opened the book. Life aboard a dive vessel allowed no time for reading. We were either underwater, preparing to go under, or decompressing on the upper deck after completing each of five dives a day. It was even difficult to take mental notes for research. I should explain that my wife and I write northern gothics under a shared pen name. We were looking for a new direction. Normally we travel the Arctic in search of settings that might lend themselves to grotesque plot twists and preternatural romance, the sort of thing where a plane crashes in the tundra and a lone woman survivor is rescued from the bitter snows by a renegade trapper who turns out to be the ghost of a reclusive innocent murdered by vigilantes who were moved to drastic measures by the man's indifference to society. One of the vigilantes would be an off-duty mounty who in remorse returns to give their victim a decent burial when he discovers the woman, delirious but alive after six weeks alone in the Barrens. She is plain but has an indomitable spirit and even in her precarious condition she radiates inner beauty. The mounty is darkly handsome and deeply troubled. The renegade ghost had been a gentleman, even when pressing his spectral nakedness against the woman's flesh under a caribou robe to save her from hypothermia. She is found by the mounty dressed in the skins of animals, a mystery he resolves when he finds the unclothed body of the trapper frozen in a grisly posture of affection, just beyond the range of her encampment. In a post-script the reified woman and the redeemed mounty retire to a cabin on the shores of a remote lake where the sun shines in perpetual spring and the spirit of the trapper sighs in the morning breeze.

Although such novels do not attract the attention of the CBC and would be regarded by Eleanor Wachtel as a sociological rather than a literary phenomenon, we are moderately successful, enough that we have underwritten an interesting marriage. I am much older than my wife; I had spent half my life in the proverbial attic garret, in my case a mid-range condo on the edge of Cabbagetown, Toronto's resuscitated slum and erstwhile upscale bohemia, from which I ventured out to an office by day to write catalogue copy for a sports-wear outfit headquartered in California and to which I returned in the evenings to re-work my novel in progress. After twenty-some years I was farther from completion of the novel than the day I started, having accumulated a seemingly infinite concatenation of random passages that demanded inclusion but yielded nothing to the coherence of character or plot or thematic development. I was not unhappy, but as living in the real world seemed to slip farther and farther into the past, I continued to write more out of habit, than because I was driven towards artistic fulfillment. I recognized myself as a desultory creator and took pride in the fact that I was not a dilettante but rather a failure.

Linda was a school-teacher when we met. She was defensive about her work, and frustrated. She taught liter-ature to sixteen-year-olds and was an expert in character development, plot structure, and thematic explication. She wrote the occasional short story in her head, dotting the i's and crossing the t's, all in her head. But she did not write any of them down because her time away from work was spent working, preparing lessons and assessing assign-ments and collating grades, and after a few years of teach-ing there was a certain amount of slippage and the stories converged, until what she held in her mind were only patterns of punctuation and slowly whirling fragments of unconnected episodes and personality attributes. Not hav-ing prepared a life for herself before going into teaching, she found it difficult to devise one once in the profession.

Putting alternative realities in print, appealing as it was, was impossible, even in her imagination.

We were a perfect complement to each other. Working as collaborators, we have taken the northern gothic just about everywhere we could imagine. Not that we made up the settings. We travelled throughout the sub-Arctic and Arctic extensively. Our honeymoon was spent at an ancient Thule encampment on the eastern shore of Baffin Island, a half-day's boat journey from the hamlet of Clyde River. We had met in the Arctic section of a Toronto bookstore, Chapters or Indigo, we disagree on which and were familiars of both. In the coffee-table pictorial monograph subsection. We were both reaching for the same book, and both of us, seeing the other wanted it, pulled away. There was a stack of copies but the presbyterian impulse held sway and each of us deferred to the other. Have you ever been there, I said, indicating the books with my palm upward to suggest she should take the top copy. No, she said, palm extended downward, letting me know the top one was mine. I'm too old for you I said, apparently out loud. I had intended it as a comment to myself. Not really, she said.

At this point he stopped writing. He felt overwhelmed by fiction; the details were disconcerting, more authentic than the world beyond the text. He had never been to the Caribbean. He read about Turks and Caicos scuba diving adventures in the travel section of *The Globe and Mail.* He had never been married but a friend of his youth had married a Linda. He travelled a lot but always as an observor, never a participant. He was an habitual tourist. He thought of himself as a tourist even when he was at home in Toronto. His house in the Annex was rented. He never felt certain enough to buy, as if somehow, even there, he was just passing through. Eleanour Wachtel once came to his door by mistake. She was looking for someone else. He was sure it was her from the voice, although later, when he had time to think about it, he was not quite as sure as he had been.

His life needed details, specifics, particularities, to be convincing. He remembered growing up in Port Credit, just west of Toronto; he remembered the name of his grade ten Latin teacher; he recalled migrating eastward as far as the city at seventeen. He moved a lot at first, from one apartment to another, one house to another, until he found his present place where he had been living for the last thirty years. Many of his belongings were in cardboard boxes that had never been unpacked. In thirty years he had never had an overnight visitor. He had never had a dinner guest. When Mormon missionaries and Jehovah's Witnesses came to the door he always invited them in, and tried his best to present a consistent and compliant personality to sustain their interest. Usually they left after a few minutes, depositing brochures on the hall table on their way out which he read assiduously, in case they came back.

He imagined himself a successful writer, someone who would be interviewed on the CBC. Not only about his own books but for quips on culture, on the passing show, the vanity fair. He imagined himself in the third person. Paradoxically, he felt more intimately connected with the character of his invention in the third than the first person. He and Eleanor Wachtel would discuss this, he thought, we could be friends. Other people would listen in on our conversations which could be taped for broadcast. Sometimes it seemed they were friends already. He would imagine being so good the Toronto literati would speak his name in quotation marks, the way people do when referring to someone of superior worth. He would write fiction about scuba diving. It would be the perfect metaphor, the writer's imagination revealed in the process of creation as it dives and drifts in the alien undersea world.

We only touched ground on Providenciales, the biggest of the Islands, long enough to get from the airport to the boat. Aboard the Turks and Caicos 'Aggressor'—an odd name given the lyrical passivity of the underwater activities it sustains—we settled in to our newly refurbished cabin and Linda retrieved her *Pride and Prejudice* from deep in her dive bag, disengaging it from compressor tubes and buoyancy control vest straps and other paraphernalia which, despite being packed so carefully at home, were now profusely entangled. She lay back on our double bunk to read, rocked gently by the quay-side swell. After unpacking *Sanctuary* and reading the information pamphlets left for us on the vanity, I ascended to the salon where there was a rack of old magazines with titles like *People* and *US,* the kind I normally read only at the dentist's, texts consisting almost entirely of explanatory captions to photographs. From behind their pages I observed other divers quietly settling in, each displaying a modicum of eccentricity beneath the bland exteriors of the newly met.

We had a great deal in common, the twelve of us. We had all come south. Some had been moving southward in increments for most of their lives, originating in Michigan and Colorado, now living in California or North Carolina. We ranged in age from Peter, at twelve the youngest, to me, at sixty, the oldest. Linda at thirty-six was precisely half way between Peter and myself. Considering the three of us together put the discrepancy of my marital relationship in unnerving perspective. When Linda reaches my age, and Peter hers, I will be eighty-four. Our relative ages did not seem as extreme when cast in the future. It was better than self-assessment relative to a twelve-year-old, even acknowledging that by eighty-four I will probably be dead.

We were all certified scuba divers. Peter was completing his open water testing. His mother Wendy had logged 250 dives in the last two and a half years. Apart from Peter, Linda and I were the neophytes of the group, having dived previously only for a period of short duration on the Great Barrier Reef in Australia, where we trained to a maximum depth of sixty feet, or six stories. We were a bit rattled at first, refamiliarizing ourselves with equipment and proce-

dures. Our first dive was ten stories down, four atmo-
spheres, one hundred feet. Despite a bit of ear pain on the
initial descent as we adjusted internal pressure to accommodate depth, we quickly settled into the gentle set of mind
and underlying mood of excitement shared by our cohorts.
Busy with details, Linda gave up *Pride and Prejudice*. I
had already abandoned *Sanctuary* and now gave up *People*.

Conversation between dives was strangely laconic. By
noon of the first day, anchored off French Cay to the
southwest of Providenciales, we were rapidly evolving
towards a singular social organism, a complement to the
way we moved around each other in the clear ocean depths
where conversation was streamlined to a few hand-ges-
tures, and facial expressions were distended to graceful
simplicity by mouths grasping mouthpieces and eyes peering unfurtively from the shadows of dive masks. Our
collective dynamic was almost familial, as if we had
known each other for such a long time the pleasantries
among us were foreshortened by common experience. We
were like a sprawling Faulknerian family without the dysfunctional elements.

That was the problem. Dysfunction is a staple ingredi-
ent of gothic romance, at least of the kind Linda and I were
there to recover from the depths of imagination through our
immersion in southern adventure. We had no doubt the
stories were inside us, but we needed a catalyst to effect
their release. Life aboard the 'Aggressor' was focussed and
tranquil, even while the air of excitement was as palpable
as tropical heat disguised by the offshore breeze. Wendy
and Peter were not promising. They got along with the kind
of indulgent affection one would expect of a single mother
and her offspring on the edge of adolescence. If it turned
out that they were not related, that she was a predatory
neighbour who had lured him into her world with the
promise of undersea adventure, they appeared so pleasantly
normal the rest of us would simply have accommodated
their eccentricity. And if Peter had seduced her, she being

not his mother but his mother's best friend, and had shamed her husband into covering the cost of this trip, they presented such a benign front to the world it would have seemed inappropriate to intervene or even to pass discrete judgement.

During decompression periods on the upper deck, Linda and I speculated about the others. We knew much about constructing romance from bare bones, having followed up our initial encounter in the Toronto bookstore with a walk-about date through the Royal Ontario Museum, where in front of the cadaverous display of Egyptian sarcophogi we wordlessly embraced with the pent-up passion of two incomplete lives finally converging. He winced at the contrivance. Carefully disengaging himself from his posture, as if physical disposition were something he inhabited and not the articulation of his genuine body, he rose to his full height and surveyed the study as if it were a battleground and he, at the conflict's end, were the soul of the unknown soldier hovering in confusion over the fields of ruin.

I do not care about the others on the ship, he thought. I do not want to swim among the fish. I do not want to dwell in an imagined world more real than the one I inhabit. He turned philosophical as he walked down the narrow stairs, through the living room and into the kitchen. He poured himself a glass of skim milk by the light of the refrigerator and contemplated the mind of Eleanor Wachtel. How can she speak with such authority about the meagre reality that consciousness allows? We live in a world in flight from our senses, he thought. We know far less than we did a thousand years ago. The stars have become a part of the time-space continuum that recedes from comprehension even as theorists grasp at its meaning. At some point the wood of my desk became atoms whirling, and before the ether filled with photons and electrons, sounds and images existed in real time. There is so much I do not comprehend, he thought, in spite of libraries, universities, and the evolution of expertise. I do not fully understand the complexities of civil power but occasionally I exercise my democratic right and offer up a single digit to the body politic. I doubt that I shall go to heaven when I die, but do not have a better option as consolation for the ultimate dispersal of my molecules. The more I learn the less I know and I am more and more unable to contain the world within my mind. He refilled his milk-glass and caught his reflection in the dark gleam of the microwave over the stove as the fridge door closed. His face was unfamiliar. Slowly, he walked through the darkness into the living-room.

He remembered reading bp nichol, writing one day he realized that he was always staring at his hand when he wrote, was always watching the pen as it moved along, gripped by his fingers, his fingers floating there in front of his eyes just above the words, above that single white sheet, just above these words I'm writing now, his words slipping thru his fingers into the written world. I live in an Escher drawing, he thought. I am a sketch of a hand sketching itself. Rose is a rose is a rose, he thought, adding a question mark as an after-thought (?). Is actual being in the word or the thing, in the mind or the mind's creation? He reached in the darkness to see if there was anyone beside him. He was unsure, if he were to turn on a light, if he would be on the double-bunk in a cabin with Linda aboard the 'Aggressor,' or a living-room in the Annex, married or single, gregarious or reclusive, a Canadian provincial or worldly, successful or a failure, and whether he would be a friend of Eleanor Wachtel, or a stranger. What, he thought, if he were someone else entirely? He kept his eyes shut tight. What if Eleanor Wachtel is a literary contrivance? A conceit? What if I am not a writer at all? Neither she nor I would really exist. What if I am neither first person nor third? What if I am the creation of a consciousness that lies outside the boundaries of grammar, beyond the laws of probability or physics or rhetoric?

We are literary characters, you and I, even if we cannot make sense of our being. I am alive in you, the second person singular. I am a succubus, a golem, invader, resident bacterium, denizen of the most abstract and obscure reaches of your secret mind, a detail of your authentic personality.

At last he had a story. Having invented someone like yourself, suddenly the future seemed possible, he came to life. He sprang from the living-room darkness, bounded up the stairs, two by two, spilling his milk on the faded runner, and swinging around the doorframe inserted himself into the emptiness of his study, sprawling just so in his chair with his legs elevated across the corner of his desk. He booted his powerbook out of sleep and the moment the cursor appeared on a blank page he began to create real worlds out of words. One day Eleanor Wachtel would read this. You have to believe in something.

Beneath Poppy Fields

Beneath poppy fields and olive groves on the southern edge of Rome, catacombs spread through the red lava rock with remarkable subtlety. Travelling along the Via Appia Antica the only indication that the ground is riddled with burrows of the departed are discrete signs inviting visitation. Otherwise, everything is much as it was when the Canadian troops stood aside beyond the city walls in 1944 so that Americans could be the first to enter Rome as the liberating force. This is how history records the painful fall of Italy as an Axis power, a country being liberated from itself. Deep within the remembering earth lies a consecrated maze of passageways, sacred artifact of an ancient conspiracy. Every surface is gouged with niches for the million souls whose bodies through the ages were absorbed into the walls of their volcanic crypt, leaving only desiccated residue. It is a place where you can see the world from the vantage of the dead.

When Harry King's memoirs were published posthumously last winter, I immediately bought a hardcover copy. I took it home in keen anticipation of discovering which version of myself he had chosen to represent as his devoted friend. We used to joke about checking the index before the table of contents in any book that might conceivably acknowledge our contributions to Canadian literature. We were complementary in that regard, not competitive; Harry was an accomplished writer and I am a critical theorist with a vested interest in Canada. Harry's memoirs were a significant literary event, born in a flurry of creative activity during the months before his premature death. With an oddly exhilarating mixture of renewed grief and excitement I opened the final pages of Harry's last book and traced the arbitrary arrangement of references to his life backwards in the index from the end of the alphabet towards the middle, slowing as I scanned closer to my own name, taking casual note of the number of citations beside various mutual acquaintances. The listing had a narrative energy that carried me through to the A's before I returned to confront the space between lines where my own name should have been.

It is commonplace to think of history as a text; what is not written never was. Revisionists in their attempts to salvage misplaced events rewrite the present. History is not the past but how the past is perceived and in Harry's version of the past I was absent. It was as if I had never been. Suddenly I was forced to question my ongoing presence in the world, a world that we had so often defined together on a thousand walks through the countryside north of Kingston, in the hundreds of thousands of words that made up our conversation over thirty-eight years.

I skimmed the book a dozen times over the next few weeks. I could not bear to give it a close reading. Even a cursory dredging for familiar references resonated from the text in Harry's voice. No-one released words on a page quite like Harry did, with their cunning blend of the flippant and profound, but as they penetrated my self-absorbing gloom their meaning became obscure despite the familiar cadence and filled me with bewildering remorse, as if I had done something terribly wrong but had no idea what it was.

Perhaps to atone for my unknown crimes I took his book with me to Italy in the spring, although I had no intention of reading it again, even quickly, or referring to it in the series of lectures I was scheduled to give in Siena on his major novels. There was no redemption possible, Harry King was dead. There would be no rewriting, but somehow I felt that having his book in hand a revelation might occur, perhaps when least expected, to explain why

I had been expunged from the narrative of his life. I had been his close friend, I was now struggling with annihilation, with the notion that possibly my life had only been through the grace of his imagination, and now that he was gone, with his refusal to bear witness to my being there, I was beyond salvation.

I mean salvation of course in a secular sense. I am a committed atheist and Harry described himself as a self-loathing Jew—I suspect us both of a certain facile affectation adopted when we were younger and cynicism was in vogue. I mean salvation as in salvaging, and redemption as a sort of exchange from one currency to another. Atonement is related to compensation; and revelation, well revelation has to do with the transcendence of knowledge between levels of awareness. Even grace can be secular, a kind of beauty, for it was the beauty of his mind that allowed me to flourish as a whole person who was otherwise, it sometimes seemed, a loose bunch of particularities adhering to a name.

The night before my first lecture in Siena, I dined by candle-light in the open air along the upper edge of the Campo, the central square which is actually a huge sloped cachment for rainwater that feeds into a maze of cisterns carved through the rock deep beneath the city. My hosts for the evening, Beatrice and Roberto, were very beautiful, the embodiment of the Italy I loved. Armani, not Versace. Dante, not Boccaccio. They had invited me to Siena to conduct an academic forum on the literary achievement of Harry King, who had never been to Siena but was devoted to Italian cooking and once lived in Bologna through a lonely and productive winter. Sitting opposite them in the rumpled linen suit I had picked up in a shop off the Via del Corso in Rome, where I had waited over a couple of days to deal with jet lag, I was enthralled by their casual elegance. Behind them, the ochre shadows of mediaeval walls that leaned in a vast arc of stone and brick to catch the light from human activities in the square formed a radiant backdrop for the superb food and quiet talk. In their presence time fell away like layers of accumulated dust. We could have been Tuscan in the middle ages or Etruscan in the evening light. The Renaissance might be flourishing or the Roman era in full swing. I think of Armani as the epitome of style-in-being that would show primacy of taste in any culture. Serene gentility; something utterly beyond the studied shabbiness of the world I inhabited with Harry, a world from which I had been posthumously banished.

As we devoured innumerable courses in prescribed sequence, savouring the evanescence of the night, we talked amiably of death. I told Roberto and Beatrice that I intended visiting the catacombs when I returned to Rome, a dimension of Italian experience I had previously overlooked. They told me about their civic ancestors in Siena, and urged me to explore the presence of a hundred generations preceding them in the wondrous concatenation of architectural design. Conversation inevitably turned to Harry King. At first, our hushed voices paid deference to the sadness of his recent passing, but soon we were exchanging animated banter about the celebrated quirks and foibles of the writer himself that informed even the darkest of his work with a kind of zany originality. In Siena at night in the company of good people it seemed for a time as if Harry and I were still friends.

Harry King lived many lives and unlike most of us he kept them separate. When he came to his rural retreat on the edge of the village where my family settled in the 1790's he always dropped in to the ancestral home to announce his arrival. My wife at the time, I was married then and had two children, would usually invite him to dinner and invariably he would decline the invitation, then stay until midnight. When he was in the throes of creation he would spend a lot of time in the country. If the novel was going well, he needed to work without distraction. If he was bogged down, he needed the clarity of country living. One evening I remember he announced that he was about to become a father. When, we asked? Next week, he said. We didn't know he had a girlfriend. In thirty-eight years I had never been to wherever he lived in the city. That time he stayed at his cabin for a month and came to dinner almost every night. Eventually he told us it was a girl, and some years later he said there was a boy.

Following my opening lecture on what I called 'the early years' when Harry's fiction made a peremptory shift from cultural dispossession in urban Canada to rural angst, I attended a lunch reception at Beatrice and Roberto's home which curiously seemed larger inside than out. It fronts on one of the narrow streets of the old town; impossible to distinguish demarcation lines on the richly textured walls from its immediate neighbours. Inside, the grandeur is subtle, each of its many rooms on many stories is scaled to enhance the domestic society of its inhabitants. Some of the furnishings in another setting might be called antique but here seem comfortably outside of time. The house has been in Roberto's family for generations. Unlike my own place where my former wife still lives although our children have now gone off on their own, it is not a reliquary, haunted by ancestral ghosts. Here, on Via Arezzo, the past and present share accommodations.

During a break between courses Roberto excused himself from the small cluster of Harry King admirers who were regaling me with arcane insights about his life and work. To my surprise, he excused me as well. Since we shared a passion for Barolo and well-aged Brunello di Montalchino, I thought he was taking me to see his wine cellar. Instead, we ascended from the cool of their summer dining room into the garden and walked quietly among the trees. These walls, he said, are Roman. That grotto is part of a mediaeval structure, perhaps an artisan's workplace, a stable or a servant's home. Why, he continued, are you not in the book?

We walked in silence among the ruins and the trees. Three tortoises slumbered on the grass. He touched my arm. Let me show you something, he said. He led me through a door and down a flight of stone steps so that we were directly below the other luncheon guests. He opened an ancient corner cabinet. Look inside, he said. Look down. A light at the bottom of a deep shaft lit a rocky ledge and a dark ribbon of water. There is a sign, he pointed downwards, with my family name. When I was a young man, I tried to find it. But it is a labyrinth down there and I was pursued by the minataur of my own fears. It was not so difficult to find my way back to the Campo and after ascending from that stygian gloom into the light of day I resolved never to return. Sometimes I dream I am down there still, looking up through that long shaft and at the top, here in this room, looking down through the cupboard opening, is a face exactly like mine.

Look down, he said with a laugh. Perhaps you will see yourself. Then join us, he said. We will talk about books. He left with a gesture indicating I should close the cabinet door when I was finished. I could feel the column of damp air dissipate around me as I leaned over and stared into the depths of the earth. It felt warm, not cool as I expected. I was not surprised when a figure stepped out of the shadows far below and poised on the ledge directly under the light. It looked up from a long way off and at first I thought it was Dante. Although I have not read *The Divine Comedy* since my student days I grew up with a gothic edition that had macabre illustrations by Gustave Doré which still animate my nightmares. I knew what Dante looked like. It was not him and I could see that it was not me. After a while the features became distinct but I did not recognize them. I knew who it was, but he looked like a stranger. Go to Hell, I said, letting the words fall in a whisper. Go to Hell, I whispered to myself.

In Rome, two weeks later, I took a city bus to Porta S. Sebastiano and walked out along the walled road to the first set of catacombs. Harry and I had been along this route when we were young, wandering Europe with the strange exhilarating sense that we were plagiarizing lives less consequential than our own. The sixties had not truly begun yet and we still looked to the twenties with a certain patronizing nostalgia. We met in Pamplona, waiting in the early morning for the bulls to be released, running side by side through the cordoned streets. By the end of a dissipated week at the Festival of San Fermin we were friends. It was not surprising when a month later I caught a glimpse of Harry in a crowd outside the Coliseum. We had not exchanged Toronto addresses or shared travel plans, both of us were hitchhiking and two men travelling together did not get rides, but it seemed natural that we would meet again. We walked along this same road in the early August heat nearly four decades ago.

After that we bumped into each other in a variety of settings; shared a small boat to cross the Bosphorus and shared a room in Istanbul. In Vienna Harry sponsored me to a lavish meal; he still had funds from a postgraduate fellowship and I was husbanding my last few dollars to get me back to London. We lived together for a while in Earls Court. We both dated Susan Hoblyn. I found a job as a packer in Harrods and Harry was broke. He wrote; in perhaps a desultory fashion but it got him through the day. In the evenings we drank pints of Watneys Red Barrel. In those times it seemed the thing to do, look after each other. I was a patron of the arts. Harry was going to be famous. When he went back to Canada he turned to writing as a vocation and when I returned a year later I took up graduate studies in Canadian literature.

None of that was in his memoir. When we met we

both described ourselves as writers. I wrote every day, on Ibiza, in Pamplona no matter how hung-over, in youth hostels and cheap hotels the length and breadth of continental Europe. Harry insisted he was writing in his head. Now he was being published and I was learning ways to celebrate his achievement. As the decades followed one another I picked up a safe academic post and moved to the country, to my forebearers' home which I brought back into the family after it had been occupied by strangers for almost a century. Harry created literature. He lived in Toronto but he bought a small place near mine on five hundred acres of sedge grass and beaver ponds. My children thought of him as family. He told them stories, some of which were in his novels; we told him stories, one of which provided him the plot for his most gothic, most authentic work. He spoke at their weddings. When my wife and I separated acrimoniously, he remained friends with both of us. When he died, we attended the funeral together.

The chapel at a Y junction of the Via Appia, where Christ's footprint embedded in stone records His enduring presence, was less exotic than I remembered, despite the name 'Domine Quo Vadis?' Harry and I had taken refuge from the summer heat in its dappled darkness, ate crispy rolls and drank a bottle of cheap wine, before abandoning our plan to visit the catacombs and turning back, to hang out and meet people in the Piazza di Spagna. Now it seemed a small and pleasant building with no remarkable features apart from the footprint. If Harry and I had been lovers, I thought, I would have been in his book. If only as an act of denial, my presence would be necessary proof that he was immune to rumours, and as fiercely heterosexual as the next guy. The truth is, Harry's sexuality was a mystery to me. We never shared secrets.

At the Catacombe di S. Calisto I joined the tail end of an English-language group led by an elderly priest from

Los Angeles coping with incipient dementia. At intervals through his opening lecture he seemed to forget where he was and treated us like a horde of the incoming dead, to be amused with vaudevillian candour while we awaited our eternal disposition. Then, solemnly, he reminded us that we were entering consecrated ground. And then, with a beatific smile he assured us this was a comical place, God's theme park. A bevy of nuns near the front giggled in unison. The old priest glowered and with a wave of his hand led us along a narrow path and through iron gates into a steep descent carved from solid rock. The gates closed behind us, signalling an end to the day's tours.We were the last living creatures to enter the kingdom of the dead.

To escape the cheerful morbidity of our leader's spiel and get the full effect of the subterranean landscape I let myself fall further and further behind. Before long his voice merged with indistinct fragments of French and German and Italian resonating in a muffled cacophony through the labyrinth of passageways. As the myriad voices of the speaking earth receded I was overcome by a sense of well-being. A sign at the entry had warned, 'Passage on These Premises Is Forbidden without Guidance,' and here I was deep underground without a mediator and quite content to be alone. I entered a small family crypt and settled against the side of a grave carved into the back wall. Soon there was absolute silence.

In the churches of Rome where I have gone to contemplate great works of art contained within the spidery depths beneath their vaulted ceilings, I have been absorbed in the contemplation of God so deeply that sometimes I would forget His absence from the world, I would forget, in the wonders He inspired, that I did not believe. Now in this sepulchre of infinite grief and adoration carved from the unadorned earth, I was face to face with my absent God. Never had I such an awareness of death, even carrying Harry's casket from the synagogue, or at the funerals of my parents. As a living conscious thing, death ran through my veins, and this knowledge, it seemed to me, this knowing is God. I was comfortable with a metaphysical equation that connected me in this place with its myriad occupants beyond the reach of chance and change.

Suddenly my reverie was broken by a sequence of snapping sounds and the illumination of my sanctuary faded. The Catacombe di S. Callisto was closed for the night, for the long Easter weekend. I began to wander aimlessly in the gloom of dim safety lights, climbing and descending stairs, turning down one passageway and back another. The air was warm and had a thickness to it, as if I were submerged in an alien element but still could breath. I was perhaps seven stories down when I chose another tomb and reclined on the dust of an open grave to sleep.

In my dreaming mind I was midway through life's journey and had gone astray from the familiar world and woke to find myself in a dark wood. After venturing through torment and despair I reached a curious silent place where nothing seemed to happen. I was content and only by great determination was I able to break free of deadly comfort and move into the clamour of incontrovertible light. As I had awakened within my dream, I now dreamed myself awake, in another world that was both inevitable and strange. It was as if, in the comical brilliance of open terrain, the journey of my life had just begun.

Rolling against the grave wall I returned to an awareness of my actual surroundings and briefly considered my predicament. Soon I was remembering the words of my dream, trying to determine how much of the verbal imagery was from Dante Alighieri and how much was my own. It is lovely to confuse yourself with a great writer,

to fall into his words. That is the genius of language, that
lives which were ages apart merge among words, shaped
by cultures as different as Dante's and mine. He lived in
a world of pageantry and superstition and I in a world of
technological splendour. But among words I can sheer
from his vision such dazzling illusions as revealed in my
dream.

I stepped out into the dull light of the corridor, disconcerted a little by the notion I had conjured that my
journey had just begun. I knew my present age and how
far I was from beginning anything except preparation for
the end. You don't look so good, said Harry King. I gazed
down the passageway towards the voice, half expecting
him not to be there. But he was, and closer to me than I
had thought. You don't look so good yourself, I said. I'm
dead, he responded. What do you expect?

We sat down side by side on the stoop leading into the
tomb behind me. We didn't shake hands. We never did
when we met, whether we'd been apart for a few days or
a year or two when one of us had been off awhile to live
in foreign places. But I could feel him against my shoulder, the strength of his presence emanating solid warmth,
and when I looked at him he looked back and it was like
no time had passed between us.

So you want to know why you're not in the book, he
said?

How did you know?

I knew, said Harry King. And of course he knew,
even while he was writing, he knew the impact of elimi-
nating me from the story of his life. He anticipated the
bewilderment, the humiliation. Harry knew me, he would
know.

Why, I said.

I don't know, he said. Do you think when you're dead
you know everything?

It's a nice conceit, I said.

Why do you think they call it a conceit, he said. How're the kids?

They've grown up, Harry. They've moved away.

You moved away too, he said.

Long before you left, I said. Jill is still there. She's co-opted my ancestral roots.

Why not, he said? ...once you made the genetic connection.

What's it like, I said? Being dead.

How should I know, Harry answered.

I looked at him and in the half-light he looked like a Gustave Doré etching. He looked like Virgil. He looked like Dante. He looked like Harry King.

Why did you leave me out, I asked? I know you had many lives, but in at least one of them I was your devoted friend. When you died I has shattered.

I died many deaths, said Harry.

I hated when Harry was cryptic. Harry, I said, I hardly knew you.

In my house were many mansions, he said. The scaffolding between them was precarious. I hated when Harry was enigmatic.

Harry, I said, was I your friend—this was not spoken in an interrogative voice. The question itself was an assertion of doubt.

My writing and my life were separate, he said. This was about my writing.

But you were dying, I said. Your writing was your life.

Yes, he said.... His features in the dull light coalesced into an expression of benign elation. I hated when Harry was inscrutable.

Harry, I said, in thirty-eight years of friendship, you were included in every aspect of my life. You were there for my marriage and my divorce. My children loved you fondly when they were young and you were their confidante when they got older. You talked writing with me, you talked books. We spun out story-lines, we plotted. We explored your beaver ponds and walked endless country miles together. We laughed at each other's pretensions, held each other's paranoia up for ridicule. You wrote from the rhythm of our intersecting lives.

Not really, said Harry. I hated most when Harry King was ingenuous. I watched clustered lines of the Doré etching shift in patterns of shadow and luminescence as Harry rose and started down the passageway, holding his left hand up to wave goodbye without turning round. Harry, I said. But my voice met only the enveloping darkness. Harry, I said to myself.

I settled back against a rough side panel of the closest grave and felt myself sink almost imperceptibly into the accumulated dust of lava walls and ancient corpses. Sadness gave way to equanimity. If this is a haunting, I thought, I am preternaturally unperturbed—the phrase turned about in my mind a bit, preening. If I have been possessed, it is by an unassuming demon. The coherance he gave my life was a gift from me to him, not something he gave me. Poor Harry, I thought with condescending affection. On Sunday, the gates above will open and a swarm of true believers will come to set me free. They will be led by a demented priest from the City of Angels. On the third day, I said aloud, I shall ascend from this place in time to catch my flight and rise above the earth and travel home.

For a while I slept and dreamed of Venice and once again I found myself in a dark wood, this time within a small park surrounded by the pink and ochre walls of houses with period windows stacked like layers of history, mediaeval, gothic, Renaissance, Victorian, contemporary, all glazed to deflect the shimmering bands of starlit night. There was neither an exit nor was deadly comfort drawing me to rest and I was long past midway in life's journey. As my eyes grew accustomed to the spangled darkness I perceived around me brick-lined canals reaching under the walls in every direction and I knew I was at the heart of a watery maze, a labyrinth of flowing streets calculated to emulate the body's blood. This living city with me at the centre dreamed itself awake and there was nothing comic or serene as I stepped away from it into a pool of incontrovertible light. Suddenly, awake, a captive of the earth, I was overwhelmed with dread.

Rising from my crypt I fled desperately from one passageway to another, sometimes running sometimes crawling, afraid that I would find nothing, afraid to stop. After what might have been hours, I stumbled in exhaustion against a wall and stopped short to see in a cavity ahead a body lying in state. I expected it to be Harry. The body turned its head and addressed me through unmoving lips. What would an Ontario Jew be doing buried in a Roman catacomb, it said? The eyes of the corpse opened and looked through me. This time, when it spoke the lips moved although its voice resonated as if it were a long way off or speaking down a well. Of course it's me, said Harry King. Welcome to my world.

Harry, I said, suddenly angry. If you're going to be dead, do it properly.

Let me, he said. Let me.

I looked at the corpse as it slowly turned onto its side. For a brief moment its line of vision pulled back from the vanishing point and looked into mine. Then, without disturbing the dust in its niche, its limbs disconnected from the torso, its head dropped slowly to the lava shelf, and as the flesh dissolved its clothing disappeared and the naked bones settled without encumbrance onto the rock. The bones gleamed briefly in the dull light and then collapsed into the dust. It was impossible to tell that anyone had been there, anyone at all.

Resisting Autobiography

An authentic autobiography must necessarily conclude with the death of the author, otherwise it is merely an interim report. That is perhaps why I have resisted writing my own story, although I have lived a full life among words and over the years have envisioned my demise from a rich variety of perspectives. Much as I would like to shape my past into a narrative that would illuminate my entire existence with an aura of significance, it would be a violation of form and a repudiation of my responsibility as a protagonist if in the end I were to avoid a simultaneous departure from both text and the world. Suicide as a literary device, however, holds no particular appeal—my dedication to the requirements of genre is not absolute—and the chance of natural expiration at the moment of closure is beyond imagining.

After my great uncle hanged himself from an oak tree in the back garden of the family home, we all went to the funeral. Following the service, there was a reception at the house. It was winter and the interment would not be until after the spring thaw. I was eleven and flattered to be engaged in a conversation with the bishop, who was very taken with the grandeur of the estate in such an obscure part of the country and with the sumptuous table laid out for the guests. Taking me into his confidence the bishop told me it was he who had cut my great uncle down from the tree. He had been summoned by my great aunt and being new in the diocese he presumed it was a matter of a major bequest. In fact she had no idea of who else to call. The police seemed a sordid option, a doctor was beside the point, and our regular minister was not quite important enough. My great aunt had heard people sometimes called the fire department in an emergency, but since she herself had tugged at his feet and knew her husband to be perfectly dead, emergency action seemed wasted. When she telephoned my mother, my mother confirmed that she had been right to summon the new bishop. By the time the authorities arrived, my great uncle was laid out on the sofa near the front door, the last rites had been given, and my mother had begun to supervise kitchen arrangements for the visitation, which would take place in the front parlour, off the library, after my great uncle was returned from the mortuary.

It is difficult to die in a vacuum. Daisy Goodwill comes close; Carol Shields eliminates Daisy in *The Stone Diaries* with so little fanfare the reader hardly notices her passing. The autobiographical format of the novel, which has been distended and distorted from the very beginning when Daisy relates the grotesque circumstances of her own birth, dissipates into trivial particularities following her death that seem to obscure the event, as if Daisy has simply run out of story to tell. The effect is paradoxically powerful, for the true story is metafictional: a sustained challenge to the limits of the autobiographical novel. Out of an ordinary life comes an extraordinary work of imagination, devised by an author who revels in the breaching of genre conventions and with sly dexterity consigns her protagonist to a minor role in her own account. Daisy does not lose narrative authority at her death—it was only a playful illusion that she ever had it. Left to her own devices, she would have been at most a figure of inconsequential pathos. She does not die so much as she falls from view as the camera pans to a higher level and the credits roll, which prove not to be credits at all but a casual obituary consisting of fragments from a life lived largely unexamined.

In writing my autobiography rather than having an author like Shields write it for me, I would have to slip away from the final scene like a victim of drowning. It would be my responsibility to dispose of the body, so to speak. The trick would be to relinquish control, embrace death, write silence, with appropriate subtlety, appropriate flare. I am uncertain about the annihilation of self as an act of creation.

When I was a student, I thought suicide a seductive alternative to reality. An arbitrary exit from the world would 1) draw my ill-formed personality into focus around the particular moment of my passing; 2) inform the random particulars of my life with the design of retroactive inevitability; 3) give me absolute control in a life where absolutes and control had steadfastly remained out of reach; 4) expunge in a singular action my innumerable fears about dying; 5) fulfill my romantic notions drawn from Scott of the Antarctic that death is intrinsically heroic if the cause is sufficiently banal, and from John Keats that death confirms genius; 6) make me the object of mourning, haunting all the young women who resisted my advances with suspicions they might have done more. I contrived termination scenarios from the mysterious to the spectacular, but I did not have sufficient discipline or resolve to follow them through.

Suicide, then, struck me as a literary device, the lives of writers and their works seemed inseparable. I thought a lot about stones in the pockets of a drowning Virginia Woolf, more than about *Mrs. Dalloway* or *To the Lighthouse,* although "A Room of One's Own" crossed gender to fill me with anger and empathy. When Sylvia Plath died in 1963 I had finished a bachelor's degree, knocked around Europe for a couple of years, and was considering graduate school. That words could etch such horrors as she endured on the nerve ends of her reader's mind, horrors that only death could finally bring to submission, impelled my application to a program of advanced literary study, a field for which I am by temperament ill suited.

I now teach at a university and have raised two children who perpetuate a few of my idiosyncrasies but I was born to be an autobiographer, not an academic or a genetic link. Like John Glassco in his notorious *Memoirs of Montparnasse,* which he began at seventeen, I have lived my life in order to have something to write about. It follows, then, that my lifelong fascination with suicide is not a predilection for death but a morbid obsession with the complexity of being alive. It astonishes me that the universe unfolded as it has to admit me. Had an ancient forbear sneezed during orgasm, I would not be here. At the same time, it is tenuous, this business of living. Right now cancer cells may be gathering momentum in my viscera, or a driver dreaming who will one day roll his truck head-on towards a place to which even now I might also be en route.

As you may have divined, mine was an indulgent childhood. My parents indulged me and I indulged myself. Not surprisingly, I learned very early to express dissatisfaction by declaring I had not asked to be born. My parents gave me brothers and sisters to soften the sting. Two of each, whom I loved in my fashion, although they diffused the focus of affection. I ran away from home twice before I was ten. The first time I sneaked out in the middle of the night but returned for my skates by midmorning. The second time I fled across the field behind our house and when my father came home from work he found me, waiting. He had brought a tin of pork and beans, an opener and some matches, and we warmed the beans over a fire of dry cedar twigs and poured them out onto pieces of birchbark cupped in our hands and ate with our fingers. Only years later did I realize how much I loved my siblings or what a good man my father was, for all that we conspired against him.

You do not grow up in a family like mine without a preternatural sensitivity to guilt and responsibility. My parents were lapsed Anglicans, which is perhaps a redundancy, but we were genetically Presbyterian. Any discussion of suicide is less a betrayal of religious decorum than of my mother's affection. The greater betrayal, however, would be not to give her appropriate status in my auto-biography—the deepest sin in my mother's cosmology was to violate the appearance of fairness. If one of her children inspired pride, then so did we all. If one fell from grace, the others did too. I know the importance of fairness; I cannot introduce my father in a text without giving my mother equal representation. If she were here now, her eyes would water and her beautiful face, even more beautiful when she was old, would resolve into a mask of forbearance, letting me know without words that being consigned to a minor role in the narrative of my life is a small price to pay for having brought me into the world.

By my time we had settled into the middle class, some-how as if it were a fallen state. The new-world fortunes of my family attenuated as they were subdivided over the most recent generations until by now I have little to leave my own children but memories, a modest academic repu-tation, and a few ancestral furnishings that survived the dissolution of successive estates by virtue of being painted or scarred or crafted in the country style, items that para-doxically are worth more now than the high style pieces that replaced them. I leave them with recollections of child-hood shaped in part by the urgency of my ongoing struggle to assimilate the imminence of death, which seemed at times my only constant witness, so much so that I held it almost in affection. Gradually it took on my personality, a doppelganger who shadowed my life, my runcible twin. My children grew up with a man who could not step away from his own shadow.

II

Contemplation of suicide is the best antidote to mor-bidity. It combines an acute awareness of death, essential to living a full life, with a sense of sovereignty over a condition that is otherwise arbitrary. It is not mortality that gets you down. Dead is dead, whether flights of angels sing you to your rest or worms consume you in a jester's grave. It is the indifference of death to your personal requirements that appals. You do what you can. Those truly engaged with being alive, for instance, usually have a vivid idea of where they wish to be buried. You may daydream of burial in a sacred place or of ashes scattered in lyric eloquence. The rhetoric of time, however, prevents your presence to appreciate the actual event. Instead of enduring the possibility that someone might decide to flush you down a drain or discard your body outside the city wall, I suggest it is preferable to reverse the order of things, bring death forward to confront the moment, contemplate on a sustained basis your own willful demise. Suicide has a purpose in the well-ordered life as much as cemeteries and premonitions of eternity.

This has been my line of reasoning for the last several years. As with most such eschatologies, I came to my beliefs through induction, not theoretic conjecture. It started when I was constructing a bookcase in my basement workshop and lost a finger to my table-saw. I did not actually lose the finger. It lay in a pile of sawdust on the floor at a beckoning angle for several moments before I realized through the shock what had happened. Jamming the stump against my diaphragm to staunch the bleeding, I retrieved the errant digit and hurried with it to the freezer where I deposited it among the blanched rhubarb. I had some idea they could sew it back on if it were adequately maintained on ice. However, by the time I drove myself to Emergency, where I passed out in the waiting room, and was revived and able to explain where my finger was, the wound had been cauterized and the stump sewn over, and I was informed that cellular damage from freezing would by now have rendered the flesh irretrievable. Two weeks later I reduced the finger to ashes in my backyard barbecue, and on a whim placed the ashes for future disposition in an urn my wife kept in the back of her closet after the dispersal of her first husband's mortal remains.

Commandeering this repository for my own ashes began as a tasteless jibe, born out of morbid jealousy and the vague uneasiness that I had thus conformed with her ultimate intention to recycle the funerary paraphernalia she had so painfully acquired before we met. I did not tell her what I had done until she asked one day with what I thought was contrived decorum if I had seen her missing urn. At first I bluffed, asking which urn that would be; this was to force the embarrassment of a clarification that would feed emotional masochism on my part as I would attempt to estimate from her tone how much she missed him more than she valued me; but she is good at disarming my immaturity with studied equanimity, and she said merely that she could not find her dead husband's funerary urn, thereby placing the sharp divide of mortality between my predecessor and myself which did not warrant further consideration. I confessed the urn was now in my possession, and solemnly requested it remain so.

My wife cuts my hair and for some time I had been gathering the clippings in plastic bags. I had an odd sense of affection for what I knew rationally were merely remnants. Perhaps as justification I nurtured a vague sense that the wisps and tufts and motley strands grown from my head might someday prove useful. Since encrypting my finger remains, however, I came to realize the value of my bags of hair was more than symbolic if less than practical. The hair although worthless had intrinsic meaning; it was me, material of my earthly being. It took some time to devise a way to transform the hair into ashes without a terrible stench but I did so by building a backyard food-smoker and then reducing the hair, handful at a time, to a dry brittle consistency that crumbled to the touch. This residue I added to the urn.

I could not help but think of Daisy Goodwill. Reading her quasi-autobiography brought my own haphazard existence into focus at about the same time that my fortuitous accident occurred. As all the fictions of her life accumulate in Shields' account, each rendering of Daisy revealing more of a ubiquitous and elusive narrative persona than of Daisy, her life merely an accumulation of intersecting arcs shed from the circles of other peoples' lives, it becomes apparent that Daisy is less than the sum of her parts. She could not ever be the author of an autobiography. Perhaps no-one can. Autobiography is an anomaly, a literary genre that succeeds in direct proportion to its violation of the conventions that define it—it will seem most authentic, most truthful and complete, when it most engagingly gathers a thematic, dramatic, schematic collection of facts adhering to one personality into a narrative design answering all the requirements of fiction. Emboldened by this revelation which I attributed to my reading of *The Stone Diaries* I determined thenceforward to live a fictional life. Without Shields to write my story, I would have to gather myself together for future disposition with assiduous care. I would mark the line of demarcation between life and death, fiction and ephemerality, with small ceremonies. Who knew what parts of me would eventually sustain my story.

Hair, perhaps? Nail parings ? I could not bear to part with palpable souvenirs of my mortal presence in the world. I took to doing all manicure and pedicure procedures over the bathroom sink, after which I would gather and sort the clippings from bits of accumulated grime and render them with my hair into ash in the backyard smoker that I had discovered also made excellent sausages, some of which we gave away as Christmas presents to friends and relatives. One day a thumbnail of considerable size slid down the drain and I had to remove the stopcock under the

inchoate particulars of my life coherent, to give them significance. I am my own semiotic conundrum. Although you cultivate my presence through the generosity of your conscious attention, this is not about you.

It is only illusion that I am in control of my story. When the words end, by reverting to my place in the temporal continuum I yield to mortality. Even though what I write may endure for eons on library shelves and in the minds of sympathetic readers, I will eventually die. Beyond the text, I will become transparent or fade to opacity, they are ultimately the same, so that readers will casually observe, oh yes, I believe he is dead; or maybe not, but he is very old; or he died years ago, if I haven't confused him with someone else, a character perhaps in one of his esoteric fictions. Readers may remember the exact point at which my autobiography concludes, but concerning my life the point of departure will seem trivial at best. There is pathos in this, from my perspective. And fear. I would rather prolong the moment of my demise interminably than achieve narrative perfection.

Daisy Goodwill has an advantage. There is no real pretense in *The Stone Diaries* that she is constructing her own account. Yet her story is not fictional biography, not an authorial imposition of narrative form on a life that has been lived beyond text. Despite the inclusion of photographs that imply authenticity in the real world, Daisy's story is a novel. It is a novel in which the author refuses to yield textual authority to her protagonist, yet fosters the illusion that the protagonist is engaged in self-revelation. Shields invests Daisy with an articulating consciousness that is paradoxically not self-aware. We read her life as innocent voyeurs, our innocence the measure of Daisy's lack of moral engagement with the world, and we are charmed. But we are never moved by Daisy, only astonished by the anarchy of her author's achievement, as Shield's defies conventions of literary form, and especially, of what is truth and what is true. Daisy has the advantage. She can recede from the text in the end and there is nothing left behind, no other Daisy who must deal with death beyond the final pages of her narrative.

If I were to write my autobiography, you would be my necessary witness. Some people find God an appropriate witness. Myself, I need you. Suppose I brought my story and life to simultaneous conclusion, you would now be more real than I. It is an odd notion, generally accepted in theories of reading, that you, my reader, enter my reality. But no, it is otherwise: in the infinite theatre of your mind I come alive. Perhaps in you I find myself quite different from what I intended. If so, it is a revelation your mind permits. I exist because you think me so. And like the God of Genesis you need me to affirm your power.

To end autobiography without the author's death is a willful plunge into the absurdity of time. Paradoxically, to bring any piece of writing to an end is a form of suicide, annihilation of the self caught up in the act of writing, sustained in the moment of creation where the past and future converge. If I continue in the conflicted moment of spontaneous engagement with language, I remain alive. But I do not know how long I can go on. I am exhausted by the discipline necessary to stay in the present. I suspect there are many who hover all their lives between yesterday and tomorrow as if today were of no consequence. But some of us, you reading this, me writing, by our conspiracy to subvert time, we affirm the absolute poignancy of being here, now.

Unlike Daisy Goodwill who thinks she is real, I know I am fiction. Although I may never write my autobiography, like John Glassco I have turned my life into an objet d'art. I am fiction because I cannot bear to be real. The only evasion that allows me to live is writing, knowing you will read this. It is like dialysis. If I cannot cleanse my system of the poisons invading from without and within, I will perish. It is not enough to write; I need to know that you will read. You will not succumb to my malaise, for the filter is virtually by definition resistant to the deleterious effects of the effluvium. But the intersection of your life with mine will allow me remission until we both reach the end. Does this seem a contrived, a narrative paradigm for the relationship between writer and reader? It is not. Trust me on this.

Consider my argument an ironic commentary on the lover-poet's ploy to confer immortality through art. The odd thing, of course, is that the beloved is invariably disguised by artifice, and the lover submerged in the art. We are left with a paradox, the poem itself as evidence that its argument is false. Only the reader is alive for sure. That is what I want, your lifeblood as a reader. My conviction that you are here keeps me alive. You cannot stop my death, but you can help me to endure the intervening hours before it occurs.

IV

When I was twenty-one, Hemingway died. The next summer I ran with the bulls in Pamplona. From Spain, Hemingway's suicide seemed both ignoble and inspired. A Spaniard was killed in the corrida; I had a fling with a flamenco dancer from New York who talked to me in Yiddish and thought I understood. After she left, I fell in love with Barbara Moxley from Palo Alto, California, but nothing came of it. Those of us who had already partied on Ibiza sat apart and drank quantities of vino tinto in honour of Hemingway, not for the writing but the man. That's what people have to understand who lament his becoming a figure from fiction, that's what we loved. It was not the writing, any more than it was Kerouac's writing, it was the way he constructed a life. As with Kerouac, his reputation was the projection of what he wished to see of himself in the mirror. We envied the authenticity of his artful deceit. This was before the sixties began in earnest, when we were in flight from the fifties, and the twenties were still the age we admired.

"Requiem" was one of my friend R.K.'s favourite words. We shared a room in West Kensington for a couple of months, hung out on Ibiza watching itinerant Americans smoke pot, and sat for hours on the main square in Pamplona talking about Hemingway's death. While we were there, Faulkner died. R.K. was the only close friend I had in those days who had not gone to university. He knew everything Hemingway and Faulkner had published, could quote terse riffs of Hemingway dialogue, whole paragraphs of Yoknapatawpha prose. He had never learned to be embarrassed by enthusiasm. This made him exotic. He would sometimes hold words up to the light. "Look," he would say; his thin face would break sideways into a grin. "Listen, you can see the letters dance," and the sounds from his lips of a single word would inscribe the clear sunlight over the plaza. "Sanctuary," he would say, "requiem," shaking his head as if saying such words brought him closer to Faulkner. "Dos cerveza," he would say to Manuel, the waiter—not because he wanted beer but because he did not understand Spanish and was gleeful each time "Dos cerveza por favor" brought beer to the table. At least twice a day we drank beer; and the rest of the time brackish red wine which came without asking. Thirty-five years later I was walking west on St. Clair near Bathurst when in a chance encounter with an acquaintance she mentioned R.K.'s death a decade ago, by his own hand, which implied a gun rather than poison or hanging. All that time, I had thought he was alive. People do not die for us until we know about their deaths.

When I think about R.K. now, he is in the ceremonial dress of a samurai, and with unwavering precision he cuts into his own entrails as he has done in his mind a thousand

times. He is in a story by Yukio Mishima. It is called
"Patriotism" and he is the protagonist. As the sword enters
his body he cannot distinguish the pain from the ritual, it is
not his pain, the ritual absorbs the shock and leaves his
mind lucid, allowing him to cut in the right direction, over
and then up, while he still has the strength to guide his
meticulous blade. His wife observes, her modest death will
follow, she is his witness. Before she plunges a small knife
into her body, she unlocks the front door so they will be
found. Ten years is a long time to be dead without notice.

One night in the Colonial Tavern on Yonge Street,
R.K. and I compared suicide notes. He had been back from
Europe for a year and I had returned home a few months
later after two years of wandering, both of us world weary
and yet strangely untouched by all that we had seen and
done, denizens of Toronto now, the world remote. We both
had ordinary jobs and often met to drink draft beer in the
evenings, sometimes bringing dates but usually alone. The
Colonial was murky and we were cheerfully morbid. Even
when he showed me the wound between his fingers which
in the dim light looked like a birthmark, and told me how
his mother had smelled burning flesh from his cigarette
after he had lost consciousness and sent him off to have his
stomach pumped, we laughed. But that was too close, and
we drank more than usual that night. Saying goodby at the
subway, I asked R.K to promise if he ever reached desperation again he would call me. It's a contract, he said with a
conspiratorial grin and descended into the subway. We met
less frequently after that, and then not at all. Neither of us
attended the other's wedding. I do not know if he had children or ever took the night courses he talked about when I
told him I was going into graduate studies.

Recently I had lunch with another friend from my
discontinuous past. He had been R.K.'s childhood neighbour. His name is H, a signal distinction in a world of
whole names and double initials—T.S., G.K., W.H., V.S.,

R.K. Usually single letters without punctuation are names only in fiction: F in *Beautiful Losers,* K in Kafka, the Countess of M-. H had shared Pamplona with R.K. and me, and Ibiza, and I had travelled with H to Istanbul and shared great adventures but we had not been in touch for a long time. And H told me R.K. used to ask about me sometimes in the hospital where he spent his last years before he died from emphysema. When I said I had been told he killed himself, H said yes, he might have done, but no, he died of emphysema. I did not think it possible to stop knowing someone, but I felt I had lost R.K. then, as if in my confusion he had slipped irretrievably away. The reality we had shared during the explosive intensity of those brief years when our lives ran parallel suddenly vanished. It was not death but the confounding of stories that did it; because each passing was as plausible to me as the other, the possibility remained that he was still alive, or that he had never been, and so his death was fiction and his life unreal. I found it difficult to reconcile my grief with an unsettling sense of disappointment—whether in myself or R.K. I could not tell.

V

Today a man I know at the University where I work died because his estranged wife had the affection of his children and they turned against him. He killed himself in a rage of despair and self-pity, both emotions familiar to me. He was not a close friend but I am in shock. I look to my own life, weigh his decision in the light of my own experience. His children are very young. I did not know his wife or the terms of their estrangement. But I do believe he died for his children; we would, any of us, die for our children.

Most of us do not have the opportunity for such appalling sacrifice. Could I restore to life my child who died or could I give my living children back their innocence I would. But even laying out my life as fiction I cannot comprehend the ways to change what having happened has become inevitable. If Daisy Goodwill could have seized control of her story, sidelined Carol Shields, she would have told it differently but it would have been the same in the end, she would have died in Florida. The plot might deviate depending on perspective as our lives unravel but the outcome is the same.

Since every conscious moment effects a reconstruction of the past, and inscribing life at the moment of our passing is impractical, it is only possible to tell our true stories by arbitrarily suspending the experience of duration, writing out of time, as if time were merely a literary device. Even then, we would need infinite autobiographies to achieve the truth. There is no library large enough to hold the books of consciousness emanating from my own unexceptional knowledge of the world. Imagine each of us an autobiographer, furiously inscribing our accounts of who we are for those few readers who will act as witness to our separate lives. We could not move for manuscripts as numerous as molecules, we would expire in a suffocation of words. If our minds were libraries, they would be labyrinths jammed with books of our own devising, the corridors stretched to vanishing in all directions. We could not move for fear of minotaurs, the monsters of imagination sprung to express finitude in the galaxies of our knowing. We cannot endure too much reality. To survive the onslaught of our myriad past in the passing moment we each select our autobiography best suited to the present, and revise as future needs reveal themselves, revising and revising until the end.

The problem is, as autobiographer you do not know what you think until you write it down, or what you feel, or who you are. I do not know the person writing until I read his story, even when it is me who invests the words with authenticity and makes them breathe. As creator I cannot tell the difference between the desire to end my account from an appetite for oblivion. I need to read the finished work.

The ambivalence of my present condition makes me suspect my own conceit. Could it be that in my recent life I am content and therefore mad, or perhaps mad and thus content. I do not want to end my life. I want my life to end. It is my autobiography I want over with, I do not want to finish writing. I want control of my story, I want to cede control; I want absolutes and absolution. I have not lived tragedy, for all the sadness I have known affects my personality but is not its emanation. I have not lived comedy, for all the joy I have known has been seized by acts of will. I have not lived romance for I am an ironic man, nor irony, for I have a romantic disposition. My life is satire, perhaps, but incomplete for it postulates neither an alternative nor remedy. Ambivalence as I write becomes ambiguity: I must consider not the story told but how to tell my present story. Rather than resolution, bear with me, let us deal with revelation, with what has been left out.

In truth, I have had two lives. Certain factors overlap and interpenetrate. I have memories and artifacts from my previous life still with me, some haunting and some affirming, some connecting me with yet another life, when I was a child and growing up among the remnants of several squandered small-town fortunes, amidst the sprawling affectations of a large eccentric family, and some reminding me of wasted opportunities and lives not lived. The mother of my children is a professional woman. Out of the crucible of a volatile relationship both she and I achieved much; not least of our accomplishments was the successful negotiation of our children's growing up. But after they were safely grown and on their own, I felt perpetually in a state of exhaustion, as if my many lives were a crowding of strangers and only the context seemed familiar and there was nowhere I could rest. I left for solitude and discovered someone waiting for me; it seemed we had both been waiting. I miss the home I built like a work of art or other self. I miss the continuity. I have broken the past and for this my children never will forgive me.

While I have courted suicide all my conscious life, it seems in times of greatest pain a misguided indulgence to consider arbitrary closure. On the saddest day of my life, I resisted the solipsistic evasions of invoking either God or death. In a fit of rational discourse between my soul and self, I determined that to call upon a deity who will not take responsibility for unhappiness is foolish, a nasty metaphysical conceit. What possible respect could I have for a master of the universe who craves adoration, demands subservience, and dispenses grace or annihilation like a madman plucking angels' wings? Suicide stood up little better to scrutiny, for if life is not bearable, its negation can hardly be preferred. Such thinking left me comfortless.

I have not recovered from the death of my infant son. Not a day or an hour, not a moment of conscious awareness, do I endure that I do not grieve. I miss the easy familiarity I once had with my surviving children but they occupy a place within me of visceral complexity that will remain until my mind goes empty. From my dear dead son, I have only the memory of holding him for a short time as his still body, warm from his mother's womb, grew gradually the temperature of air; and memories of our single winter as a family, the three of us, me touching his movement through his mother's flesh, him reaching to the sounds of our affection.

I wrote poems to him that winter. I sang to him with my crooked voice. Nothing can shatter the love that we wrapped around the three of us like a cocoon, not even his death. But there was no metamorphosis, only an absolute end. I miss him so much, I sometimes think I am broken. Then his lovely mother, my beloved, takes me in her arms, and breathes into my broken heart, and not shamed but moved by her courage I come together and we share gratitude that we had him even so briefly. She carried him, and it must be unutterably sad to remember his birth, yet they were so much part of one another for the whole of his living that she can remember with joy the promise of his surging inside her. I did not know him as well, but in his mother's eyes I see all that I miss and all that I will love as long as we remain alive.

For them I abandon equations of autobiography and being. I resolve not ever to write myself out of the story, I will not submit to despair. That does not mean I won't sometimes stare at an oncoming truck and as it goes by wonder that it could have been over with a swerve of the wheel. I will probably never cross a bridge without looking down to imagine my trajectory and feel the thud like a premonition in my bones. But these are vain thoughts and I will let them vanish like voices in the air. Each new moment will declare my autobiography subject to revision. It is an impossible genre, but inevitable for those of us who cast our lives in letters and sometimes confuse the written word with being alive.

Anne of Green Gables and the End of the World

In the end is our beginning—I could not have said it better. As the world spins off its axis and the mind opens to its own ephemerality, we are born again. The death of metaphysics has been long in coming, although its span was brief in relation to four billion years of evolution on this small planet. Even in the human story, the severance of meaning from experience was of short duration, measurable in mere millennia. The savagery of recent times has set our minds to break beyond the bounds of thought, that we might now resume our place as molecules in the chaos of the universe. All this, I think while holding in my hands a pristine copy of Lucy Maud Montgomery's *Anne of Green Gables,* a book I have not read but know with that kind of awkward familiarity normally associated with literary critics and undertakers.

The truth is, despite astonishing changes in human society, the new order has not broken our conviction that knowledge is the measure of reality. Obscured by revolutionary fanfare is the simple fact that we have merely traded one mode of knowing for another. Those of us, and it is only conjecture that I am not alone, those of us who believe the present dispensation no better than the age of print we left behind, are dangerous. We feel—I should accept that I might be a solitary voice—I feel everything that has happened is proof we can modify quite radically our apprehension of the world but has done nothing to make us relinquish our assumptions of existential primacy. This position undermines those who believe Armageddon has been circumvented, despite the horrors we endured, and the time of revelation is upon us. My conviction that absolute humility, the annihilation of meaning, is essential to the well-being of the world is unpopular. Thus, I am confined to this place with a single book for solace and as torment, and my personal continuation is precarious at best.

When I was first brought here, I was given the opportunity to choose from among a residual cache of books one volume that would be my sole companion for the duration. It was much like a heretic in the dank bowels of an Inquisitional dungeon being offered a table of gleaming geometrical instruments from which to select a preferred method of torture. When I did not at first see *Anne of Green Gables* I asked for it but my keepers responded with looks of such virulent disinterest I was, despite my nakedness, more ashamed for them than for myself and kept on looking. Just as they were about to haul me away empty-handed I discovered a pale green copy of *Anne* in a mouldering pile. I wiped the soiled cover against my bare flesh and clasped the book to my heart as a sort of amulet to ward off their indifference. They marched me out a door adjacent to the one I had entered and along a series of blank-walled passageways that periodically intersected with other passages that were equally nondescript, until at last we faced a doorway at the end of a hall which opened to an empty cell. Clutching *Anne* to my withered chest, as a condemned man might grasp at the swaying rope to hold it taunt while it is drawn against his throat, desperate to make the surreal a visceral event, I entered my sanctuary triumphant—for that is how I try to see my cell, a sanctuary, and in finding Anne I had the instrument in hand that while it might not deliver me to a merciful death would make my remaining life more tolerable.

Exhausted after the ordeal of the preceding months, and in pain from lack of food and exercise, I lowered myself to the floor. Using the book as a pillow I curled into a fetal position in order to hold as much of my nakedness against myself as possible and preserve my body heat. When I awoke a shutter had been removed on an outer wall and a book-shaped window was revealed that looked onto a lush garden several stories below, a curious phenomenon because I did not remember ascending stairs. My reading glasses had been placed on the floor beside my head. Over the next few days, during the dark hours while I slept, food appeared inside my cell, and clothing, and after a fortnight I awoke to find the cell-space diminished by the furnishings of a bed and a wooden chair. On a subsequent night, placed over the hole in the floor through which I expelled my personal waste I found a vintage chamber-pot. Since this could have been shattered and the shards used to slit my veins, I assumed my keepers had decided I was not a danger to myself, even if, as my extreme isolation testified, I was considered so to them.

I have no visitors and my keepers remain out of sight. It is ironic that I am an advocate of thought which they find dangerous, and they have provided me with circumstances where the only occupation open to me is thinking. It is not the thoughts I think that frighten them. Their orators could demolish my ideas in a single drum roll of syllables, a flourish of semantics. What strikes terror in their hearts is that I refuse to subordinate the complexities of thought itself to the simple rules which for ages now have shaped perceptions of ourselves in speech and print. When reading was still ascendant, they argued that written language was the model of the human mind, and therefore what was written was *de facto* how we were. Subsequently, after a brutal interregnum, the Derrideans who enforced the primacy of speech equated the ephemerality of the voice with a sort of existential urgency that signified our fleeting eminence. My insistence that reality is independent of the human mind threatens with the prospect of inconsequence, of finding ourselves once again integrated within the cosmos and not by intellectual fiat its Prime Observer.

The institution in which I find myself confined is a cultural construct. I am no longer a denizen of the campus, nor a familiar of the church, nor of the courts of law or governance. I was a professor once but this was not a permanent condition. Little of my old life remains with me. It is easier to endure the present if you have no past. Anne Shirley animates perhaps the only narrative that spans the reach of memory. She seems always to have been there, inside my mind. She arrived long before the change, when books were still revered and the dominant reality was textually determined. I recall specific incidents in our developing relationship but not the primal encounter. When I was a child I think my parents read passages of L.M. Montgomery to me, but never the whole of anything; when I had children of my own, they must have read Anne stories to me at bedtime, to prolong the day. Anne's trajectory and mine periodically intersected over the years. I recall reading an essay about her iconic status in Japan; another time I mistakenly attended her musical apotheosis in a summer tent theatre; and not long before the old ways ended I fell almost in love with a pastel rendering of her likeness in one of the last tourist brochures to come out of Prince Edward Island.

As a figure of popular culture, Anne shaped my sensibility in which she lived. Like Huck Finn and Rebecca of Sunnybrook Farm and Lassie and Alice and Tiny Tim and Heidi and Nancy Drew, she seems for me to have preceded self-awareness, as if she were a fixture in my mental pantheon, I almost said asylum, before I was, myself. I can summon her now with such clarity that on certain of our recent encounters my solitary confinement has become strangely crowded, and I am forced to send her away by screaming nonsense syllables against my pillow, in a curious display of glossolalian dementia.

Of course, there is no-one to observe my behaviour. The only evidence that my keepers exist is that the door remains locked when I am awake and food appears while I sleep. The only indication of personality in my reluctant witnesses is in the idiosyncrasy of the chamber pot, a relic that perhaps is meant to remind me of what my ideas signify, that I have defined myself according to the basic functions I share with my ancestors, and also in the provision of my reading glasses as a reminder of the civilization we left behind, and a taunting incentive to open my one book and lose myself among its written words.

Sometimes, exercising a childlike affinity for the perverse, with Anne clutched in my arms, I reminisce about reading. It is not something you forget. But it is such appalling self-abuse, the debasement of the mind for access to vicarious pleasures, that I limit myself to remembering. Years ago, I condoned the drive against literacy, despite my occupation as a literary specialist. My conviction, however, that in breaking from the bonds of print we might resume our natural status as a peripheral phenomenon in the universe, this threatened the new order. They said, echoing Descartes, I speak, therefore reading is irrelevant. But I think it is we who are irrelevant, for we have not yet broken from the tyranny of thought.

The age of print is missed by no-one. From the time of Heraclitus writing history and Moses etching God in stone, we dwelled among books, endured through the ages in a vortex of intertextuality. We could not conceive life with value except through transcendent meaning drawn from the written word. We could not valorize the present moment except as the interface of what was written and what is yet to write. But we had reached the point where of all the volumes that comprised our culture, none were left whose passages could serve as an index or concordance to the rest. Words were no longer something to believe in; irony reigned over us like fallout. Under the dispensation of one text or another we had killed millions of our kind in trenches, in tenements, in gas chambers, in the marketing of tobacco. Absolved by an absence of moral coherence in the reality we had written into existence, we forgave ourselves.

With the breakdown of righteousness that followed, the least among us were filled with apathy and the best lacked definition. There were some who thought we had only to set down the old texts, stop reading ourselves into significance, and we might retrieve our lost capacity for innocence. Because we were the creatures of language, however, our best thinkers could not conceive a reality beyond the reach of words. It is ironic that print has become an eerie artifact, signifying the lingering malevolence of a past that placed human consciousness at the centre of the known universe, since language as the source of knowing, a model for the known, is once again the informing principle of the philosophies that govern us.

Anne Shirley has red hair. She has freckles. She has an infectious enthusiasm. She has an Aunt Murilla and an Uncle Cuthbert who die. Anne never dies, no matter how many times her story is considered. Anne lives between writing and speech. She is not an object of consciousness but a subject. I know she is not here. She dwells within thought. I know she is here. She is not waiting in books to spring into life. She is waiting in books. I know her already and I have never read her author's writing. Anne occupies a world within me, waiting to happen and happening, as real as memory or imagination.

There was a time, it was when I was still teaching literature at the university, after reading had fallen into disrepute, or disrepair is perhaps a more appropriate term, before anything coherent took its place. Spoken thought only achieved ascendancy after a transition interval of considerable violence known retroactively as The Fukuyama Disruption. What this means, no-one can say, but it was suitably arcane to endure. During this period the walls of reality crumbled and it was several years before their rebuilding was undertaken, on the same foundation but to a different set of plans. People lost the ability to discriminate between various types of experience invading and occupying consciousness. Did that happen to me or was it something I read? Did that happen ever or was it devised for entertainment? The Holocaust was brought to ground as *Schindler's List,* D-Day was contained by *Saving Private Ryan.* The special effects on CNN were provided by the U.S. military, the dying extras by lesser foreign powers. Commercials on television conveyed more inventive authenticity than the programs they delivered. The subversion of editorial content to advertising layout pioneered by *Vogue* became the standard of the transient print industry. Theme parks proliferated like churches, offering a purity of experience more genuine than private lives. At first it seemed that books, such as those I taught my students, offered worlds more coherent than the worlds of private memory they displaced. Who would not rather be Ahab or Moll Flanders than a mewling sophomore awash in beer? This phase of the transitional period soon passed.

My own youth had been lived by Holden Caulfield, my memories of small town Ontario were created by Alice Munro. My mother was June Cleaver more indelibly than were the disparate particulars of the woman who bore and raised me. I do not recall when critical mass was reached, the point where empirical experience came crashing down. Suddenly, but at no identifiable moment, consciousness superseded the reality of its antecedents. Everything was real within the mind, wherever it originated. Since being in the world was more confusing and less antiseptic than the packaged realities of artists and entertainers, we abjured the world. We gave up any notion of individual presence as, *a priori,* necessary for experience to occur. I remember only fleeting anguish that my mother was displaced; she was assimilated into larger patterns gleaned from diverse sources, and only a shard of grief remains.

Inevitably, books, which at first seemed obviously a diversionary medium as potent as the others, were shunned as profligate progenitors of individuality. I had thought my professorial sinecure secure, for in a civilization determined by texts what could be safer than work so wholly removed from actuality as that of the literary academic. Yet hardly had conceptions of objective reality collapsed when I noticed my students no longer bothered to prepare for my lectures but expected me, instead, to present the texts to them in a mixture of précis and analysis. Before long, they wanted only character and story, finding explication unacceptably intrusive. Then they stopped attending lectures. Lectures interfered, they said when I accosted several representative miscreants in the corridors on their way to film-studies' showings, with their synaptic capacity to receive from more generous media. Books demanded individual engagement which they were not prepared and perhaps were no longer equipped to undertake. Books were talked about occasionally by older faculty as the source for other media to draw upon, but lecterns in the lecture halls were soon replaced with screens and amplifiers. Library stacks became mazes where students could play at war, acting out scenarios from video games. Internet terminals in the undergraduate cafeterias allowed students to eat without having to make conversation and before long the more progressive faculty members were eating there as well. In the larger world beyond the university, the notion of a larger world had broken down: "The Young and the Restless" "Coronation Street" and "The Advertising Award Show" were looped on universal media displays with periodic intervals of Allie McBeal and Jerry Seinfeld reruns inserted to remind people who they were.

As the perimeters of personal experience turned transparent, and the boundaries between virtual realities became obscure, acts of random violence escalated. It became impossible for the majority of people to distinguish between what was happening to themselves and others, or whether what was happening was real. Violence became epidemic as an expression of sensibilities desperate to connect, without regard to how or with whom. Minds became video terminals. The only proof of being was pain. Pain became the medium of human intercourse. Inflicting pain made others real; receiving it affirmed personal reality. Minds became video terminals; pain was the medium of human intercourse.

Inevitably, those few who had been philosophers resisted, holding consciousness the higher authority, and violence a mere diversion. Gradually, deconstruction took control, undermined the chaos. A new order of stability was born. Survivors were relieved to find themselves again. The past was declared unconstitutional; the future a discredited literary device. The human voice displaced memory and imagination as the criterion of intellectual excellence. Print was deemed the source of instability and utterly reviled.

As for myself, I survived the brutality of the Fukuyama Disruption relatively unscathed. Having lived so long in a world defined by books even after I had lost all inclination to read, and perhaps because I have a revolutionary set of mind, or perhaps because I am an anarchist at heart, I had long-since determined to live out my interior life among literary figures. The character who predominated in my private pantheon of written familiars was Anne Shirley. Even as others faded from significance, Lear and Pip and Prospero and Kurtz, Cordelia and Estella, Miranda, the Intended, Anne whom I had never actually met in print lingered. In the emotional dissonance of the times I had lost track of my wife and children, the latter as I recall were married and with children of their own. Anne became my confidante and other self. Despite the brutality surrounding us, we had lovely conversations and great adventures. Sometimes we went skinny-dipping in the Lake of Shining Waters and, while I was younger than I really am, I was not aroused; and Anne was never bored.

When the deconstructionists rose to power and the Derridians proposed to do away with print entirely, on the argument that speech was the authentic voice of thought and writing an evasion of temporal consciousness, I hardly noticed. Like most people, I had reached the point of dissociation where I was content to !et the thinkers rule. It was a relief from the chaos and a radical departure from the orthodoxy that had seen us through recorded time, where thinkers thought and rulers ruled and seldom did their spheres converge. After the Derridians declared the authority of writing obsolete and the spoken word paramount, they showed devastating subtlety. Books that had survived the bad times were not burned; the books of common law and common prayer, the holy writs and learned documents, were merely acknowledged to be inconsequential. As computers learned to talk and listen with perfect fluency, writing was reduced to a residual function in binary code, the unspoken word became an electronic hieroglyph, familiar if encountered but strange. Within a surprisingly short time the general aptitude for print was virtually extinct.

Assembly of those known to have been readers was banned. Literary allusions were the new obscenity, references in speaking to print were profane. So thoroughly had Anne broken free from her origins, however, to establish herself as an icon of popular culture, that I found her the frequent subject of discussion among scholars with whom I occasionally met in secret colloquia to discuss the importance of oral discourse. Several of my superannuated colleagues allowed themselves to remember reading Lucy Maud Montgomery but could not connect the Anne we now discussed with the narratives from which she had sprung. This might have been because the mode of apprehension, namely reading, had been so compromised that to protect themselves from humiliation they subliminally repressed their true recollections of the text, thus diminishing the writer's achievement while simultaneously enhancing their conception of Anne as an integral part of their present lives. It could also, I suggested, be that Anne came not from good writing now forgotten but that, conceived with brilliant vitality, she had risen above the ordinary prose of her author to become an emanation of our innermost desires. She lived, in other words, not because Montgomery shaped her out of words but because we invested so much of ourselves animating what the words became in our imagination. This latter suggestion was treated with derision. Anne was real, my colleagues said, and it is we who are ephemeral.

That was the turning point, the beginning of my end. Much as I enjoyed Anne's company I knew she was imaginary. Intimate though we might have been, I knew she was a creation of the mind, resident among neurons in my brain. Such a confrontation with the nature of being provoked an infectious restlessness on my part that, magnified by the tenor of the times, made me a dangerous offender against the state of equanimity we were now obliged to foster and endure. My former colleagues expressed a preference that I not join them for their colloquia, which had heretofore been secretly conducted in the fast-food court of the local mall.

Because I was dangerous I gathered a following. Mostly they were young people, with only societal memories of the past and no residual memories of their own, who in another era might have joined the IRA, the SLA, or the FLQ, thugs for the most part with enough idealism awash in their systems to make them collectively a pathological menace. At first we had little trouble holding meetings since these consisted of fiery speeches and sloganeering banter. Ah, said the Derrideans, seeing us as a fundamentalist sect. Ah, they intoned, they are the vanguard, and yes, they added, the rear-guard as well. In a world where the spoken word defined reality, we seemed the essence of what was currently deemed real. Briefly we were lionized.

Then someone chanced to listen. Suddenly, we were counter-revolutionary deviants.

Our outlaw status spurred us on. We took to holding rallies in library reading rooms, each of us brandishing unread copies of *Anne of Green Gables* in the air as a salute to virtual anarchy. Every time we were routed and our books confiscated, our determination intensified, we dug deeper in the stacks and came up with alternative volumes, variant editions. Old as I was, I found these heady times. Then two things happened. One, the powers-that-be decided the best way to contain our movement was to ignore us utterly. That was remarkably depleting, but the second thing that happened brought us to our knees. This was the spontaneous realization that seemed to sweep through the movement like a runaway virus: nihilism even with the best intent was pointless.

Redundant, paradoxical, contradictory. Absurd. The word absurd echoed through our ranks and anarchy collapsed. As with all such movements, ours contained within its ideology the seeds of its own destruction. We believed that neither print, nor speech that superseded the terrifying confusion of actuality and imagination at print's demise, were true measures of the world. We believed that human consciousness expressed in present time through vocal modulation and aural apprehension, like human consciousness put on hold in print, did not convey the reality of human thought: print is not encoded thought; consciousness made articulate in speech is not the equivalent of thought. Thought is not reality. These are difficult concepts to inform the mission of an activist ensemble. But what ultimately did us in was the notion that followed from all of this that thought, freed from print or speech, led inevitably to the conclusion that we as humans are not significant. I did not preach the death of God but the end of revelation, the resumption of our place in the unimagined world.

It was not enough that my acolytes deserted me. It was

not enough that I appeared demented, desiring we abandon assumptions of privilege in the universe. It was not enough that I acknowledged my only friend was an imaginery foundling. Apparently, I could not be ignored. After trying to break my spirit by confining me to a retirement home for bridge-players and golfers, where the conversation was a barrage of arcane words like trump and bogie, bid and birdie, they offered me the sanctuary of this cell, for the good of all. They find it necessary to keep me alive. I am sad, but not bitter. Whatever oppression I endure comes from within.

The garden below is a visual retreat for constricted sensibilities of those like me, looking out our narrow windows. The flowers run riot among the trees and shrubbery so as to seem untended, although in fact I know enough of gardens to realize it is a well-planned illusion, the gardeners working unseen when we sleep. Sometimes I envision Anne seated by the lily pond with its tall grasses on the far side. Occasionally she looks in my direction, towards the huge wall with all the windows. I assume there are many windows just as I assume the wall is vast. As the sun passes overhead and a veil of shadow slowly draws across the garden, Anne disappears. One day I shall throw my book into the darkness. Then at least one of us will be free.